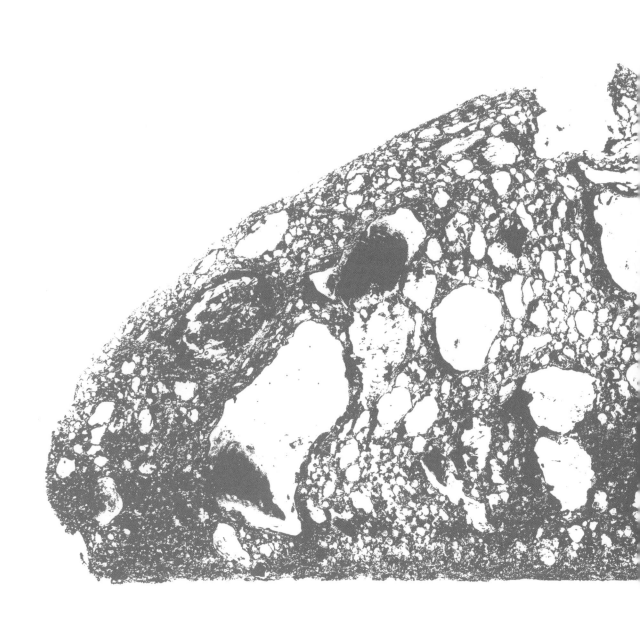

SUPER SOURDOUGH

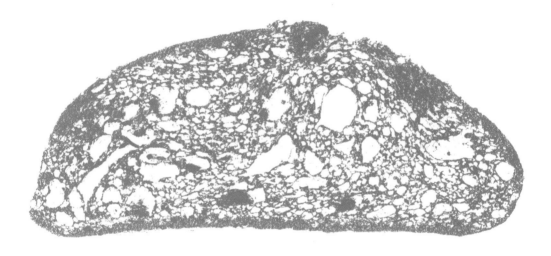

JAMES MORTON

Hardie Grant

QUADRILLE

Publishing Director **Sarah Lavelle**
Design & Art Direction **Will Webb**
Photographer **Andy Sewell**
Copy Editor **Eve Marleau**
Production Director **Vincent Smith**
Production Controller **Sinead Hering**

Published in 2019 by Quadrille,
an imprint of Hardie Grant Publishing

Reprinted in 2019, 2020 (four times), 2021 (twice), 2023, 2024
12 11 10

Quadrille
52–54 Southwark Street
London SE1 1UN
quadrille.com

Compilation, design, layout and text
© 2019 Quadrille
Photography © 2019 Andy Sewell

Cataloguing in Publication Data: a catalogue record for this book is
available from the British Library.

ISBN 9 781 78713 465 2

Printed in China

MIX
Paper | Supporting
responsible forestry
FSC™ C020056
FSC
www.fsc.org

CONTENTS

INTRODUCTION   7

10 TENETS OF SOURDOUGH   15

INGREDIENTS AND EQUIPMENT   21

PAIN AU LEVAIN   39

UNDERSTANDING DOUGH   75

UNDERSTANDING STARTERS   91

BREAD TROUBLESHOOTING   105

RELAXED RECIPES   113

WHITE BREADS FOR SHARING   131

LITTLE BREADS   153

DARKER BREADS   173

BITTY BREADS   191

ENRICHED   217

LEFTOVER STARTER   237

INDEX   248

ACKNOWLEDGEMENTS   254

SUPPLIERS   255

INTRODUCTION

I THOUGHT ABOUT MAKING YOU A PROMISE. I never decided exactly how it would go, but knew it would be similar to the mission statement of my first book. Something along the lines of, 'This will give you the tools to produce loaves without failure or fear of disaster.' I do not doubt my own sincerity back then, but now, writing such a statement makes me a little uneasy. To include it would be reassuringly confident, but dishonest. In truth, I'm not always happy with the loaves I bake and I ruminate over how I can improve every single one. I still have semi-regular dough catastrophes, and through the work I've put into this book, more bread has ended up burnt or in the dog's bowl than I'd be comfortable admitting.

In contrast, I don't want to jump on the idiotic bandwagon of suggesting that sourdough is really difficult and you need to take it really, really seriously, and you're definitely going to fail if you don't follow every single step exactly. That's not right either. I don't take baking seriously. I'm no more talented than anybody else. I've just been shown a way once that clicked for me, and then I appeared on telly and found I was expected to teach people who certainly knew more than me. Then, I learned from them.

I'm still an amateur. If I have a skill, it's in talking to you as an equal, hopefully with enthusiasm and (very) occasional wit. This particular piece of work has been a joy, and is my way of paying back the people who have inspired me. This is how I have chosen to pass on our collective understanding.

So, instead of a promise, I will begin this book with a request: treat your loaves with respect. Sourdough, and the making of it, tends to attract personalities with a level of perfectionism, and each loaf baked is an attempt to improve on the last, with inevitable (if occasional) disappointment and eventual disenfranchisement.

You'll see beautiful loaves through these pages with magnificent aeration, scored with intricate patterns made by the bursting of the crusts as the loaf rises in the oven. It's okay if yours doesn't look like the ones shown here. Mine don't, mostly. These only look like this in a particular light from a particular angle, and you haven't seen the ones that didn't quite make it. And besides, a picture tells way less than half of the story: your first ever loaf might taste better than any of the ones we've made for this book.

Most important is that each loaf is yours. Each loaf is truly unique. Your yeast, or the magical blend of yeasts and bacteria and other things that we call your **sourdough starter**, has never been used by anyone else in the history of the world. It is yours. The flavours it creates are yours, and the breads it rises are yours. Pay your loaf, and yourself, the respect they deserve.

And if you're already past that, and you're an addicted, pedantic purist looking to drive out the imperfections in your perfect loaves? Well... well done. Let's do that, then. Just be sure not to skip anything.

GLHF.
(Good Luck; Have Fun.)

James

WHAT IS SOURDOUGH?

Flour, water and salt. Mixed, left and baked.
At its most basic, this is sourdough.

Sourdough, or sourdough bread (*pain au levain*), is what civilised Western man ate before the advent of commercial baker's yeast. Instead, the various wild yeasts and bacteria that rise the bread are cultured spontaneously. The vast majority of these come from the flour itself, where they sit in a dormant state.

The word *sourdough* can refer to the baked loaves of bread, but also to the sourdough starter (levain) – this is a dough of varying wetness that is kept by the baker as a continual fountain of yeast. This makes starting a new **fermentation** a simple and predictable process. Some call this a **mother dough**. And some people name theirs Boris and ask friends to look after it when they go on holiday.

These loaves, compared with ones made using a commercial yeast, usually take longer. Far longer. This has led to a wariness that hangs over even experienced bread makers – sourdough is seen as complicated, involved and with a high risk of failure. For some, this is a turn-off; for others, an allure.

Sourdoughs can usually be identified by the tang that gives them their name, but before then, by their anatomy. Note the smooth and shiny, golden **crust** speckled with tiny bubbles and with a magnificent tear where it has been scored. As you slice through them, you'll witness the **crumb**. This is the word for the pattern of the holes through the middle of your bread. Naturally leavened breads often have large, irregular holes that bounce back when pressed.

The word **sourdough** isn't a protected term. Like craft beer, gin and yoga, it has become an expression of one-upmanship among the hipster elite and something of a middle-class, sabbatical endeavour. It's trendy. It has therefore been jumped on by multinationals; a buzzword for selling upmarket lines at a vastly inflated price. Don't assume 'sourdough' means 'quality'.

A Manifesto

The subject is filled with jargon. I'm sorry. I'm bad for it, but I hope not as bad as some. It seems that the primary aim of sourdough recipe books is to further insulate an already nerdy community. In this one, if you're not getting things and it all seems a bit off-putting and complex, don't worry. I'm going to go through things from the most basic steps and build bit by bit. Everything will be repeated again and again and again, so that soon, the words that were unfamiliar won't be.

By building this understanding, my hope is that this guide can take someone who's either never made bread or only dabbled, and bestow an ability to make unbelievably good bread almost straight away. When you show people how to make bread in person, it works. I've been really quite annoyed when their first loaf is better than mine have been for weeks. Let's hope it translates to the page.

If you're already an experienced baker then, rest assured, this is not solely a beginner's guide. You might find my point of view useful, or you might not. If you find your way works better, great. But I hope you'll click with something. Here's to ironing out all the flaws that were bugging you, or that you didn't even know were there. Hopefully, we'll take your bread to the level you want it to be.

There may be many guides out there promising similar things, and indeed my methods are mere suggestions. There may be better ways of doing things, but I just don't know them yet. I hope you will come to trust me.

That's because I'm a home baker. This means all of the techniques and processes I'm outlining were crafted at home; and it means I'm free to admit my own mistakes because I don't have a product to sell except bound documentations of my own failure, cut with recipes. I've resisted every opportunity to go professional: I did that with another hobby, brewing, and it enveloped all the nice hours of my life in return for very little spiritual gain.

I continue to moonlight (full time and more) as a doctor. Because of this, I have the opportunity for down-to-earth, horizontally levelled conversations with lots of normal, non-media, non-professional-baker people about baking. Not just because I can relate to having to fit the baking of bread around a busy life, but because I think I'm as close to normal as people who write books about bread are.

> Work Colleague: *"Oh, I hear you're the bread man. I like making bread, too. I've got a sourdough starter. His name is Frank."*
> Me: *"Awesome. How's that going?"*
> Work Colleague (pursed lips, scowling forehead): *"Really well... (pause)... but I had to make three starters before I got one going. And then my first few loaves weren't great, but now they're much better. They're still super-sour, and they're a bit chewy and dense, but the crust is amazing."*

This recent conversation demonstrates the self-critical nature of the average sourdough baker. There's the irritation of having to make multiple starters – but the resilience to keep trying again; the acceptance of numerous issues and the desire to fix them. What stands out, though, is pride in the results and the delight at finding a kindred spirit (and the urge to talk about it).

A more common conversation is with the person who's tried to make sourdough once and the starter didn't work, or the loaf deflated or spread into a dense pancake. And then that's it. Time wasted, self-worth slightly dented. Move on.

This is the fault of people like me. Many guides, including my own, haven't been intuitive or exhausting. There are so many factors outside of our control, and I should have told you about them, and how to control them. Going forward, my aim is to aid as many people as possible to get it right from the off. I want to eliminate the uncertainty in something that is, by its very nature, unpredictable: **spontaneous fermentation**. This means the act of letting whatever yeast and bacteria happen to reside on the grain in the fields, in the combine harvester, in the hoppers, driers, grinders, chutes, bags, bowls, spoons, water and air, ferment away in their own unique way. This is the basis for sourdough.

I'll be concise, honest. (Concise for *me*.) Actually, I won't. Practical, then, rather than theoretical. I will, of course, explain the science behind things because I find it interesting, but understanding the science isn't necessary for making the best bread in the world. You'll have to skip past the bits that you don't like or when I go into more detail than you're interested in, and that's okay.

My Sourdough

If you don't know me, I'm James. This is my fifth book.

The first time I heard of sourdough was when I landed my first and only job in a bakery. Nineteen years old and during my first summer at university, I applied for a job in a pre-hipster Glasgow café, about five minutes by fixed-gear bike from my flat. The job was for waiting staff, and I didn't make the cut. The owner, though, was kind enough to note my experience in washing dishes and called me up, asking me to come for a trial shift as a kitchen porter.

I didn't nick anything, and so I was hired. Here, I spent my time with massive sinks of garlicky dishwater, scrubbing down trays and becoming intimate with the minutiae of the Brillo pad, scourer and sponge. I developed a passion for the Victorinox serrated knife and an immunity to onion-tears. This was the first time I listened to BBC Radio 6 Music in earnest and came to hate the Fleet Foxes.

The set-up was a large, stainless-steel food prep area, a washing-up area and a bakery area, with four deck ovens (stone-based bread ovens), shelves and shelves of trays and various fridges. I worked in my washing corner. David, the head baker, worked on bread in the bakery, and one of the many gigging chefs played with soups and fried arancini in the kitchen.

Occasionally I'd be allowed to make the soup, or David would let me weigh out dough into precise portions. He'd hand me the empty bucket in which the dough fermented, and then he would start shaping them. I liked David because he conscientiously removed all the dough he could from the bucket before handing it over for washing – others would toss the bucket at me with the contempt of what seemed like a full loaf's worth of dough spread across its entire surface.

The biggest perk was my exposure to sourdough. There were two massive white buckets kept under the shaping bench – one contained a rye-based starter and the other a white one. I remember the smell and the sting of the acid as I stuck my head in to take an ill-advised sniff. I was repulsed.

I resisted the lure. I baked my own bread at home, and felt my yeasted aspirations were well above this sour silliness. I sceptically stuck to my own recipes and humoured David with his evangelical affection for the sour. But like all who are forced into the constant company of someone who has true conviction, I could not help but be infected. From time to time I'd take the little loaves we made with leftover dough home to share with friends. I liked the sweetness, the chewiness and the soft acidity. I liked the story of the starter – this one was three years old and had never missed a day of feeding in its life. I started to look at who else made sourdough and, at that time, only two other bakeries in my city of over a million people were doing so.

I'd been a keen and poor bread baker until this point; baking bread at home was economical, and a good way for a student to forge lasting friendships. Washing dishes transformed my technique, because afterwards I borrowed David's copies of Richard Bertinet's *Dough* and *Crust*, and started making **high-hydration doughs** (those using lots of water) for the first time.

My first attempts at sourdough were lousy. Flat, dense. Always over- or under**proved** (rested, or fermented). For something that took so long, it seemed hard to hit the timings. My starter, propagated from the one at work, was fed with the religious regularity to which it had become accustomed in the café for the first few days, maybe weeks. Then I left it to fester as my enthusiasm waned. I'd try to revive it at infrequent intervals with varying success.

It took a long time for me to get it right. The step up was taking notice of the most important idea in Chad Robertson's *Tartine* book – baking in a cast-iron pot. Before I understood the art of shaping, this stopped my stupidly wet doughs from spreading pancake flat in the oven. Baking inside a pot also gave my breads a chance to rise in the presence of steam, and the deficiencies of my oven were balanced.

I baked two sourdough loaves for my audition for *The Great British Bake Off* – I picked the better of them and left the other at home for my brother and my then girlfriend (now wife) to pick at. It was round, scored with a 'cross' shape, with a few smaller secondary slashes around the border, and baked to a chestnut brown. I wrapped it in baking paper and took it with me on the five-hour train journey.

At the audition I sat opposite Faenia, who I'd soon come to know as Home Economist Supremo at *Bake Off*. She sliced my loaf straight down the middle in front of me. As the tightest of Scots, I'd been hoping to take most of it home to eat later, and I tried to hide my grief.

"Well, James, this is the best crumb I've seen all day."

I looked at my savaged loaf and nodded with humble acknowledgement. I had no idea what 'crumb' meant. The other bake I'd brought down, a cake made with home-brewed IPA and a spun sugar decoration, was fine. It was in a solid second place.

In the second week I became the first (and so far the only) person to complete a full sourdough within one of their stupid time restrictions. I was proud of myself, but that doesn't make the time restraints any less ridiculous. Bread should take time, and never be rushed.

Later, Paul Hollywood was prowling, and he wandered over and asked me to shape some left-over dough into a *boule*. I did so, and he smiled. Then he said shape for a *baton*, and I was confused because I'd already shaped it for a boule. My black-and-white mind thought it couldn't be re-shaped.

He brought his thick baker fists down hard onto the dough several times and said, "There, try now." I did, and we repeated it for a few more shapes, and then he showed me his way. I didn't like his demonstration – the smashing of the dough – but the feeling of the dough after he had re-shaped it was enough to pique my interest in *rheology*: the understanding of dough characteristics. While it would be years before I'd learn that term, I knew there were things I needed to discover.

Fast-forward 18 months and I'm on stage at the massive *Cake & Bake Show* in London in front of hundreds of people. I'd written a well-received book on bread. Standing next to me is the man who wrote the book that started it all – Richard Bertinet. I'm gatecrashing his stage.

I shamelessly plug my book over the microphone: "If you can't see what we're doing, my new book contains pages of detailed step-by-step photos." Richard looks at me, smiles and calmly states: "My book comes with a DVD." The audience applauds and I go red.

Back then I was doing shows in theatres, town halls and marquees across the country, teaching bread making. The big sell was 'no-knead' bread, and the way bread can be shaped around a busy life. There was a buzz around baking then – everyone was so enthusiastic to learn, and just so joyful at doing so. Now, I think there is a change.

People's aspirations and expectations are higher. A sense of competition can be quite nice, sometimes. But you don't need branded bakeware or the latest stand mixer.

Baking is awesome, and bread is a gift for you. It's for your families and your friends to enjoy. Becoming better at it is a personal journey. By all means, be proud and post your loaf on Instagram – but take pleasure in your closeness to it. You and the people you love are the ones who can taste it.

A Note on Heartache

Baking is supposed to be a calming escape from the mundane and the insane of everyday life. But it can be stressful, and nothing in baking (apart from filming for *The Great British Bake Off*) is as stressful as slowly watching the thing you've spent the last week crafting fail miserably. I've baked sourdough for about 10 years, and the countless times my own enthusiasm has been dented play on repeat in my head.

It's important not to shy away from this. To my publicists' and editors' dismay, I like to be honest. Your bread will work, eventually. And if it doesn't, don't worry. Even following every piece of information in this book, there's still a chance that things won't happen the way you want. It's not your fault.

The key is to march on, don't give up and don't make it personal. Be a scientist, if you will, and look back, examine each step individually and decipher anything that didn't feel right, or didn't match up. Re-read the recipe and then compare it with others and look for the consistencies. Then Google it. Then, if you're still not sure, get in touch and I'll try to help. I'm @bakingjames. If I don't get back to you for whatever reason, the lovely guys on thefreshloaf.com forum will help.

10 TENETS OF SOURDOUGH

If you're new to making bread, its vocabulary might cause some trepidation. Lots of stuff will be new. Keep reading: I've made a commitment to going over things again and again and again, and so I will. The following hundred pages will be dedicated to baking one loaf – **your best loaf.** In its production, there are lots and lots of processes, and lots of ways of doing each one. I'm going to touch on just a few of them now, to explain some of the more important principles.

If you already make bread, then use this to consider how your practice can be improved. Follow all of these rules with rigidity, and you will have amazing bread. World class. Light, massive bubbles, an amazing crust, a great rise in the oven, complex flavour and mega-Instagrammability.

Do I follow them all, all of the time? No, because I'm lazy. In these instances I still, for the most part, produce good bread, and occasionally bread that's very interesting. Perhaps, then, view the 10 tenets not as rules – they're more like guidelines.

THE BASIC PROCESS

1. A Very Active Starter

Creating a sourdough starter – the thing used to rise your bread – is easy once you know how. We'll cover that.

If the starter is misbehaving and simply will not rise your bread as it should, don't be sentimental. We'll fix it using science, or dump it because of science. Don't get hung up on keeping it alive if it is suffering. It's very simple to make a new one. And while some bakers will tell you a nice story about the aged nature of their starter, time actually bears no resemblance to quality.

A good starter should always be doubling or tripling in size when fed. If you're not baking bread every day or two (and that's most people), you should keep your starter in the fridge between uses. It can be used as soon as it's warmed up to room temperature again. If you have any doubts about its bubbliness, then you can take it out the night before you use it and give it a good feed.

2. Wetness

For massive bubbles and a soft, light texture, a wet dough is key. Soon after mixing the ingredients together, it is quite sticky, but will become more sup-ple over time. A wet dough means a dough of **high hydration**, where water makes up a higher propor-tion of your ingredients. This helps the dough stretch, and allows your bubbles to expand enough so that the dough holds together, but only just.

More importantly, though, you want a dough that is manageable for you. As you become more practised, thus more skilled, what is manageable will become wetter and wetter. The feedback I receive regarding the sourdough recipe in my first book is that the dough is ridiculously wet to the point of being a splodge that sticks to everything; a loaf that unfortunately ends up as something more akin to a pancake, with loads of bare flour folded through it from numerous unsticking attempts.

I was guilty of 'hydration-shaming' – my method suggested that people were somehow inferior bread makers if they couldn't handle a wet, wet dough.

I apologise to those whose relationship with sourdough was tarnished as a result. The truth is that the best bread is a bread that works.

3. Good Dough Strength

Gluten, the wonderful matrix of protein in flour that gives dough its gas-capturing abilities, is developed and sculpted through the stages of bread making. Gluten is often developed by kneading, but this is just one of the many ways, and it certainly isn't the only one we'll use. Sometimes kneading is recommended, but many times it's not. Kneading develops the structure of the gluten, but it doesn't necessarily develop it in the right way.

This property of being able to maintain a shape or structure without degrading is known as **strength**. You should notice your dough is **elastic**, or springy. Leave your dough to rest, and as the gluten slides over itself, it will lose its strength. You'll notice your dough is more **extensible**, or stretchy. If you've made your dough too stiff, with not enough water, or with lots of wholemeal flour, it will be overly **tenacious**, or firm. Every dough is a combination of **springy and stretchy and firm**, and the balance of these three together defines the strength of the dough. I'm geeky about this stuff, and if you want to be too, it's well worth getting into it (see page 76).

By developing good strength through a combina-tion of **mixing**, **stretching**, **folding** and **shaping**, you are avoiding that 'flop' sound you get when bread made from a wet, under-kneaded dough that's poorly shaped hits the work surface. Saying that, we don't want to over-work it either – the aim is a beautiful, open crumb and fantastic oven spring. Too much strength and you'll have a dense bread of small bubbles and thick, hard crust that doesn't rise much in the oven.

4. Think Temperature

Sourdough goes through the same **proving**, or rest-ing, stages as any bread. After you've weighed and mixed your ingredients, your finished loaf could be four hours away, or a day, or anything in between. This is your choice. The rests allow the yeasts within your

THE CIRCLE OF (SOURDOUGH) LIFE

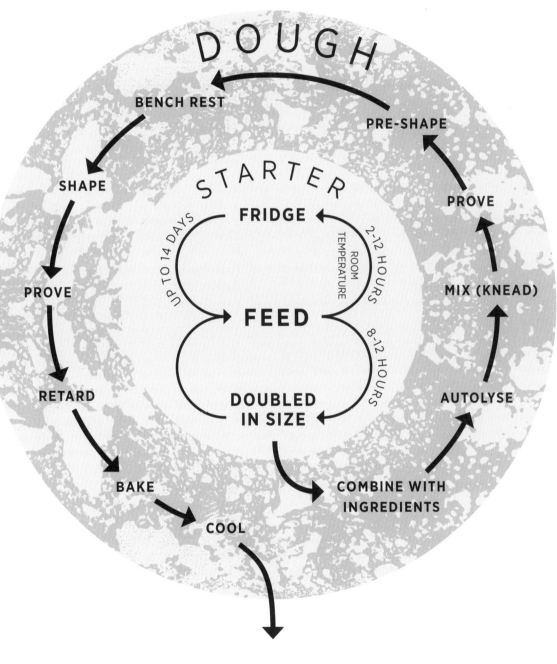

DOUGH

BENCH REST

PRE-SHAPE

SHAPE

PROVE

STARTER

FRIDGE

PROVE

UP TO 14 DAYS

2-12 HOURS
ROOM TEMPERATURE

MIX (KNEAD)

PROVE

FEED

8-12 HOURS

RETARD

DOUBLED IN SIZE

AUTOLYSE

BAKE

COMBINE WITH INGREDIENTS

COOL

BREAD

sourdough starter to produce carbon dioxide gas, which rises your dough.

On average, sourdough takes two to three times as long to prove as standard yeasted loaves. The first prove takes **three to six hours** at room temperature, depending on what your room temperature is. After you've shaped it, there's at least another **hour or three** of re-filling with bubbles. Despite being a very long process, it should take up only **half an hour of your time**. This means that a busy person can still churn out a lot of bread around a demanding job and family.

It's important to think about **temperature** and how much it is going to influence your dough. While in my first book I maintained that proving dough in a warm place (airing cupboard, or near a heater) was a bad thing, this is not the case for sourdough. My house is quite cold, so I use warm water and put it near a heater to ensure a decent prove. The rapidly expanding, tense bubbles are the architecture that provides your dough with great strength. Without this, your dough will need extra work to keep it together.

Alongside this, you will see the allure of **retarding** your dough in the fridge, overnight or longer. I often do this on the second prove, because this allows me to bake it whenever I feel like it. I'm in control. More importantly, retarding either prove helps develop a lot of flavour and leads to a softer, more irregular crumb.

5. A Gentle Touch

Between the proves, we use our hands to **shape**. In my last book, I advocated a very traditional, heavy-handed method of shaping, based on old British prejudices. Sourdough shaping and strengthening, however, requires a very light touch. Under no circumstances should one ever 'knock back' the dough, expelling all that precious gas.

If you hit that sweet spot and manage to keep all those big bubbles in there while creating a tight (bouncy) dough, it will appear to have layers of smooth sheets protecting it from sticking to anything. You're going to have bread that rises magnificently in the oven and a beautifully contrasting crust: between the smooth edge and rough '**ears**' where it has expanded.

If your dough doesn't have the strength to hold itself up, you can **pre-shape**, and indeed I recommend this extra step in nearly every recipe. This is an even more delicate shaping process done about half an hour before the main event, and can really help if you've had pancake-shaped loaves in the past.

6. A Shallow Score Releasing Tension

Once your bread has been shaped and it's ready to go into the oven, you should score it. You don't have to, but making a cut controls the way it is going to rise in the oven. If you don't score, you'll get random bursts and cracks all over the place.

The key with scoring is to keep it simple, especially when starting out. You just need to make one or two cuts, using something very sharp. And crucially, they need to be shallow, or you'll simply open a crevice that may or may not get filled as the bread rises in the oven. The angle at which you score matters less than people think.

You'll get the most amazing tears and rises in your dough if you score along the lines of tension: for example, in a long thin dough (like a baguette), you want to score in slashes down its length, as these cuts will open up magnificently in the oven. If you score using little horizontal cuts, none of them will open and you'll have a flatter, denser loaf. The key is always to cut in a place that will release the tension you've created.

7. Steam

The key to amazing **oven spring**, the rise of the bread in the oven, is steam. It's also the key to a golden, shiny crust that's deliciously crisp for the first day, and chewy in the days beyond that. When you bake your bread in the oven, you should find a way to introduce steam.

I used to advocate chucking a glass of water inside the oven, and I'm sorry for the fuses that have been blown as a result. I've since learned that the single best way of introducing steam is by baking your bread under cover – either inside a lidded cast-iron pot, or beneath a cloche or bread bell (a metal or ceramic dome). These trap the steam produced as the loaf bakes until the oven spring is complete, and then you can remove it to develop the crust.

Some shapes of bread don't fit inside a round pot, of course, and so baking on a flat stone or tray is necessary. In this case, I stick a cast-iron griddle pan to preheat on the oven floor and pour water into it as I slide my bread onto the rack above – just remember to remove the pan when you vent the oven if there is any water left in it, so no more steam is created.

Use what you have – I have some old Le Creuset cast-iron pots that my parents got as a wedding present, so that's what I use most often. The lid stays on for the first 20 minutes, and comes off for another 20 minutes to crisp up the crust. For a supremely even crust, I will often bake my bread straight on the oven shelf for a final 10 minutes.

8. A Routine

All of the best sourdough bakers I know rely on a routine: that of doing the same things over and over again. Gradually your technique is refined as you see what works and what doesn't, and we all develop our own path to a better loaf. This doesn't mean baking bread every single day, but it might mean baking bread once a week. Frequency is much less important than consistency. If you change something, make it one thing and measure it.

The need to feed a starter enforces this – if you're having to pour away a starter because you've got too much, think about baking a little more. The only issue with this is that it can become rather addictive. Neighbours, colleagues and family will always be very appreciative, though.

9. Ingredients, Not Equipment

When I wrote my first book in 2012, even big supermarkets didn't stock rye flour. Now my local shop stocks about eight varieties, as well as about 50 different sorts of wheat. Flour companies are one-upping each other by breeding new cereal strains and rediscovering ancient ones.

You can make the most of their hard work by experimenting with new sorts of bread. Some of these flours can be tricky to work with, but there's very little precedent for comparison. Yours are even more unique than before. You can get away with anything.

While great bread can (and should) be made with any flour, a special mention should go to the independent growers and millers out there producing amazing ingredients. Switching to well-sourced, stoneground, unbleached white flour will vastly improve your bread's flavour and texture, and using fresh flour will also make a massive difference to the health of your starter.

I'd also recommend trying some blends of ancient grains.

I'd rather spend money on posh flour than expensive equipment. Proving baskets, cast-iron cloches and electric mixers are awesome things, but they're not necessary. You can bake amazing bread with a bowl, your hands and an oven.

10. Every Loaf is Unique

It makes me very happy that no two loaves baked from a single recipe in this book will be the same. They're not designed to be. They might not look anything like the pictures. Don't worry about it. Your loaf will be *yours*. In truth, I've made a special effort for the loaves we photographed; I don't take quite the same care when not under a watchful, photographic eye. I have fun with the flours and the fermentation, as that aspect of the process interests me, but more often than not, I just bake to have something to eat, and that bread is invariably sourdough.

Hopefully, we'll manage to avoid any true disasters, but it's important to accept that you *are* going to bake loaves that you aren't particularly happy with. The better you get, the higher your standards become, and success is more likely. You'll have to adapt to conditions; learn from mistakes. Hopefully, they will still be delicious mistakes.

Keep going. Don't lose heart.

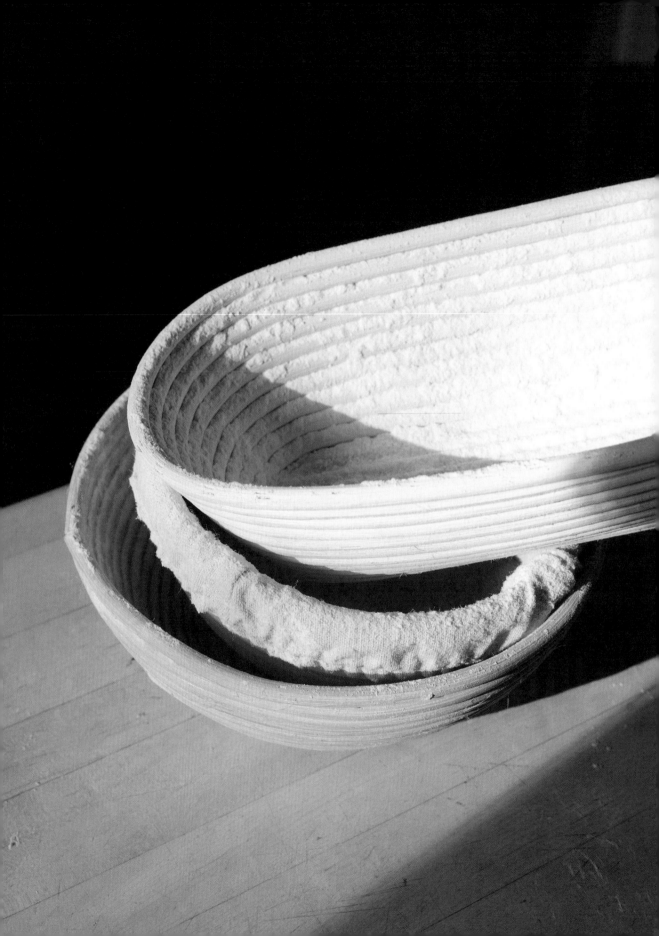

INGREDIENTS AND EQUIPMENT

I'll try to break up this chapter as much as I can, because this isn't just a simple list of all the things you must go out and buy in order to make great bread. I'll talk you through each ingredient and piece of equipment, and then we'll explore what they are and why you might want to get hold of some, or what the alternatives are. You can come back later to check details if you find this all a bit dense.

FLOUR

What is Flour?

Flour is an inclusive term: it can mean anything that is ground to a dry powder. Usually this means ground grains, but flour can be made from anything that has been suitably dried to the point that it can be ground up into something 'floury'.

Having said that, for the purposes of sourdough crafting, flour means any ground-up, gluten-containing cereal. Whether wheat, barley, spelt, rye or ancient related breeds, they all have a similar structure. I do appreciate that some people do whole PhDs on the anatomy of single grains, so I'm sorry if the simplicity of the following explanation offends you. The husks of these grains are the hard 'bran', and contained within is the white stuff that provides the energy and the building blocks for future life. This white stuff is made up of the tough 'germ', and the soft, starch-rich 'endosperm'.

After milling, or grinding, lots and lots of these individual grains together, you are left with **wholemeal flour**. This means that the whole meal is left in. Simple. And if it's wheat that's the cereal used, that's **wholewheat flour.**

Following this, most flour goes through a refining process of some kind; this makes it whiter. Refining the flour involves removing some of the bran and the germ. The simplest way of doing this is by using a sieve. Larger grades will remove just the big bits of bran and leave you with a flour that is somewhere between brown and white. Using a very fine sieve will not allow any of the brown stuff through, and you get something akin to white flour. Most white flours are then bleached to make them even whiter and accelerate their ageing process, leading to more consistent products.

The more of the bran and germ that is removed, the lower the 'extraction rate' of the flour. For example, a true wholemeal flour will have an extraction of 100%, as 100% of the grain has been extracted after the original milling. A really refined white flour has an extraction of about 70% – this means pretty much all of the bran and germ has been removed. Cheaper supermarket 'brown bread flour' is usually a mixture of white flour and some of the by-products of refining.

The reasons for refining are twofold: first, while flour is a store-cupboard product, bran tends to hold a lot of moisture, and therefore wholemeal flours tend to perish much more quickly than refined white flour. Secondly, there's the product and there's the consumer. While using whole grains gives a huge variety of flavour and texture, a bread made using only wholemeal flour is difficult to work with and inevitably dense. Then there's the fact that all-white bread is magical. And not just the baked loaf – the dough itself is a pleasure to handle.

While bran does contain moisture, it also absorbs a lot of additional moisture. Therefore, if you do use wholemeal flours in your breads, you should be adding significantly more water when formulating your recipes. I also like to do a long rest (called an **autolyse** – we'll come to this on page 79) when using more wholemeal flour, to give the bran time to soak up as much water as possible.

Gluten

Good bread is normally made with **strong flour**. This means it has more of certain proteins – two of these proteins, called glutenin and gliadin, form a complex, sponge-like matrix when tangled together. This matrix is **gluten**, the wonderful pantomime villain of the 'wellness' industry. If you understand gluten, you will understand bread.

Gluten is wonderful. It is the building block of bread. Making truly good gluten-free bread is difficult because the gluten provides a structure that can be manipulated into something that can then be shaped and moved without losing aeration – it has resilience. Indeed, as the initially random gluten structure is stretched and folded through the process of kneading, it becomes

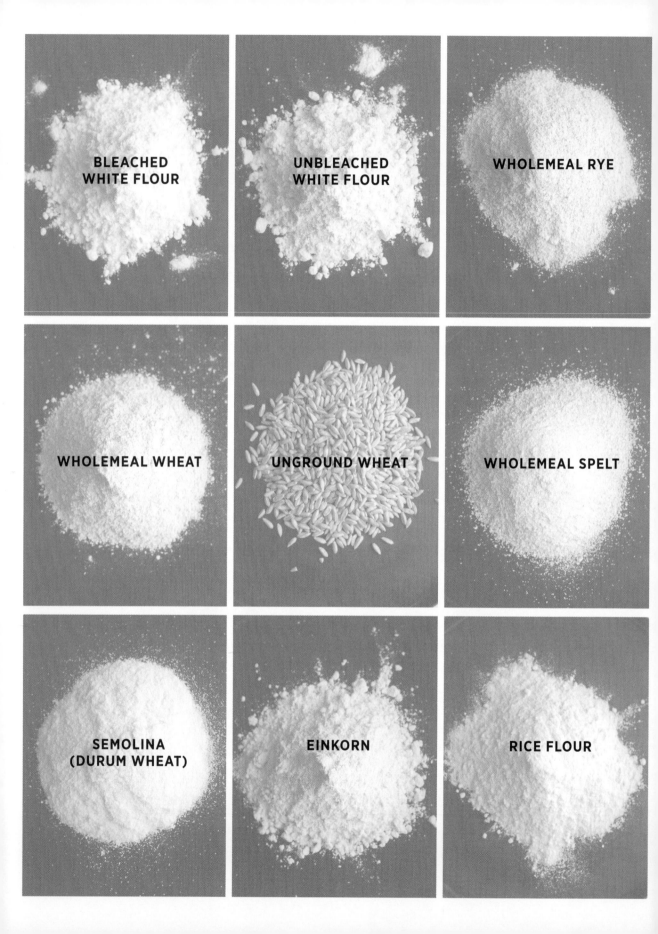

BLEACHED WHITE FLOUR

UNBLEACHED WHITE FLOUR

WHOLEMEAL RYE

WHOLEMEAL WHEAT

UNGROUND WHEAT

WHOLEMEAL SPELT

SEMOLINA (DURUM WHEAT)

EINKORN

RICE FLOUR

more organised, moving from a random sticky mess into thousands of overlapping, flexible sheets of protein.

As your yeasts munch away on the starch in the flour, they produce carbon dioxide gas. This gas would simply escape from the dough if it wasn't for the gluten – but instead it is captured by these organised sheets of protein and contained. The pressure from the gas further develops the structure of the dough and can aid in reinforcing its structure. Too much pressure, though, and the bonds that help form the gluten matrix collapse, leading to burst bubbles and a flat loaf. Put simply, strong flour means more gluten, and therefore more matrix.

The strength of a flour is determined by the grain, first and foremost. It is defined by its total **gluten-forming protein** content. For example, you might not think it, but wheat is stronger than rye. Wheat is also, despite having a lower total protein content, stronger than spelt. Within wheat, myriad factors affect flour strength, including species and growing conditions. Artisanal flour millers would argue (rightly so) that the pursuit of high-gluten flour might help you build wetter, easier-to-handle and more aerated doughs, but that in doing so, you sacrifice flavour.

Just as you make adjustments for extraction, you can make some adjustments depending on your flour strength – all the recipes later in the book are fairly standardised to (good) supermarket strong white flour, but if you're using a weaker local artisan flour, you'll need less water. This is both because the proteins absorb water, making the dough stiffer, and because the more gluten there is, the better the 'scaffolding' to support your bread.

Bugs

There's one more thing to think about when buying flour: the way it has been ground. There's roller-ground flour, and then there's stoneground flour. People who sell flour will only ever mention this if their flour is stoneground.

Stonegrinding flour is a labour of love – it's high-energy work using expensive or very traditional equipment. It produces a flour that is a little uneven, and is therefore most suited to producing whole-meal flours, where you're not having to worry about removing all of the bran and germ.

A roller mill is a precise and easily industrialised piece of equipment, and the only practical way of producing most of the wheat flour we use. The issue is that the rollers are made of metal, usually stainless steel, which conducts heat very well. As the grain is forced through the tiny gap between the rollers and crushed, this causes a lot of friction. Thus, heat.

This heat might have a bit of an effect on the essential nutrients in the flour, and indeed on the proteins, but what I care most about is the effect on something else found in the flour – **bugs**. Flour is full of micro-organisms, millions and millions of wild yeasts, bacteria and more. The variety and the quantity are both greatly reduced in roller-ground flour compared with stoneground. There's some, certainly, but sometimes not enough to get your sourdough starter going.

And that's important. The vast majority of bugs that ferment your bread come from the flour itself and, ultimately, the field in which it grew: the soil as it emerged from the ground, the wind, the gentle touch of other sheaves of wheat and the landings of innumerable insects. All of this contamination results in the bubbling mess in your kitchen that we call a sourdough starter.

I'm not going to rush into how these yeasts and bacteria interact to give us amazing bread. The important thing is that they do. There's a chapter on that coming up, page 91.

CEREALS

Wheat, or common wheat, is the third most widely cultivated grain in the world, after maize and rice. Wheat is wonderful. It doesn't just provide an enormous proportion of the world's nutrition, it forms the basis for nearly all of my recipes because it has been the backbone of the bread that has built the Western world.

While you can now buy white spelt and white rye flour, when I say 'white flour', I mean wheat. I love it. Some people have certain aversions to wheat and, if they aren't in the 1.5% of the population with a genuine medical reason to avoid it, they're probably listening too much to what other people are saying rather than their own body. There's a huge variety, and white flours range between 8% protein (sponge flour) to 16% protein (very strong Canadian-grown flour). Some are even fortified with further gluten to facilitate greater structure and easier handling.

Durum wheat is the species of wheat used to make **semolina.** Durum has a very hard endosperm, meaning that it is difficult and time consuming to mill it into flour. Semolina is therefore usually sold as coarse granules and is very useful for adding texture and acting as tiny, crispy ball bearings that stop your bread doughs sticking to surfaces, or to each other. If incorporated into a wet dough, or if you can get hold of **semolina flour** (re-milled semolina), then it can help provide some extra protein.

Spelt is a subtype of wheat. Its popularity has been driven by its nutty flavour, but also by the people who cling to the idea that it has been consistently cultivated for at least 7000 years, without significant genetic engineering during this time. Proponents of spelt argue that the natural goodness of wheat is somehow lost by breeding it, which is unproven in any kind of rigorous way. Either way, spelt is tasty, and so I use it. Spelt is high-protein, often more than 20%, but contains less gluten than wheat.

I use **rye** an awful lot – not alone, but to complement wheat. It has a deeply earthy, spicy and slightly astringent flavour that works well with the light flavour of wheat. It's difficult to make a 100% rye bread with good aeration, as it has a thick bran and a very low gluten content. When I wrote my first book, you could only find rye in some of the bigger and posher supermarkets – now I'm delighted to say it's a staple.

The above are the big ones. But you can find a selection of other flours available to play with, and I encourage experimentation. **Barley** is used to make beer, but you can use it equally well to make bread. In small quantities, it adds a nuttiness. Adding ground **malted barley** designed for brewing – or indeed any other malted grain – can rather speed up proving times and lead to a very golden crust, as the malting process involves leaving the picked grains to sprout before drying them, producing lots of enzymes that help to break down the starch into sugar.

Einkorn and **Khorasan** (Kamut) are a couple of the more commercially well known of the many varieties of ancient wheat available. **Buckwheat**, confusingly, isn't wheat – it's a dried seed from a rhubarb-like plant. It's good for making noodles, pasta and, of course, crêpes, but also for adding a little into your bread. Don't use too much, though – it's got bitter and acidic qualities.

Buckwheat, **dried potato flour**, **corn flour**, **rice flour** and **tapioca flour** make up the majority of the gluten-free lot. These flours are useful for dusting onto proving baskets or cloths to stop sticking. Personally, I don't make bread with them; that's why there are no gluten-free recipes in this book.

WATER

There's everything and nothing to say about water. Without water, your dough can't ferment, and your gluten can't form. Water is good. Sometimes it's a helpful endeavour, for the sake of simplicity, to set certain rules around water; for example, to always strive to use more of it ('wetter is better'). Or use water that is only cool to tepid, and never hot. Follow these rules if bread making is new to you or these are unfamiliar concepts, and your bread may improve. The truth is that these are only true up to a point and there are no rules except one: **use your tap**.

No matter how filthy your tap water is, no matter how hard, no matter how much it has been recycled through the digestive tracts of other human beings and no matter how many self-righteous blogs tell you to use bottled water – use your tap. Tap water is fine for making bread. How 'hard' your tap water is will affect the structure and the fermentation a bit, but not much. The traditional teaching is that hard water helps with yeast growth and fermentation and adds to dough strength – and this is correct. But it isn't something that can't be dealt with by waiting a little longer or giving your dough an extra fold. I can assure you there is not enough of a difference to require your giving much thought to it, presuming you are working at a sub-industrial scale, as most of us are.

If contamination of your water is an issue, this will not matter because the bread is going to be baked and any worrying bacteria will be dead. If the opposite is true and your water is very chlorine-heavy and sterile, equally, don't worry. Even when present in massive quantities, the only effect it might have is to slow down your fermentation, but I find that the bugs that thrive in my sourdough starter don't seem to mind too much.

Hydration

I've written and given innumerable talks where I've pronounced: "If there's only one thing you take away from today, make it this: wetter is better." In sourdough, I'm not sure this is wise. Now I say, "Use as much water as you are comfortable with." It doesn't quite have the same ring to it, admittedly.

We'll talk later on about the concept of **hydration**, or how wet your dough is, and the impact this has on your dough strength, but the important thing is that there's no point in struggling to shape a super-wet, batter-like dough, especially when you're starting out. It will inevitably end in frustration.

If it feels too wet to handle, that's okay – when you see the amazing results that you can get from really wet doughs, you'll want to persevere and take more risks, but if it's just sticking to everything, don't lose faith. It's fine to add a bit more flour or a bit less water next time.

Water Temperature

I mentioned the temperature of water briefly – you'll find that a lot of my recipes demand 'tepid-warm' water. This is an advancement on my previous bread book, which suggested 'tepid' water.

Tepid means water that is not warm and not cold; it has the chill eliminated from it. It is below body temperature – usually 18–22ºC (65–72ºF). The best test of tepid water is to stick your fingertips in your measured water, and if you can't tell whether it's hot or cold, it's tepid. This might be a strange thing to say, but you only need to try it once to feel the difference.

Tepid-warm means water that is a little warmer than this. It should feel as warm as putting your hand in a swimming pool or the bath, but still below body temperature: we're talking 25–30ºC (77–86ºF).

Of course, we can use water of any temperature to adjust the desired temperature of our dough. For example, if my flour has been stored in a cold place, I'll use properly warm water to bring my dough to a temperature just above room temperature, or about 25ºC (77ºF). If I want to kick-start a fermentation and get it going quickly because I've started late and want to bake my bread the same evening, I'll use warmer water still.

Increasing the temperature of your dough has some downsides. In commercially yeasted dough, your yeast can become a bit stressed and start to blow off flavours that aren't desirable. This smells like Hovis or Greggs. If you go higher again, into the high 30ºs (90ºs), you will begin to kill your yeast altogether. The bugs in sourdough seem a bit more resilient and off-flavours happens to a much lesser extent, but you will still lose some of the complexities of a long fermentation if you prove warm.

Going too cold, unsurprisingly, has the opposite effect – your yeast will lag and splutter into a slow growth when they get their feast of flour, and you'll have a very slow ferment. While this might give you excellent flavour and good sourness, your dough's strength will gradually fail and you'll be left with a dense, floppy dough that never fills its bubbles.

SALT

In bread, salt is first a flavour enhancer, as it is in all food, but its second effect is on the preservation of your dough. Salt preserves because it attracts water – this means that any troublesome bacteria or moulds nearby have less water in which to grow. This water-holding capacity also maintains moisture in the bread; a salt-free bread stales within a day.

Salt adds strength – in part because it competes with the flour in attracting water, but also because it strengthens the bonds between the proteins that make up the gluten. While this strength makes the dough a bit easier to handle, it can also lengthen mixing and proving times. The increased resistance of a stronger gluten matrix from the start lengthens the process of flattening out that gluten into nice sheets ready to be filled. This makes mixing harder and longer, and as a result many bakers choose to leave out the salt for the first part of the resting and even some of the kneading process.

For dough, use cheap salt. What we want in bread is something that is dissolved easily and quickly, and the cheap, small-granule industrial stuff is perfect for this. We want the sodium chloride and we don't want any of the impurities that allegedly give extra flavour in posh salt.

However, for scattering on top, use posh salt. It is the shape of the crystals in those expensive sea salts that is the primary driver of their pleasantness – the crystals are wide and flaky, with comparatively little salt to surface area, thus giving extra bursts of flavour without being too overpoweringly salty. Because we want our salt to be dissolved in dough, though, the shape is irrelevant. However, on focaccia or pretzels, use the expensive flakes.

SUGAR

I don't add sugar to any of my savoury bread doughs, and find the idea of adding it routinely to sourdough a little strange. Adding table sugar, or sucrose, is a cheat used by legendarily bad British bakers in order to obtain a golden crust in as little time as possible. In sourdough, the long fermentation and mix of organisms mean that lots of starch is broken down into sugar naturally. There's plenty to help caramelise our crusts and leave that sweet tang that helps sourdough taste so good.

You might think that adding sugar has a beneficial effect on the yeast, but it doesn't. The yeasts that predominate in sourdough can't metabolise it – meaning they can't grow and reproduce. The lesser yeasts (including baker's yeast) can, but there isn't nearly as much of this in your starter. It doesn't like switching between the sugars broken down from your flour and the sucrose.

Adding extra sugar therefore means that the majority does indeed remain as sugar, instead of being broken down into carbon dioxide and alcohol. This keeps your final bread very moist and it does remain sweet – so I make an exception for enriched doughs.

FAT

Adding oil, butter or other fat-containing ingredients will have a profound effect on the structure of your dough. Add too much or too early and they will make creating your gluten matrix an absolute pain – how oil lubricates a car engine is exactly how it lubricates between the protein molecules. Rather than getting an ever-expanding gluten matrix, you get an ever-sliding mass of fatty globules.

You can overcome this with lots of mixing, but it will take a fair while. Therefore, if you are adding lots of oil or butter to your dough, add it after the mixing is complete, or at least towards the end of it. As a general rule, if the weight of fat is less than 5% of the weight of flour, it can be added safely at the beginning. If it's above this, it's best to leave it until the end.

CHUNK AND BITS

The great thing about bread is the freedom for experimentation. Once you're happy with the basics, you can go one of two ways – the first is to get really, really into the science of it and absolutely perfect your crust, your scoring or crumb structure. The second is to go wild by customising your bread with various flavours – nuts, seeds, dried fruit, spices, herbs and so on.

I'm not going to try to give an extensive list of all the effects of every possible ingredient, because it will inevitably be inadequate; my suggestion is to look online. Let's instead look at the guiding principles that govern how and when you should incorporate additional flavours and textures.

The issue with extras is that they physically get in the way of the structure of the gluten. For larger ingredients such as dried fruit and nuts, this isn't so much a problem because the matrix holds them in suspense and expands around them. Incorporating these is pretty easy – add them all at once at the end of the kneading or mixing stage, or during your lamination (see page 56). If you add them right at the start, they do get in the way, impacting on the formation of those nice regular sheets of gluten.

Smaller ingredients, such as the more hardy herbs, whole spices and small seeds (like poppy seeds or sesame seeds) cause a bigger issue. Adding them too early in your bread making process prolongs the gluten development. Adding them too late means they won't be mixed in properly, or you'll remove any dissolved CO_2 in your dough in the mixing process. And these extras do rather get in the way, leading, inevitably, to slightly smaller, thicker bubbles compared to a dough without them.

If spices, ground or otherwise, are being used, you've got to think about the effect this is going to have on your dough structure as above, but also on your yeast. Some spices or flavours have suppressive effects, meaning that your yeast works much slower and you've got to prove your dough for longer. Cinnamon is the most common example of this.

Don't ask me how to incorporate softer fruits or vegetables without their breaking down into mush. There isn't a way without having an exceptionally wet dough. But most importantly, why would you want to? If you want a flavour, its almost always better added on top. Think of it like cheese: you wouldn't add fruit to it except to sell something novel to tourists. Instead, concentrate on making an awesome cheese, and if it pairs well with a certain fruit, serve it alongside.

EQUIPMENT

You don't need much kit to make bread. The items required for good, consistent sourdough make for a short list: an oven is a solid start, followed by a bowl, a set of electronic scales, something sharp with which to score the bread and a tea towel (dish towel). The only other thing you'll need is a surface to bake on, which could be anything from an oven tray to a heatproof pot. Most people have all of this in their kitchens already.

This wee section will go through each piece of equipment that you might want and some minimum requirements to look out for, along with a few entertaining musings, if you're lucky.

Oven

Ovens can be separated into a few categories: gas or electric, fan or conventional. Whichever you have doesn't matter, as great bread can be made in any oven. They all have their advantages and disadvantages.

I have two electric fan ovens within a range cooker. These are popular for their fantastically even heat distribution, but as the hot air passes over the bread, it dries it. A skin forms and, eventually, a crust; this often restricts the bread's oven spring and prevents proper caramelisation.

The ways to modify a fan oven for better bread are numerous – the best is to bake your bread inside a **cloche** or **pot** (see page 34). The next best is to use a **baking stone**. A granite slab will even out your heat distribution and help your loaves expand from the bottom up, but radically increase your preheating time. They can have truly transformative results: one friend had an oven with its heating element on its floor, which caused minor fires whenever fat dripped onto it and burnt his bases at the best of times. His bread and his entire baking repertoire changed for the better when he installed a granite slab on the bottom.

In fan ovens, you should preheat your baking stone for a good 40 minutes before baking. Then, when you slide your bread onto it, your oven will have relatively little work to do. Ideally, you want to turn your fan off, if you can. If you can't, like me, and your stone is at least 2cm (¾in) thick and properly preheated, then you can get away with turning your oven off completely for 5 minutes. Combined with the use of water to create some steam, you'll get fantastic oven spring.

In gas and conventional electric ovens, bread is still best baked in a pot, and second best is on a stone, but for a slightly different reason. Gas ovens are bottom-heated and notoriously variable in heat; up and down, and back to front. The stone regulates and evens this out. If baking over two levels using two surfaces, then you'll still want to swap your loaves over and turn them around half-way through for a completely even bake. Don't worry, the bread can take it.

If you're lucky enough to have an Aga or Rayburn, you can bake great bread by sliding it onto the floor of the hot oven. If you find that your bases burn too easily, then place a baking stone directly onto the floor of the oven.

Dough Scraper

Almost as essential as the oven, the dough scraper is a wonderful thing. You might have one already, or a selection. Some of you might have soft silicone things that resemble dough scrapers – these are rubbish. You want to stick to hard plastic, and if you can, have one that's stainless steel, too.

The latter is known as a 'Scotch scraper' and is good for dividing large batches of dough into individual portions and for scraping surfaces down after kneading or shaping.

The former – the plastic, mildly malleable but mostly rigid device – can be used for the above, but doesn't do quite as good a job. But if you're going to have one dough scraper, then make it a plastic one, simply for the sake of something that's multipurpose. It's excellent for scooping dough from one place to another, for kneading, and for scraping clean bowls, or scales, or your hands, for that matter – it's your tool to help you rule the bread making world.

Scales

My gran had a set of balancing scales with individual brass weights in pounds and ounces. It is pretty, but useless. It's very slow and it is not precise.

Get yourself some basic electronic scales. This isn't so that you can get your hydration (wetness) bang on – this doesn't matter much. It's so that you can get accurate salt levels; often in bread we sail quite close to the threshold of 'too salty' because we want the maximum flavour and strength possible. That means that even half a gram or one gram more in a loaf can taint it.

Standard electronic scales from the supermarket or your local homeware shop aren't that accurate, but they are good enough. They also tend to come with a fantastic warranty, so stick the receipt in the box and keep it – I find they often break within a year or two.

For salt I use scales I bought from a dubious supply store on eBay that measure to 0.01g. I hold my hands up and admit that this is another hipster indulgence. You don't need to be that exact.

Proving Basket

A basket is there to support your dough, to add a pretty pattern and to allow you to cover the dough and stop it drying out.

It isn't an essential, but it's very much recommended. The main reason is that a basket helps to regulate the structure of the dough – as your loaf rises, more gas forms in bubbles towards the top of the dough. When you bake the dough, the bubbles on top tend to expand more than the ones on the bottom. The proving basket means that your dough is flipped upside down just before baking, regulating the above phenomena.

Baskets aren't expensive, but you can make one out of a tea towel and a bowl if you're feeling tight. If you choose to invest in one, you'll hear a few names bandied about, such as **_brotform_** and **_banneton_**. To some, these are interchangeable (they're the respective German and French names for equivalent devices), but they can actually refer to different forms. To most of the English-speaking world, a _brotform_ is a spiral of cane or bamboo (or horrible fluorescent plastic) that's wound into a hemisphere or any number of oblong shapes. These don't tend to use a cloth liner, and so leave a nice spiral pattern of flour on top of your loaves. These are my _least_ favourite proving baskets because they are unforgiving: if your dough is lacking in strength or it's a bit wet, you'll find that they stick badly. As your dough expands into the many nooks of the basket, it becomes engrained. The thing that's taken you all day to make is ruined at the last minute.

The same does not apply if it is lined with a linen cloth, nor does it apply to my _favourite_ kind of proving basket – the **wood-fibre brotform.** These aren't as aesthetically pleasing or cheap as the wound-cane sort, but your bread never sticks, and they can give the same nice pattern.

Linen-lined wicker baskets or bannetons are arguably the prettiest but usually the most expensive option. The bread almost never sticks to the rough weave of the linen, so as you turn the basket to remove the dough, the weave just peels away, which is a very gentle movement. And they're super easy to clean – for those of us with a common-sense approach to cleaning, you can just bash the excess flour out after each use. For those of you with obsessive tendencies, you can remove the linen liner completely and wash it.

Any proving basket can be used with a linen liner, and the liners can be picked up for almost nothing. Therefore, if you're in doubt about what type of basket to buy, I'd suggest getting a couple

EQUIPMENT

PROVING BASKETS

PEEL

STEEL DOUGH SCRAPER

SCALES, PLASTIC DOUGH SCRAPER

of cane or wood-fibre baskets of different shapes, and some spare liners. Whilst pretty, the wicker baskets can't be used without the liners, and so this limits your options.

Couche

A couche is a heavy piece of linen distinct from a proving basket liner. It is used in a similar way to a proving basket in that it supports the sides of dough. It must be dusted heavily in flour. A couche is used primarily with baguettes and batons – these long cylinders of dough are lined up in parallel with a fold of floured material in between each, so they support each other as they prove. They work well for very wet doughs like ciabatta, too, but you've got to make sure they're properly coated in flour.

Thick, coarse linen is good because it has a tendency not to stick and its stiffness provides some support in itself, but you can create your own just by using any large piece of material – a heavy tea towel will also work.

Trays, Tins, Pots and Cloches

You'll need something to bake your bread on, or in. The ideal item for baking bread retains as much heat as possible, and then transfers this directly into your loaf, without burning it. Therefore, the baking tray is probably the worst object for the job because they're made to be as thin as possible so that they heat up quickly when placed in the oven and your biscuits or cookies don't end up with soggy bottoms.

The traditional baking surface is the stone, and it is one that I've used on and off for many years. The idea is to try to emulate the conditions of a traditional baker's oven; the stone absorbs a lot of heat, meaning that even through the opening and shutting of the oven door and the placing of a cold slab of dough on top, it stays hot. This surface transfers heat directly into the dough, giving an awesome base and good oven spring.

You can use a baking stone to even out the temperature in a temperamental oven, but it does takes ages to heat up. If you don't preheat for 40 minutes or more before using it, the sub-temperature stone will actually cool the dough compared to the rest of the oven, giving you a soggy, dense base.

A compromise, then, is what we call a 'Welsh' baking stone, which isn't a stone at all, but a large, thick piece of cast iron or steel. This does a similar job to the baking stone but heats up far more quickly. That means that when you pop your dough on top, the transfer of heat is far faster in turn because of metal's high conductivity.

A few Welsh-style baking stones are made with companion metal domes: this is where it gets interesting. These domes, or cloches, are amazing pieces of equipment. The bread is baked with the dome in place. As the bread is heated, it creates steam, and this means that you get a very moist environment surrounding your baking loaf. This moist environment inhibits the formation of a crust, giving your loaf a chance to rise magnificently. This moisture also helps to caramelise the sugars on the surface on the bread, giving you a properly shiny and crispy crust.

The idea is, again, to re-create the professional baker's oven, which has a steam injection system. However, you don't need to fork out for a new range of cookware to get baking. If you have a **cast-iron pot** or **Dutch oven**, it will do exactly the same job; Le Creuset or any knock-offs will do. Be wary, though, that temperatures over 220ºC (430ºF) will cause the outer enamel of your pots to darken.

Preheated, your loaf will take 20 minutes with the lid on and then 30 minutes with the lid off. I find you get a more even crust by splitting it 20-20-10; 20 minutes lid on, 20 minutes lid off, and then finish it directly on the oven shelf. Choosing **not to preheat the pot** is legitimate, and this is a technique you can use to further save energy and help bake multiple loaves in succession. I do find that oven spring and dough flavour is slightly better using a hot pot, though.

You'll see **ceramic cloches** advertised, and these do a good job. But not, in my experience, quite as good a job as the cast-iron ones or cast-iron pots, in terms of crust colour and oven spring. These are also fragile: you should preheat them in the oven, as placing a cold ceramic cloche in a hot oven can cause it to crack.

Some recipes will call for **loaf tins**. The majority of these can't be used in a pot because they don't fit. But if you do have a stone or a thick metal baking surface, you should still preheat your oven in the usual way and stick your tin on this. This helps stop the compressed 'concertina' effect at the bottom of tin-baked loaves. Make sure any old loaf tins you use are as thin as possible, so that the heat is conducted through them quickly for a good crust. If you do notice that the enclosed part of your loaf isn't quite as crusty as the rest of it, you can bash your loaf out of the tin when it has 10 minutes or so to go, and finish it off directly on your stone or tray.

Lames

Scoring bread is an art, and we will get onto that, but first, you'll need something with which to score it (see page 37). To begin with, your sharpest knife will have to do. If you're an obsessive Japanese knife enthusiast with razor-sharp blades, you need look no further, as these will be more than adequate. If not, serrated 'tomato knives' are a pretty good place to start, as they slice through the skin of a dough with minimal tug.

If you or a loved one shaves using a traditional safety razor with a double-sided blade, this is the perfect blade for scoring bread. You have to be careful, though. They do make excellent tools, but they are dangerous. I once left one lying around, wrapped loosely in its paper wrapping. My mother grabbed it thinking it was a scrap of paper, slicing into her palm and several fingers.

These razor blades can be transformed into safe(r) scoring devices known as a *lame* (it's French, pronounced like 'lamb'). This is a handle that holds your blade securely. It's worth picking one up, if not for the safety guard alone, but you can also make your own by curving your razor blade around a chopstick or skewer.

Peel

A peel is used to transfer dough from one place to another, and sometimes used to retrieve loaves from deep inside ovens. Traditionally, they have very long handles for reaching inside commercial or wood-fired ovens, and if you've any experience baking pizza outdoors, you'll probably know all about them.

You don't need a long-handled peel for baking bread in a home oven. But if you bake using a stone or hot metal surface, you will need something to transfer your dough onto for scoring, and then to use for sliding the dough into the oven and onto the hot stone. While there are a great many purpose-designed peels available for home use, they aren't necessary. And actively avoid a peel made of wood; you want them to be metal and as thin as possible, for sliding and scooping with minimal disruption to the dough. A **thin baking tray**, while not good for baking bread on, makes a great peel. This allows you to slide right underneath your dough without causing any trauma.

Whatever form your peel takes, it should be dusted with a little semolina, rather than flour. The roughly ground durum wheat acts like little ball bearings for sliding and gives you a very crispy crust.

Mixer

You definitely don't need an electric mixer, but it can be quite a nice thing to have, especially if you have a health condition that makes kneading difficult, or you're lazy. Lots of us have one sitting pretty without much use, so it's nice to be able to put it through its paces.

Mixers develop gluten through the use of a dough hook. The idea is that the twisting action of the hook winds the dough around and around itself, working it in a similar way to a commercial mixing machine or traditional baker's hands. Except most mixers do this job more slowly and poorly than your hands. If you try to counteract this by turning the speed right up, you'll find the hook can rip through your dough creating a lot of friction, a lot of heat and not much else.

I've used most sorts of mixers – from the cheapest supermarket own-brand, hand-held devices with a couple of spindly dough hooks, to massive commercial models. Avoid the former; thick doughs will eventually cause the hooks to shear with the force of kneading. The most common stand mixers – KitchenAid and Kenwood – are fine. They do the job well. But after mixing with all of them, I still like to get my hands in and do a few folds.

I've recently switched to a scaled-down commercial mixer called Teddy, which deserves a mention. It's made by a Danish company called Varimixer. The difference compared to other mixers is night and day, and it has converted me (on a day-to-day level) back to electric mixers after years of avoiding them.

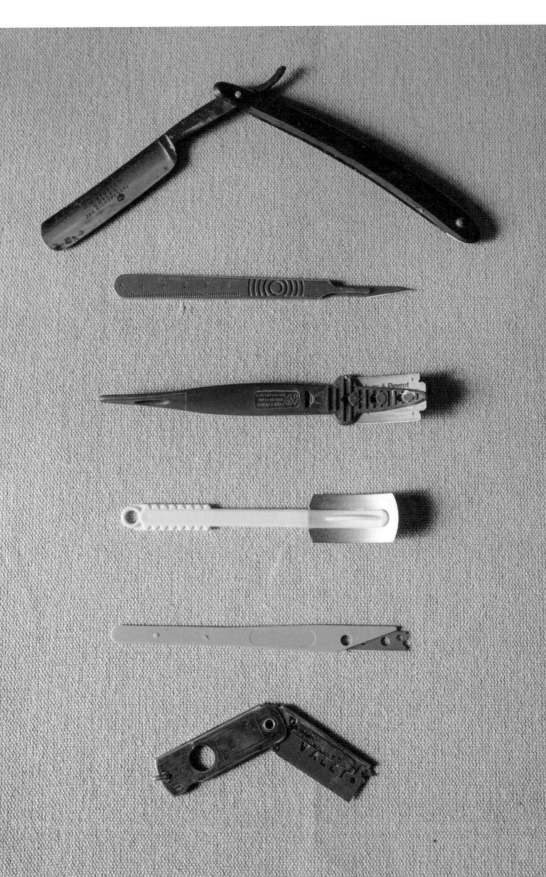

PAIN AU LEVAIN

Or, the longest and most important recipe you'll ever read.

THE PRINCIPLES

I'm about to outline the basic processes of bread making – again – but this time, I'll go into why they exist. Each step contains a very concise summary and then a detailed explanation of what it means, or how to do it. I've tried to be restrained. More detail will come later for those who crave it.

The following pages are dense, and some might say a little dry, but read them, and hopefully your loaves won't be. These steps will become naturally engrained in your mind; there are relatively few, and you'll go over the same ones every time you bake a new loaf. Soon you'll be a past master.

For the sake of detail, I'll talk about optional steps that you can take, and show a few different variations on certain techniques. This should allow you to pick and choose; these are all useful tools to have in your arsenal. You can figure out which ones you like, and I'll do my best to keep jargon to a minimum, but I'm afraid some is inevitable.

We'll start with basic starter starting and starter care – I'd strongly recommend that, if you have time and the interest, or if you've ever had any issues starting a starter before, read my detailed notes beginning on page 92. But this will get you going.

HOW TO START A RYE SOURDOUGH STARTER: CONCISE

FLOUR AND LIQUID

Mix about 100g rye flour and 100g fruit juice (pineapple, grapefruit, apple or orange) in a container and wait. If you don't have juice, just use water.

MIX AND WAIT

Mix daily for 5 days until it starts to become very aerated. Don't add more flour. Ignore any bubbles in the first couple of days.

FEED

When the aerated starter begins to contract, add equal weights of rye flour and water. Leave it for a final half day until it rises again. Now, move to the fridge and feed weekly.

You can't make sourdough without sourdough starter. This is the microbiological gift that rises and flavours your bread. The simplest way of starting one is getting one from someone else. But then it won't be yours. It won't be unique. Start one yourself, at least once.

This process takes about a week.

When you create your starter, you're reawakening the multitude of bacteria and yeast lying dormant within the grain. They start to break down the starch into sugars, which they then use to grow and multiply. The yeast works intimately with the bacteria to produce **carbon dioxide** (CO_2), which rises the bread, and some alcohol and some acid, which sours the bread. With these, there are loads of flavourful compounds – some desirable, and some less so.

I really wanted to suggest that you use only flour and water to make your sourdough starter, and 95% of the starters I've made using these two basic ingredients have turned out well. But if 1 in 20 people are disappointed with their starter after buying this book, I'll get a lot of angry messages. I've therefore been converted to using fruit juice instead of water, and we'll go into why overleaf.

HOW TO START A RYE SOURDOUGH STARTER: EXPLAINED

1
FLOUR AND LIQUID

Mix about 100g rye flour and 100g fruit juice (pineapple, grapefruit, apple or orange) in a container and wait. If you don't have juice, just use water.

Your choice of flour is crucial. For most consistent results, use good rye flour. **Organic, stoneground, wholemeal rye flour.** The majority of posh rye flours you'll find in the supermarket will fit the bill. Ideally, support someone local and independent who gets the flour straight from the miller, and who can assure you it is fresh.

Find a receptacle in which to store your starter. A Tupperware, a Kilner (Mason) jar, a sturdy drinking glass covered loosely with cling film (plastic wrap): anything. My humble favourite is the jam (jelly) jar – just make sure you leave the lid loose, or it might explode. It helps if your receptacle is glass or transparent plastic so that you can see what's going on.

There's no great need to weigh – the quantities of flour and liquid should be roughly equal. I'm deliberately vague here – it matters little the scale, and it matters less the exact ratio. For those who feel more comfortable with an exact quantity, follow the measures above.

I'm suggesting fruit juice because I've had more consistent results by doing it this way. The science is interesting – the acid in the juice suppresses some unwanted fermentations and so you've got a higher chance of culturing the right bugs first time. It's nothing to do with the sugar in the juice. In my own (albeit crude) experimentation, juice has been especially helpful when using cheap supermarket flour.

When mixed, stick a loose-fitting lid (or lay cling film) over your starter receptacle and leave it somewhere at about room temperature. 18–22ºC (65–72ºF) is perfect. If it's hotter, then things will happen faster, but don't stick it on a radiator or in the sunlight. If it's colder than 18ºC (65ºF) at home, you might need to add a day or two onto this entire process.

2

MIX AND WAIT

Mix daily for 5 days until it starts to become very aerated. Don't add more flour. Ignore any bubbles in the first couple of days.

After a day or so, give it a stir. You might notice a few bubbles. Ignore these. They're probably a little air incorporated from stirring. Don't add any more flour.

On day three, give it another stir. If you used water instead of juice, you might notice an exciting number of bubbles at this point, or this might take another day. Ignore these, too. **These bubbles are caused by an early bacterial fermentation that is no good for making bread with.** These are not the bugs you want to grow. Do not add more flour. Stir away the bubbles and then leave it.

Days three and four are generally the same. A few more bubbles, maybe, but the bubbles might stop altogether when the bacteria that caused them starts to falter as the starter becomes more and more sour. The mixture will appear wetter. Do not add any more flour or water. Continue to stir gently daily, or twice a day if you can be bothered.

On roughly the fifth or sixth day (but it might be anything from the fourth to the seventh) you'll notice a distinct rise in the number of bubbles and big jump in the volume of your starter. Now we're getting somewhere, and you can move to the next stage.

If you don't notice this increase after a full week has passed, or if your starter turns **black** or **pink** or **blue** or you notice a very strong, unpleasant smell, dump it and begin again. This doesn't usually happen if you use good flour. If you're really struggling, consult the starter troubleshooting guide later on (see page 101).

3

FEED

When the aerated starter begins to contract, add equal weights of rye flour and water. Leave it for a final half day until it rises again. Now, move to the fridge and feed weekly.

Feeding is the process of keeping your starter alive in perpetuity by adding more flour and water. Don't use juice again – tap water is fine. Your starter can be kept at room temperature, and in this case it will need to be fed every day or, as a maximum, every two days. If you keep your starter in the fridge, it should be fed weekly to keep it active, but it will easily survive several weeks between feeds.

Once your starter has made its big jump in volume, try not to feed it straight away. Let it get used to this new environment. Let the bugs grow. Feeding it with new flour at this stage will radically alter this new ecosystem. When you notice the walls of the bubbles begin to collapse or the volume start to diminish, that's when you can be confident that you've got as much yeast as you're going to and you can feed it.

Feed it with equal quantities of rye flour and water. Stir well. A few hours after, you'll notice some new bubbles. It will begin to rise again. Over the next 12 hours it will rise to at least double the size of where you started after adding the extra flour and water. Make sure there's plenty of space for this, or transfer to a more suitable jar or receptacle.

Your sourdough starter is now ready. As a rule, it should be fed in proportions similar to those aforementioned – the **new total weight** of starter should be at least **double** that prior to feeding. You can go as high as triple or quadruple comfortably. Much higher (for example, if you use all the starter and re-start it just from what's stuck to the sides) and you'll notice that your starter takes a long time to kick off its fermentation – it might take a couple of days at room temperature to get going properly again after this.

If you feed it only in small volumes, your starter will use the new flour in a short time, and will gradually become more and more acidic. To maintain good activity, you'd need to feed more regularly. Rather than pouring it away, save leftover starter and use in the recipes from page 238, or make bread more regularly.

A final note about storing in the fridge: when we use our cold starter, we let it warm up to room temperature first. This allows the yeast to acclimatise. When feeding, it also helps to do this at room temperature. It's then good practice to leave your starter out of the fridge for a few hours so that the fermentation can get underway. When you notice the first bubbles, you can safely stow it cold.

HOW TO MAKE BREAD:
CONCISE

If your sourdough starter seems in good health following the first feed, then you can use it to make great bread without any manipulation or delay. If it has been sitting about in the fridge for **anything over a week** without being fed, it's best to take it out, let it rise to room temperature and give it a good feed the night before you're planning on baking.

Some bakers formalise this process by feeding the required amount of starter in a separate container to create a *levain* (which is just French for sourdough). This misnomer of a pre-dough is made 6–14 hours before you mix your initial dough. Either making a separate levain or giving your starter a good feed the night before ensures that your starter bugs are extremely healthy prior to use.

INGREDIENTS FOR 2 LARGE LOAVES

900g strong white flour, plus extra for dusting
600g tepid-warm water
300g rye sourdough starter
20g table salt
semolina, for dusting

WEIGH

In a bowl sitting on top of your scales, weigh your flour, water and starter. Mix together and leave to rest for 30 minutes.

MIX

Add your salt. Knead your dough for 5–10 minutes, or until supple, stretchy and elastic.
If you don't want to or can't knead, instead you can do extra stretches and folds (see opposite) through the first prove.

FIRST PROVE (BULK PROVE)

Allow your dough to rest in a covered bowl in a warm place for about 4 hours, or until increased by at least 50% in size. This can be extended, after a couple of hours, by placing the dough in the fridge for up to 1 day.

STRETCH, FOLD AND LAMINATION

Increase strength by stretching and folding your dough within its bowl once or twice during the first prove. Alternatively, avoid kneading altogether by carrying this out four or more times during the first *prove.*

SPLIT, PRE-SHAPE AND SHAPE

Turn your dough out onto an unfloured surface and split it into your desired number of loaves (two in this instance) using a scraper. Pre-shape into rough balls and leave them to rest for 20–30 minutes. Form into your final shape and place each loaf in a floured proving basket.

SECOND PROVE

Rest your dough for a further 2–3 hours. Alternatively, you can prove for 1–2 hours at room temperature and then 8–12 hours in the fridge.

SCORE

Turn your dough out onto a semolina-dusted peel (tray) and score using a very sharp knife, razor blade or lame.

BAKE

Bake each loaf in a very hot preheated oven by sliding into a pot, cloche or Dutch oven, or onto a baking stone. Add steam or bake with the lid or cloche on for 20 minutes before removing the lid and baking for another 20–30 minutes.

COOL

Place your loaf on a cooling rack or wooden board. Allow to cool to just-warm before slicing.

HOW TO MAKE BREAD: EXPLAINED

1

WEIGH

In a bowl sitting on top of your scales, weigh your flour, starter and water.
Mix together and leave to rest for 30 minutes.

The first step is to weigh your ingredients. Our demonstration dough quantities make **two large loaves** of a *pain de campagne* (country loaf) style. I pop a bowl onto my electronic scales, weigh my flour, zero it, weigh my water, zero it, and finally I weigh out my starter. I usually feed the remainder of my starter at this point, too, so I don't forget to replenish what I've taken from it.

The quantities above mean that, in total, you have 1050g flour, and 750g water, including the quantities contributed by the sourdough starter. Because 750 divided by 1050 is 0.714, this formula gives a dough of just over 71% hydration.

That is pretty dry by most standards, and even more so compared to a white loaf, as the bran of the rye absorbs quite a bit of water. However, this means it should be manageable. As you progress, you can increase the hydration gradually to 75%, or perhaps a bit more. How wet a dough feels will vary based on what flour you're using, so if you think you need to add a little more flour, then that's fine.

I'll use any number of implements – often my right hand, often a wooden spoon, often a dough hook that's going to get dirty soon anyway – to roughly mix the ingredients together. This is less kneading, more amalgamating into something resembling a very sticky dough.

Next, a rest. Just a short one. Known as an **autolyse**, this rest is something we'll get more into later because it makes some bakers very excited. This really increases the stretchability (or extensibility) of your dough, and shortens the time it takes for it to come together. The effect of this rest appears to be rather heightened if you leave the salt out, so that's what we do. Give it 30 minutes, or up to an hour if you can, covered with a damp tea towel.

2

MIX

Add your salt. Knead your dough for 5–10 minutes, or until supple, stretchy and elastic.
If you don't want to or can't knead, instead you can do extra stretches and folds (see below)
through the first prove.

First things first: don't forget to add the salt. This is probably the most common mistake at this point, and it is often not realised until the loaf is baked. To avoid this, I leave my salt next to my mixing bowl to remind me.

Great sourdough can be made without any kneading; however, I will say that it's fun and enlightening and good for the bread if you do get your hands dirty and give your dough a slap around. At this stage, you can use your electric mixer – if you do, give your ingredients about 6 minutes on the slowest speed, and then 4 minutes at speed setting '2'. For the most common mixer brands, these numbers equate.

If you don't have a mixer and can't (or can't be bothered to) work the dough, see pages 55–6 for the **stretch and fold** method during the first prove. Personally, I'd recommend you stretch and fold anyway, even if just once or twice, but completely replacing the need to knead is a very popular method for building strength in your dough.

If you are kneading by hand, you can do it a couple of ways. The first is my old chum, the **slap and fold**. This is now often referred to as the **Bertinet method** after legendary baker and top bloke Richard Bertinet; it's an old French method of kneading that allows you to handle really sticky doughs, as most in this book are. The second method is a variation on a traditional **English knead**. This works a little less well with wet doughs, but if you keep the dough moving, it won't stick too much. Both methods require a dough scraper.

There's one important rule of kneading, or stretching and folding. **Never, ever add flour**, unless you realise you've made a mistake with your quantities. Adding flour makes the dough drier and the final bread tougher. When flour is added later in the knead, it isn't fully hydrated, and so this interrupts your gluten network and reduces the stretchiness of your dough. This is bad. If your dough is sticking to everything, that's okay. Just use your scraper to scrape it all back together into a lump.

You know you're done kneading when your dough has changed from being a sticky, lumpy mess to something that is very smooth, supple and a little bit rubbery. We'll go into dough properties later on, but a handy thing to know is the **windowpane test.** This is when you take a pinch of dough and stretch out four corners. If it forms a smooth, translucent window, there's plenty of gluten development. This indicates a very well-developed dough that may not require any stretching and folding.

Following kneading, scrape your dough and any straggly bits back into your bowl. The dirty bowl from mixing is fine. Cover with a damp cloth, or a piece of cling film (plastic wrap), or a plastic supermarket bag. This is just to stop the surface drying out too much.

To clear your hands of dough, grab a bit of flour, rub it between your fingers and then rub all over your hands. The dough will flake off, then your hands can be washed clean more easily.

KNEADING: THE SLAP AND FOLD

1. SCRAPE YOUR DOUGH OUT OF YOUR BOWL ONTO AN UNFLOURED SURFACE

2. SLIDE YOUR FINGERS UNDERNEATH THE DOUGH

3. LIFT THE DOUGH IN THE AIR

4. TURN IT OVER AND SLAP IT DOWN

5. GRAB THE END THAT'S FACING TOWARDS YOU

6. STRETCH IT TOWARDS YOU AND FOLD IT OVER

7. TURN THE DOUGH AROUND A QUARTER
TURN AND REPEAT

8. USE YOUR SCRAPER TO INCORPORATE ANY EXCESS

KNEADING: THE ENGLISH KNEAD

1. TURN YOUR DOUGH ONTO AN UNFLOURED SURFACE

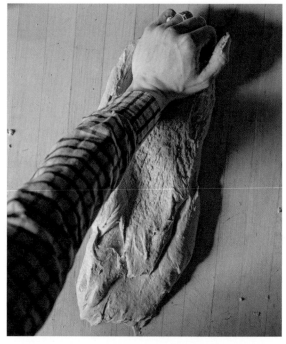

2. STRETCH THE DOUGH AWAY FROM YOU

3. USE THE SAME HAND TO SCOOP AND ROLL THE DOUGH TOWARDS YOU

4. REPEAT, OCCASIONALLY TURNING THE DOUGH 90 DEGREES

3

FIRST PROVE (BULK PROVE)

Allow your dough to rest in a covered bowl in a warm place for about 4 hours, or until increased by at least 50% in size. This can be extended, after a couple of hours, by placing the dough in the fridge for up to 1 day.

It is likely that the recipe on the back of your flour packet does not recommend proving your dough twice. But I do, and so does every other sourdough baker. The first rest, or prove, following kneading and before shaping, is absolutely necessary for reasons including, but not limited, to the following:

– It gives a great, golden crust. The extra time proving prior to shaping allows the bacteria and yeast to break down more starch into sugar, giving a sweeter, softer inside, or **crumb.** And this means that there are more sugars at the edge, too, so more to caramelise on the crust when the bread is baked.

– It makes the bread taste awesome. The yeast and bacteria, and a huge number of other bacteria and yeast that live in symbiosis with their domineering cousins, all produce certain flavours – so give them a chance to.

– It develops the gluten. This is the primary reason for giving your bread a chance to prove twice. Kneading will develop the gluten into nice linear sheets, but those sheets need to fill with the carbon dioxide produced from your yeast. These bubbles tighten the gluten and give it structure, as well as passing it over its neighbouring strands and further improving the immense matrix.

– It gives you an open structure. A good, long first prove is crucial for achieving a really nice, aerated crumb: the signature of sourdough. This is why when we shape our bread, we do it very gently indeed, so as not to destroy the bubbles we've created following the first prove. The preservation of these, with the added strength of shaping, allows them to grow rather large.

How long the first prove will be is usually determined by the temperature. A good rule is to prove it at a warmer-than-room temperature of 25ºC (77ºF) or so, for 3–4 hours. The traditional teaching is that it should double in volume, but this is a very difficult measurement to make, especially if you're stretching and folding as below. And if you're waiting for a dense wholemeal or rye dough to double, you'll be waiting all day. An increase in size of roughly 50% is more than adequate for most loaves.

The great thing about bread, though, is the malleability of the process, meaning you can make it as and when to suit your lifestyle. Say, for example, you want to extend that 3–4 hour prove, as you're out at some sort of social engagement for 6–7 hours; no problem, as you can mix your dough with cold water instead of warm to delay (retard) your fermentation.

Bakeries use large **retarders** to delay their fermentations; these are expensive, many-shelved fridges. You can use your own fridge, and doing so will have a tremendous effect on the flavour of your bread. I heartily recommend it. It's a good idea to give your dough an hour or two of proving at room temperature before sticking it in there, so that it's at least starting to inflate, and if you do this during the first prove, it will extend the length of your second prove quite a bit. Otherwise, if it's cold outside and you've got somewhere that's down to about 10–12ºC (50–54ºF) – for example, near a window in a Scottish winter – then you could safely leave a dough overnight there.

4

STRETCH, FOLD AND LAMINATION

Increase strength by stretching and folding your dough within its bowl once or twice during the first prove. Alternatively, avoid kneading altogether by carrying this out four or more times during the first prove.

If you can't or won't knead, or despite kneading your dough is flopping about all over the place, there could be one of several things going on. The most likely is that your starter isn't active enough – get it healthier or use a levain. But the other option is that your dough doesn't have enough **strength**. Strength is gained by developing gluten and then shaping it into the right arrangement.

The essential tool in upping your dough strength is stretching and folding (see opposite). This is such a big deal that most bread books now don't even mention kneading or mixing at all, because this method works so well on its own. I'm often asked how to stop a dough from splatting everywhere following its second prove, and the answer is almost always a few stretches and folds through the first prove. This is especially true if it has been proved cool or cold, as the lack of activity will make your dough weaker.

If you choose to rely on the stretch and fold as your sole method of kneading, then you've got to be around. By that I mean in the house, rather than carrying a bowl around with you and constantly thinking about when it might need another stretch. Personally, I like to mix and forget. Then, if I'm passing through the kitchen, the dough might get a quick fondle. But you should do whatever suits – almost all of my doughs are a hybrid of an initial development with a few stretches and folds through their first prove to enhance strength.

You can take the dough out of the bowl and give it a really good stretch on your work surface, and this will be more effective, but that gets everything (including both hands) dirty. One particularly effective variant is the **lamination method**. If you're struggling with the technique or despite stretching and folding, your dough still flops everywhere, try this approach (see page 56). Whichever you choose, try not to add any additional dry flour, as this will interrupt the structure we're trying to create.

Stretching and folding can make it a bit less obvious when your dough is done and ready for shaping, because by repeatedly folding you'll have rid the dough of some of its gas bubbles. A dough that is ready should feel aerated and bubbly regardless of whether it's been handled. Don't worry – you'll get a feel for it. Rely on arbitrary timings if you're unsure.

STRETCH AND FOLD

1. WET YOUR FINGERS WITH A LITTLE WATER AND GRAB THE EDGE OF THE DOUGH

2. STRETCH IT TOWARDS YOU, BUT NOT ENOUGH SO THAT IT TEARS

3. GENTLY FOLD IT TO THE OTHER SIDE OF THE DOUGH

4. TURN THE BOWL AND REPEAT, WETTING YOUR FINGERS IF THEY STICK

LAMINATION

1. ON A DAMP SURFACE, STRETCH YOUR DOUGH INTO A BIG RECTANGLE

2. EVENLY SCATTER ANY FILLINGS OVER THE DOUGH

3. FOLD IT OVER LIKE A LETTER, SO THAT IT IS A THIRD OF THE ORIGINAL SIZE

4. ROLL YOUR NEW RECTANGLE UP SO THAT IT FITS BACK IN YOUR BOWL

5

SPLIT, PRE-SHAPE AND SHAPE

Turn your dough out onto an unfloured surface and split it into your desired number of loaves (two in this instance) using a scraper. Pre-shape into rough balls and leave them for 20–30 minutes. Form into your final shape and place each loaf in a floured proving basket.

The importance of shaping bread cannot be understated, and it is the most difficult and most technical aspect of bread making to learn. In short, it's annoying.

The problem is this. If you decide to simply chop your proved dough into lengths and roll them into sausage shapes before baking, you won't get something that resembles a baguette (and you'll probably end up with a sticky mess over your hands). If you stick it in a loaf tin without shaping, you'll get bread that's welded into the corners of the tin and with a poor, limp crust. Bake a badly shaped loaf on a baking stone and some bits might burst open, but others will be dense. The crust will be shoddy. And that's if you can even get it out of whatever you've proved it in.

Shaping is important. In sourdough, we often shape in two stages. First, there's the splitting of the dough into however many loaves you're making and **pre-shaping** it – this makes your dough strong. This has to be followed by another rest, preferably of at least 20–30 minutes, to allow your gluten to relax enough to let you shape it again.

Second, there's the final shaping into whichever shape you want your loaf to be. This controls how it rises in the oven and dictates how you're going to score the loaf. If you want those beautiful tears in the surface of your bread, it's got more to do with the shaping than the scoring. I'll take you through the various shapes with some step-by-steps on pages 60–3. Recipes that require specific shaping techniques – such as baguettes – will be shown separately.

Shaping sourdough is a little different from shaping conventional yeasted breads. It requires more care – you want to be gentle. If it feels like you're having to force your bread into a certain shape, don't. Gently roll and pull until it goes as tight as it wants to, and that's it. And shaping, like kneading, should be done with as little added flour as possible. Splitting and pre-shaping should be done with none, ideally. Anything added now will only interrupt your final structure.

SPLITTING AND PRE-SHAPING

1. USE A SCRAPER TO DIVIDE THE DOUGH INTO YOUR REQUIRED NUMBER OF LOAVES

2. WEDGE YOUR DOUGH SCRAPER UNDERNEATH A PIECE OF DOUGH

3. DRIVE YOUR SCRAPER FORWARDS SO THAT THE DOUGH CATCHES AND CURLS UNDERNEATH

4. TURN YOUR SCRAPER 90 DEGREES AROUND YOUR DOUGH AND REPEAT UNTIL SMOOTH

SHAPING A BOULE

1. SCOOP YOUR DOUGH ONTO A FLOURED SURFACE, SMOOTH-SIDE DOWN

2. STRETCH ONE EDGE OF THE DOUGH TOWARDS YOU

3. FOLD IT INTO THE CENTRE

4. WORK YOUR WAY AROUND THE DOUGH, REPEATING THIS

5. STOP WHEN IT FEELS TAUT AND BOUNCY

6. FLIP YOUR DOUGH OVER

7. SCOOP CURVED HANDS UNDER THE DOUGH, MOVING
ONE FORWARDS AND ONE BACKWARDS

8. REPEAT 3–4 TIMES, UNTIL
TIGHT AND SMOOTH

SHAPING A BATARD (OR FOR LOAF TINS)

1. SCOOP YOUR DOUGH ONTO A FLOURED SURFACE, SMOOTH-SIDE DOWN

2. STRETCH THE TWO SIDES OF THE DOUGH AWAY FROM EACH OTHER

3. FOLD THEM OVER EACH OTHER IN THE MIDDLE

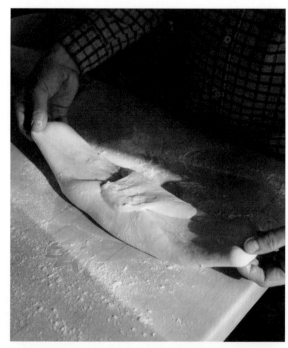

4. TURN THE DOUGH BY 90 DEGREES AND REPEAT

5. NOW DO THE SAME WITH TWO CORNERS

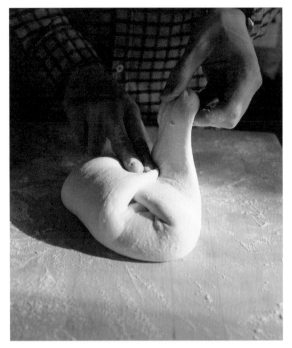

6. IT SHOULD FEEL VERY TIGHT

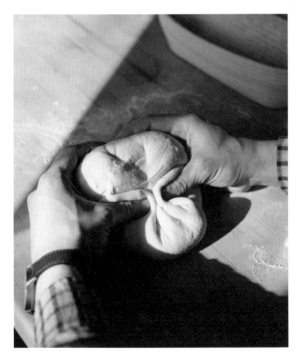

7. FROM ANY ANGLE, ROLL THE DOUGH TOWARDS
YOU LIKE A SWISS (JELLY) ROLL

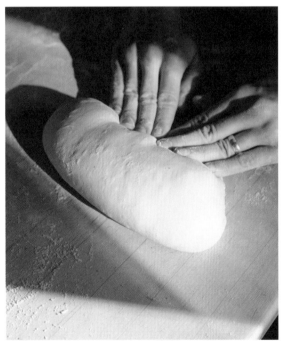

8. PRESS DOWN AT THE SEAM TO SEAL

6

SECOND PROVE

Rest your dough for a further 2–3 hours. Alternatively, you can prove for 1–2 hours at room temperature and then 8–12 hours in the fridge.

The second prove isn't required in every bread. Pizzas and flatbreads, for example, often miss it out, because they rely on the striking heat of the oven and any residual gas to aerate them. But in most breads, this stage is required for lightness and consistency of structure.

The second prove is often shorter – as a rule, half to two thirds of the time. Therefore, I'd suggest proving these loaves for **2 hours** at room temperature. Be wary of this rest – it's a little more sensitive. If your bread becomes overproved during the first, it's no big deal: shape it and prove it again. If your bread is left for too long at this stage, you get very fragile, overinflated bubbles that will burst, if not with the slightest of touches then inevitably as your loaf is slid into the oven. This leads to a denser, stodgier loaf.

Because **bread can be baked just as well straight from the fridge**, retarding this prove allows you to control rather precisely when your bread goes in the oven, as well as adding loads of flavour and further enhancing those big beautiful bubbles. Using the fridge is convenient. Don't have time to finish your sourdough off tonight? No problem – stick it in the fridge and forget about it overnight. Don't have the oven space to bake two at a time? Stick one in the fridge 45 minutes before they'd be ready and bake them back to back.

If you decide to fridge, do consider the time it takes for the dough to cool down. It will take a while for the cold to penetrate the centre of the dough. In fact, much of your dough probably has up to 1 hour's close-to-room-temperature proving **after** being placed in the fridge. Thinner loaves cool quicker. And once it is cool, activity doesn't cease: proving in the fridge overnight is roughly equivalent to an extra hour of room-temperature proving. Therefore, if you tuck the dough in the fridge for the night after more than an hour into the second prove, expect a slightly overproved loaf in the morning.

If you're making a loaf in a loaf tin of any sort, the second prove is carried out within the tin itself. This can give it, especially if it's very wet or shaping has been a trial, ample chance to weld itself to your tin. Always heavily grease a loaf tin, right to the corners. Use butter, or some other hard fat. Do not use oil.

If your loaves are to be hand-finished, it's best to prove your dough in a **proving basket.** As discussed earlier, this is a wonderful device that supports the structure of your dough and allows you to slide it into or onto a preheated surface. I cover it in a plastic bag to stop the surface drying out; if the exposed dough is allowed to dry, you'll get a thicker, less tasty quality to the base.

So how do we know when the second prove is done?

You can test a dough's doneness by pressing on it and assessing whether your finger leaves an indentation. If it springs back with no indentation, then it's underproved; if it springs some of the way back but leaves a bit of a mark, it should be fine. And if it leaves a finger-shaped divot in your dough, it's probably overdone. The critical among you might note the number of variables and vagaries, and you'd be right. It isn't the best test.

The decision to end a prove can be a difficult one, and proficiency will come with time and experience. If you've left your bread overnight and you've only got a rushed morning before work, then you'll be at the mercy of when you can bake it, and this is fine. Let it dictate how things are going to go, and if in doubt, do what feels right. The bread will be different from the bread before and you will have learned from it.

7

SCORE

Turn your dough onto a semolina-dusted peel (tray) and score using a razor blade or lame.

Whenever *you* think the second prove is done, it's time to score. First, though, you need to turn your loaf out of your proving basket. Because we're making so few loaves at a time, we can turn our dough straight onto a peel, or whatever substitute we are using to slide our bread onto our baking surface, or into our pot. Make sure this is well dusted with semolina, and flour can be substituted if you don't have any. If you're baking inside a pot from cold, you can turn your loaf straight out into the pot for scoring.

If your loaf is stuck to the basket, lift it a few centimetres above your tray. Be patient – your loaf will slowly unstick itself. If it was stuck, it's probably about to flop into a large pancake, because loaves usually stick when they're lacking a little in strength. Next time, stretch and fold a few more times, shape a bit tighter or use more flour on your basket. Or all three.

Anyway, I hope you used lots of semolina. Once it's out, give your tray a wiggle back and forth to give the base an even coating and make sure it isn't stuck.

Use a knife, razor blade or lame to score the bread. How you score it will dictate how it rises: your bread will rise in the oven perpendicular to your scores. This can be a hard concept to explain, but the first time you see it, you'll get it. It means that, for example, if you've made a loaf that's perfectly round and you give it one almighty score, your bread will *widen perpendicular to this score in the oven*. This means that a round dough with one score (or several parallel scores) ends up as an oval-shaped loaf.

If you want to keep its round shape, you could score with a perfect cross or '+' sign; this means your loaf will open up preferentially on the top of the bread. Or if you score with overlapping lines creating a square, you'll get an even rise all the way across its surface.

You'll figure it out. When scoring, less is more. If you want a beautiful, rustic gash (called an 'ear') contrasting with totally smooth sides, one very gentle cut down the entire length of your *baton* or *batard* will suffice. Scoring it all over with lots of smaller cuts will result in none of these opening up in the same way.

Finally, while we might feel like we have a lot of creative freedom with scoring, we should always score considering the way the dough has been shaped. Scoring helps to maximise the aeration of the bread.

Because we've introduced tension by shaping, this tension directs how the bread wants to rise. With a perfectly round loaf, it's simple because there is even tension all over. With a baguette, baton or batard, we've intentionally introduced lateral tension down the length of the dough. This means that if we score across the dough, side to side, we aren't doing much to release that tension. A dough scored like this will rise poorly.

If we score down the length of the dough, we release tension in a fairly major way and this allows the bread to expand, which as a knock-on effect releases more tension, and allows for even more expansion. It is in this wonderful situation that you can get truly great rises in the oven, known as **oven spring**, and those wonderful 'ears' of exploding crust.

8

BAKE

Bake each loaf in a very hot preheated oven by sliding into a pot, cloche or Dutch oven, or onto a baking stone. Add steam or bake with the lid or cloche on for 20 minutes before removing the lid and baking for another 20–30 minutes.

If you've made it this far (whether wading through my prancing prose or having followed my somewhat lengthy instructions), then good. But you've still got one of the most important parts to go.

You cannot bake a bad dough and make it good. You can bake a good dough badly and make it bad.

Baking is carried out immediately after scoring – don't leave your dough to rest again. This means you'll need to have preheated your oven according to what baking method you're going to use. You should almost always preheat your oven to as hot as they go – usually about 250ºC (480ºF)/230ºC (450ºF) fan/Gas 9 for a domestic oven. Then, when it is time to bake, turn it down to about 220ºC (430ºF)/200ºC (400ºF) fan/Gas 7, but this will vary depending on your recipe and your preferences. If your oven has an option to turn its fan to slow or off, use this feature.

The short heat-up times of the iron is one reason I really like using it, and this has led me away from baking stones. I don't need to guess when the bread is going to be ready and preheat the oven ages before, and then leave it on for another half an hour, wasting energy when the dough isn't quite there. With metal, I can see when the dough is imminently ready and then just turn the oven on.

During baking, there's a big change in the size of your loaf – this rise is called **oven spring**. Lots of things contribute. You might have heard that the warmth of your dough causes your yeast to become more active, producing more CO_2. This is true, but it produces a tiny amount. Once the dough hits just over 40ºC (104ºF), those yeasts are dead. Yeasts contribute very little to oven spring.

OVEN PREHEATING REFERENCE GUIDE

Cast-iron or heavy baking tray	20 minutes
Baking stone	40 minutes +
Cast-iron pot (Dutch oven), preheated	20 minutes, with the pot inside
Cast-iron pot, baking from cold	10 minutes, or as long as your oven takes to heat up
Ceramic cloche	10 minutes, or as long as your oven takes to heat up

What does happen is that CO_2, which was dissolved within your semi-liquid dough (the same way, though to a lesser extent, that CO_2 is dissolved within a beer or in Coca-Cola), moves out of that dough because it becomes less able to contain it the hotter it is. Some of this gas is lost into the oven, and some makes its way into the bubbles. Wetter doughs can store more CO_2 within the dough itself, which is one of the many reasons that being wetter does tend to give you larger, more irregular bubbles and can be more forgiving if your rises haven't been as good as you hoped for.

As well as this, gases expand as they heat up. There are lots of bubbles already contained within your dough, and the CO_2 within these expands rapidly with the heat of the oven. Add to that all this extra CO_2 from your yeast (minimal) and from your dough (some) and this rise can be dramatic.

But this rise isn't without resistance. Gluten, during the early stages of baking, turns to a mushy, even more extensible mesh, but then it begins to set. This happens from the outside in – the parts of the dough that will become the crust set first, and the middle (crumb) takes a bit longer.

The crust can form very quickly, especially in fan ovens, leading to a hard shell through which even the force of the expanding gas cannot break. This is especially common in poorly scored loaves that don't allow the centre of the dough to properly expand. This leads to a loaf that may still be delicious and golden, but will be considerably denser than a well-baked counterpart.

One way of counteracting this is with steam. Moisture is an essential part of the baking process and without steam, the crust dries out too quickly and becomes a greyish brown colour. Think of the difference between burnt sugar and luscious caramel; this is what separates a loaf baked in a dry environment and a wet one.

Of course, if you have steam all through the baking process, a crust will never develop and you'll end up with some large steamed dumplings. This is partly why the technique of baking within pots and cloches has become so widely used – taking the lid off is so easy. You can control the time for which your loaf is steamed, and then remove the lid (or indeed the entire pot) to allow (often astonishing) crusts to form. Baking in a pot is basically the only time I'll use non-stick grease-proof baking paper for a single large loaf, just because it helps when lowering it in.

Most flatbreads, tinned loaves, ciabattas, focaccias and baguettes can't be baked within a pot. Here, you should do your best to add some steam into the oven. When baking with stones, I have a cast-iron griddle pan that sits in the bottom of the oven. When I pop my bread in, I fill this with water. Because of the grooves in the pan and how it maintains its heat, the steam is impressive. Furthermore, because my oven is a fan oven, I turn off the fan for 5 minutes to help it rise even more.

You can just chuck a glass of water onto the side of the oven and at once close the door to enclose the steam, and I do this if I forget to put the pan in. Sometimes, I'll mist my dough directly using a hand-held sprayer, but this is nowhere near as effective as filling your oven with steam. If you decide to use an old detergent bottle as a DIY sprayer, please make sure it is thoroughly rinsed first. Please.

9

COOL

Place your loaf on a cooling rack or wooden board. Allow to cool to just-warm before slicing.

This is the smallest, most frustrating and probably most controversial step of the whole process. Cooling. Let your loaf cool properly before even thinking about cutting it.

The reasons for this are many. When it is still very hot, your bread is still soft and setting, and if you squish it down with the pressure of a knife, you're likely to crush and permanently damage the bubbles you've worked so hard to craft.

The second is that, quite simply, it's difficult to cut hot bread; your knife will stick to the soft dough-like centre and you'll get a poor, crushed slice. Yes, you could tear your loaf like the pre-millennial heathens we all are, but then you've got the squishing problem again. Then there's the fact that if you eat a whole loaf of just-out-of-the-oven bread, you're going to end up with a big clump of very dense, poorly digestible starch and protein that's going to make you feel a bit rubbish, if not cause you any true harm.

Instead, wait. Listen for the crust to crack as the softer dough contracts, and think about something else. After at least 30 minutes, but preferably 1 hour, slice. It will be worth the wait.

Your sourdough, because of the acid, alcohol and the salt content, has an extremely good shelf life compared with shop-bought bread, and will be quite considerably longer than homemade yeasted breads. It will still be good for toast after a week, and you almost never have to worry about it going mouldy. There's no great secret for storing it – I leave each loaf open to the elements, cut-side down on the chopping board, surrounded by its accompaniments.

You can freeze it, too; par-baked loaves freeze especially well. Par-baking involves cutting the total baking time short: for example, baking in a pot for 20 minutes with a lid on, then a mere 10 minutes with it off. You can then bake your par-baked loaf straight from frozen, straight on the oven shelf, and have the equivalent of a freshly baked loaf of sourdough within 20–25 minutes at 220ºC (430ºF)/200ºC (400ºF) fan/Gas 7.

NOVEL PROVING SCHEDULES

I thought it might be helpful to include some schedules I regularly use to bake bread around a busy life. Some of these are weekend schedules, some weekday, and all are interchangeable. I start my bread whenever the whim takes me.

THE WEEKEND OF A NINE-TO-FIVE WEEK

If you're up by 9am on a day off, you can have very good bread by 5pm if you're not out and about.

9.00am	Weigh ingredients, mix and autolyse
9.30am	Knead for 10 minutes. Prove with a stretch and fold or two
1.30pm	Pre-shape and bench rest
2.00pm	Shape and basket
3.45pm	Preheat oven
4.15pm	Score and bake

SUNDAY MORNING BACON SANDWICHES

A lack of bread on a Saturday doesn't have to mean a lack of bread on a Sunday, if you remember early enough. Nor does it mean missing out on your Saturday.

Saturday

Around lunchtime	Weigh, autolyse and mix
Around dinner time	Pre-shape, bench rest and shape
	Prove for 90 minutes
	Retard in the fridge

Sunday

Earlier than anyone else	Preheat the oven
	Bake

THE WORK CYCLE

Colleagues at work most appreciate this one, as you become more and more cajoled into bringing loaves in.

7.00am	With half the recipe's flour and water, make a levain
	Mix the other half together to autolyse
	Leave both at room temperature
6.00pm	Add salt and mix together the levain and the autolyse
	Stretch and fold 4–5 times throughout the evening
9.00pm	Pre-shape, bench rest and shape
	Leave at room temperature
10.30pm	Retard in the fridge
7.00am	Bake before work

LONG FIRST PROVE

This schedule is proof that you don't need to check the temperature of your dough, and that sourdough is forgiving. You can easily prove dough around your busy life.

6.30am	Get up 5 minutes early. Mix the ingredients
	Autolyse
	Use the electric mixer to develop the dough while eating breakfast
	Cover and leave somewhere cool, such as by the window
6.30pm	Get home from work
	Pre-shape, bench rest and shape
	Leave the basket in a warm place (on the heater)
8.00pm	Preheat the oven
8.30pm	Bake

SPEED SOURDOUGH

Some of the best loaves I've made have been through using a similar method to this one. Because you don't develop much flavour from the fermentation, use more earthy flours or a less frequently fed starter.

6.00pm	Weigh and combine using warm water, autolyse
6.30pm	Mix for 5 minutes
	Stretch and fold three times during the first prove
8.30pm	Divide into small loaves and pre-shape
9.00pm	Bench rest
10.20pm	Preheat stones
11.00pm	Bake

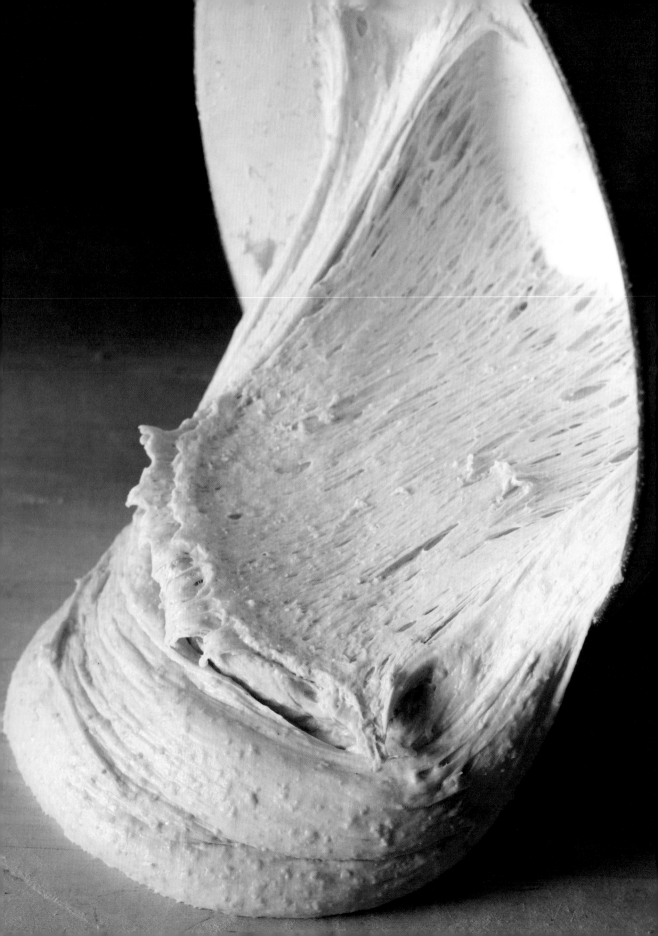

UNDERSTANDING DOUGH

It would be a con for me to promote this book as some kind of bread bible. It is certainly not perfect, though we have tried to make it so. It is simply a collection of advice I've taken from many other great people that really works. If you'll let me, I'd like to take things a level higher. I want to delve a bit further into the aspects of dough craft, and hopefully you can take all I've said to develop your own ways of doing things.

There's time for consistency, but the theme of the following is flexibility. Anyone can make awesome bread – the key is figuring out the way that you *will* make awesome bread. More than once. This involves a little bit of understanding of dough, the same way that understanding a little of the microbiology of sourdough starters can help you keep it in tip-top health.

I want you, midweek and a little exhausted, to use this understanding to be able to whip up a world-class sourdough around the busiest of lives.

THE PERFECT DOUGH STRUCTURE

We've touched on gluten. Now let's pick it up again, and maybe our hands won't stick this time.

When you mix flour and water, you enable a whole load of chemical reactions, as well as the micro-biological events we talked about in the previous chapter. First, I want to chat about the proteins that you hydrate. Namely, two proteins: *glutenin* and *gliadin*. These proteins stick to each other as they come into contact, and as more and more bond, they form one massive matrix. This matrix is gluten.

Gluten will make up less than 10% of the dough. The rest of the dough is mostly starch. Starches are long carbohydrate chains that, like gluten, attract water, and thus act as a thickener. Starches don't stick together well, though – and so it is gluten that provides the structure of your dough.

The manipulation of gluten is something a lot of people struggle to get their head and their hands around. Just when you think you've got a grasp and great bread is flowing, something changes to make you doubt all you've learned so far. This still happens to me.

Gluten can be talked about in the general terms of 'how developed' it is, and this is useful when starting out. As soon as you've roughly mixed your hydrated dough, the gluten is there and formed. You've got lots of irregular bunches of protein that create lumpy clumps. They'll contain some gas, but they aren't particularly efficient or effective at containing it. Some bubbles will be very thick-walled, tough and don't expand; some bubbles that are fragile will burst, leading to a dense, irregular dough.

By kneading or by stretching and folding, we develop the gluten. This involves repeatedly tearing apart these original clumps and stretching them over and over each other. This causes the formation of layer upon layer of thin films. As gas is produced from the dough, these films are pushed together, thus creating membranes.

It's easy to tell whether the gluten within a dough has been developed in this way because it will appear smooth and shiny. If you stretch it thin, it will pass the 'windowpane test' (see page 49) – this is a test of your gluten's ability to form thin films in order to create the membranes of your bubbles.

Lots of variables affect gluten development. High hydration levels, for example, will space your proteins further apart and lead to fewer links being formed between them. Equally, if you have a very stiff dough, it's difficult to stretch the gluten out and, as a result, far harder work to develop the gluten.

The addition of fat to your dough interrupts the bonds between the gluten – think of it as a lubri-cant that, rather than allowing you to stretch and tear the gluten, allows your clumps to slide over each other again and again. This causes a more tender, flakier bake.

While gluten forms best at an only slightly acidic pH, further acidity reinforces the gluten matrix and gives dough a slightly improved strength. Therefore, sourdoughs have stronger gluten strands than commercially yeasted breads. As you leave your dough, though, enzymes called *proteases* break down the matrix and start to use it for energy. This hybrid of goings-on causes the thick-walled, strong and huge bubbles in sourdough.

The key to excellent sourdough making is to balance this protein degradation with its concurrent formation during the dough's fermentation. And that's my favourite sentence of the book – I'd read it again and again. This is why I recommend, during at least one of your fermentations, to get the dough up to a decent temperature. You get more acid production and more fermentation, and so the dough is strong.

Rheology is the study of dough's strength, or lack of it. I've touched on the key terms briefly before, but I've found a few home guides that delve deeply enough into this to practically show you how to manipulate dough for optimum results.

Extensibility describes the 'stretchiness' of the dough. A dough that is highly extensible is a weak dough. This dough will be easily stretched while not springing back when pressed. A very wet, unshaped dough is extensible.

Elasticity is nearly the opposite of extensibility. This describes the springiness of the dough. Try to stretch an elastic dough and it will spring back to its original position. A relatively dry dough that's been very heavily worked is very elastic, almost rubbery.

Tenacity is subtly different from elasticity. A tenacious dough is a resilient dough. You can't stretch it, and if you try, it resists you and then breaks. Very dry doughs that have been pounded are tenacious.

Tenacity is a property that, for the most part, one wants to avoid in sourdough making. A little is required, but a highly tenacious dough will not expand properly and will give you a tough, dense crumb. That's why we tend to avoid dry, low-hydration doughs. It can be done, but it requires a very long autolyse (see opposite).

Therefore, the trick is to balance extensibility and elasticity, both of which are required for a decent dough with a soft and open crumb.

First, we choose a relatively high-hydration dough: you get the dilute formation of gluten as described above. Then we autolyse: your enzymes start to break down a few of those bonds and the gluten begins to spread out, especially at the weakest points. This, without any work from yourself, creates a more sheet-like structure to the dough. It creates a highly extensible dough.

We then build some elasticity into the dough by mixing or kneading. How we mix very much depends on how much extensibility or elasticity we add to the dough at this point. Mixing by hand, you're breaking and re-forming your sheets of gluten, but you're also then curling them around each other. This twisting action in turn adds elasticity to your dough that gives it strength.

This is what a dough hook is designed to do, but most (especially those in home mixers) don't carry out this function very well. They tend to develop the gluten into nice sheets without contributing much to elasticity; therefore, you've got a developed dough but with rather huge extensibility. These doughs need quite a few stretches and folds to give them structure.

Either following mixing or in a no-knead scenario, the aim is to turn your dough from a weak, highly extensible one into a relatively elastic one. This allows it to hold its shape and burst open in the oven, while retaining a great softness and open structure. The four ways we do this are: with an **active fermentation**, by integrating a few **stretch and folds**, by **pre-shaping** and finally by **shaping**.

A very **active fermentation** causes your gluten sheets to pass across each other, further developing those cross-links and cementing them in place with acid. As gas is pushed into the bubbles, the walls of each neighbouring bubble will be pushed together, creating strength.

A stagnant fermentation will only contribute to extensibility – that means that if you retard your dough during the first prove, for example, you'll want to do some extra **stretches and folds** to maintain your dough's strength. In any fermentation, if you think your dough looks very wet and floppy and uninviting, you should try stretching and folding a few times prior to shaping.

It's important to leave some time between stretches and folds. Once you reach a certain point of tightness, you just start tearing your gluten matrix rather than stretching it. Leave it and those proteases will begin to break down the bonds under tension again. Half an hour later, you'll have an extensible dough once more – just not quite as stretchy as it was before.

Pre-shaping is not common practice among non-sourdough home bakers because it is not seen as necessary, and many people perceive it to be quite difficult. It isn't difficult if you've got a stiff dough scraper, and are happy using a little water or flour to stop the dough sticking to your hands. It is simply the act of curling your sheets of gluten around each other some more, giving your dough strength. The 'bench rest' following the pre-shaping allows for some relaxation so that there is just enough malleability for shaping.

Shaping will decide your final dough strength – your balance between extensibility and elasticity. Despite all the science behind it, this is where I like to get a bit creative. With experience, I firmly believe that the dough tells you how it wants to be shaped. Not which shape, but how tight. Shape too tightly and you'll destroy much of your delicate matrix and push your gas outwards. Shape without conviction and your dough will flop during its final prove and have poor oven spring.

Gently does it. Feel what stretch you get and use all of it, but never so much that you feel it give or tear. As you fold and tighten, the dough will begin to support itself. As you gently roll it into its final shape, you can easily overstretch things, so take it very slowly and very gently. Keep all those delicate bubbles. The dough shouldn't stick, but don't get stressed if it does: just use your scraper to unstick it.

Following all of this, we can still wreck things by allowing a dough to stagnate. Either overproving or leaving it in a retarded state without fermentation for too long will again break down your protein structure. The tense structure of the dough is destroyed, and your oven spring will be terrible.

It's easy to cut corners or to forget. I do both all the time and I'm often left with substandard bread as a result. Don't lose perspective: I'm talking *relatively* substandard. Follow 90% of the above, and you will have world-class bread. Follow half of it, and you're going to have very good bread.

Don't lose heart if things don't go well: just make the choice. Do everything as it should be done with scientific, obsessive precision, or embrace the uniqueness of every loaf. The choice is yours.

AUTOLYSE

Sourdough bakers demonstrate they've been taught by the way in which they **autolyse** (for reference, it's pronounced *auto-lees*). I've kept the concept simple so far and only mentioned two methods: the first is where you introduce all the ingredients together and rest your dough for 30–60 minutes before mixing – this is the traditional way. I've also talked about leaving out the salt during this time, and mixing it in during the knead. However, this is but scratching the surface.

Some people don't autolyse at all, and this is fine. This is a legitimate choice, and especially so in sourdough – the slow-rising dough is so extensible as it is, is it really worth spending extra time making it even more so? Conversely, some people become obsessed with it, leaving only flour and water to meld and melt for up to a day at a time, creating a dough that can be stretched and stretched until it is metres long.

This particular fascination I'm not too keen on; I believe in a law of diminishing autolyse returns.

If you choose not to knead or mix at all, and go only for stretching and folding, a good autolyse melds into the time between stretching and folding, becoming one of the many times you allow the dough to become lax and floppy and then tighten it again. Effectively, this method involves curling your sheets of gluten around and around and around each other, creating a stronger and ever-tighter dough. This leads to a fairly irregularly and lightly developed dough, but tends towards a very irregular open-closed crumb and big oven spring.

Wholemeal doughs benefit especially from an autolyse. This is because it takes a while for the bran to become properly hydrated. As a result, a wholemeal dough that seems horrifically wet will feel very manageable after 30–60 minutes of patience. For most of my loaves, I don't have to worry about this too much, as I use a wholemeal starter, which has been well-fermented and fully hydrated before mixing.

When Should I Add Salt?

Adding salt does affect the autolyse, but to what significance is hotly debated and utterly unproven. There are numerous theories, but they are just that: theories.

The salt will cause the flour to be a little less hydrated. As it holds on to water, salt reduces the total water available to the starch and gluten. This means that in a dry dough, salt could be detrimental to gluten formation during an autolyse. But salt does help gluten form, and enhances the number of links between the gluten molecules for a stronger structure. It's not known exactly why this is, but it has been proposed that the salt alters the shape of the proteins in gluten to help them tangle more easily. Sourdough – especially high-hydration doughs, as anyone who has baked a loaf after forgetting to add the salt – depends on salt for its structure.

My own theory is unproven. I think that adding salt *after* an autolyse causes a subtly uneven dispersion of the sodium chloride within the dough. This causes irregular formation of gluten, leading to an enhancement of the characteristic thick-walled bubbles we see. You can test this by taking random needle aspirations of doughs and breads autolysed with or without salt and comparing the salinity of each. Please do.

The bottom line: an autolyse without salt seems to contribute to an even more extensible dough that may require more stretches and folds to reach adequate strength. It also leads to a more irregular and subjectively creamier, chewier crumb. Autolysing with salt leads to a more regular-bubbled dough, and reduces the chances of forgetting to add the salt.

To Add Starter?

You'll have noticed that I, controversially in some pedants' eyes, have thus far not recommended mixing only the flour and water and leaving them together. That's because I don't believe it is necessary.

When mixing commercially yeasted doughs, there's an argument that a really soft, extensible dough can't be achieved without a long, yeast-free autolyse. The reason for this is that any yeast is so active that it develops the gluten at quite a rate during this time.

In sourdough, there's a change in environment from a very acidic starter into a mild, unfamiliar environment, and so your yeasts take a little time to get going. And even then, your yeast activity is much lower, thus resulting in far lower dough strength.

As we've already discussed, though: acid reinforces gluten. Your starter is very acidic, and this will instantly bring down the pH of your dough, reducing the extensibility of it. But you have to balance this with the excess enzyme activity going on in a sourdough starter: after all, the starters themselves are very wet, stretchy things indeed.

The bottom line: sourdoughs are very extensible doughs, and there's little yeast activity towards the beginning of the prove. Subsequently, autolysing with the starter makes minimal difference to the final product.

BREAD FORMULAE AND BAKER'S PERCENTAGES

This is just a brief word, with the aim of aiding in the understanding all the mad stuff written online.

Bread formulae are useful as guides to help you compare recipes or scale up to commercial levels, and that's it. I much prefer recipes: this much makes one loaf of this size. Double it or triple it and you'll have three loaves. Simple. The bread formula gives you only the **baker's percentages** of each ingredient, usually set out in a table.

Baker's percentages are calculated based on the total weight of flour in the dough, regardless of its type. Stupidly, they don't include the flour volume contained within your sourdough starter.

As an example, a recipe including

wholemeal flour	100g	33%
rye flour	100g	33%
white flour	100g	33% .
Total Flour	**300g**	**100%**
white sourdough starter	**150g**	**50%**
water	**200g**	**66%**

would have a formula of **33% wholemeal, 33% white flour, 33% rye, 50% starter and 66% water.**

The above formula might give the impression of a dough that's 66 percent hydration, but it isn't. It's actually 73% hydration – this is because the extra flour and water within the sourdough starter mean that the total flour is 375g and the total water is 275g. 275 divided by 375 is 0.73.

This overall number becomes even less relevant when you look at the combination of flours we're using. Who knows what 73% hydration actually means when it comes to this particular mix? All I can tell you is that it will be very stiff. It's easy to compare like-for-like when using a standardised white flour, but not when blending. This is when the whole thing becomes a very rough tool, and sometimes altogether meaningless.

The health and stage of your starter affects the wetness of your dough, too, and thus the dough's subsequent rheology. An over-fermented starter will be wet with broken-down gluten and high acidity. A recently fed starter will combine into your dough much more like flour and water, but might not yet have the number of yeasts required to adequately ferment your dough.

The bottom line: call out anyone who boasts about high hydration levels a 'hydration wanker'. Then, ask them how much wholemeal there is as a percentage of the dough.

LEVAIN

You'll read, if you wish to, about many people who add in an extra step when making their sourdough. This involves separating the sourdough starter from the dough to create a *levain*.

This is the American perversion of a French term, and is equivalent to a pre-dough or a pre-ferment that is fed from your sourdough starter and then incorporated into your dough. This step will add an extra 6–12 hours to your total proving time, depending on how long you leave this ferment to rise.

This does ensure a very active starter. And because you can quite considerably increase your yeast count by including this step, you can get away with using far less starter to begin with, reducing waste. Having such fresh, active yeast leads to a more active fermentation and thus greater dough strength, with lower acidity. You can create large volumes of dough from small volumes of starter, and indeed, when making really large volumes of dough, stepping up twice or even three times to gain the required number of yeast cells for a decent fermentation might be necessary.

As well as reducing waste, it reduces the space needed for storage (and thus life partner annoyance). It's especially good for infrequent bakers who keep their starters in the fridge and want to feed them minimally to keep them alive. Creating a levain allows you to revive and build up a starter to ensure health prior to fermentation. You can watch how it behaves.

A very popular method involves the combination of a levain with an autolyse of flour and water over the same time period. This creates a very extensible dough, followed by a very active fermentation and good strength. It works with any sort of kneading or stretching and folding that suits you.

I don't use levains because an active sourdough starter does the same job, and in all honesty, my brain can't process an extra step in my bread making.

GRAINS AND HOME MILLING

The final stage in the classic journey of bread-making self-fulfilment is buying a mill. This might seem off-puttingly indulgent, and you can come back to this later if it seems too much. I'm not going to provide a super in-depth guide to all the mills available; I'm just going to preach about flavour.

Mills have swollen in popularity thanks to a greater awareness of the different grain varieties. You may have seen Chad Robertson's third *Tartine* book, which not only stands up as an entire book on the subject, but does so as a mainstream, best-selling cookbook. Bloggers, too, have influenced things: many have been sent awesome (expensive) electric mills as 'gifts' from online bakery stores, and so a huge audience is now seeing them used on a daily basis.

Reasons to Mill

The thing that attracted me to milling my own grain wasn't flavour, per se. Or rather, it wasn't the direct flavour of the loaf it was used in, but the flavour from the **bugs** that live in the grain. If you can get good, fresh grain of any sort, then it is full of bugs. When milling with my archaic hand mill, I take special care not to go too fast, so that the grain stays cool as it comes through. This means you can begin new sourdough starters very rapidly, and you can see some massive variations in their flavour.

Some would argue that **freshness** is key to some kind of nutritional nirvana. And true, milling your own unsifted grain means that you won't lose any bran or germ in the process, and your moist, oil-rich flour won't have time to degrade. I think the perception of any positive effect on your body (apart from this process encouraging you to eat more whole grains in general) is most likely placebo. I don't think it's going to make you live longer. It might, but it probably won't.

Instead, I think **provenance** is up there with the decent reasons to invest in your own mill. If you've got a great farm shop or health shop nearby that sells good-quality, fresh and organic whole grains, you're laughing. If you don't, you might be able to befriend a farmer. And then, if you're not very sociable or don't know any farmers, there's the Internet. You can buy grains of any sort and know exactly where they come from, and exactly how they have been cultivated.

Provenance should be considered alongside the single most important factor – the sheer number of **varieties** available. I'm not just talking 'wheat' and 'rye'. You can get all sorts of strains of each, or blends of many. In fact, loads of varieties of wheat that have never been bred for commercial cultivation are now being cultivated commercially, for the benefit of people like you and me.

They're given names to help distinguish them or promote them as something different from wheat, but you should think of these varieties as all related. Spelt is perhaps the most well known, but Einkorn, Kamut, Emmer and Rivet are also common. They all can be used to make great bread alone without adulteration. And while this nomenclature is useful for comparing the flavour of one wheat to another, you're unlikely to change to one of these flours as your primary provider of your bread. It's largely for personal experimentation, which usually fizzles out.

The most interesting work is being done on blends and mixed crops. These biodiverse fields grow under whatever conditions are available – every year, different strains will do better than others, and no matter what the conditions are, yields will be good. This seasonal variation is particularly enchanting, and absolutely captures the spirit of this book. Just as no sourdough is the same, no season will be the same, and even different batches of flour from the same field could be wildly different. And this is a good thing. Rather than strive for Instagram ideal, let yourself be carried away by the flavour.

You should check out the work of the charismatic John Letts, who has achieved amazing results by blending hundreds of varieties of ancient wheat and planting them together. The flour he makes, sold under the brand Lammas Fayre, is exceptional. There are plenty of his inspiring interviews online.

It is worth pointing out that good sourdough can also be made from other gluten-containing crops. Barleys can be treated much like ryes; they tend to be dense if used to make bread on their own, but can be a great addition in small quantities. This includes interesting varieties, such as the hardy Bere, which is grown in Orkney.

When it comes to **mill shopping,** you get what you pay for. I'll skirt around the vast number of considerations and straight away suggest that you want an electric, stone-burred mill. With hand mills, the action of twisting it puts quite a lot of lateral stress on the burrs, giving you an uneven grind. Use stone, as it can produce a very fine product without too much heat. The KoMo Fidibus mills are very good. I've never used NutriMills, Schnitzers, Hawo's or Mockmills, but have heard positive things about them all. I've heard fewer good things about the KitchenAid mill attachment.

The smallest KoMo will set you back around £300 ($390), so it isn't for everyone. It's the sort of thing I'd recommend investing in if you've got access to some really exciting grain, or if you enjoy one-upping your neighbours in the game of 'interesting kitchen appliances'. If you want to start out, you can pick up some very cheap mills indeed. Check eBay and Gumtree – many that are designed for crushing corn, for example, can be used to mill flour.

My own cast-iron thing, which cost a tenner and was produced cheaply in China, has broken twice in its life, but the main structure of it is sound. It can't finely mill wholemeal flour in a single pass, but it can do it in two passes. The effort and the loudness only add to the experience.

A NOTE ON WHAT DOUGH DOES TO YOU

Here, I want to tackle a few personal points. You can take this or leave it – this knowledge won't make you a better bread baker, but maybe it will make you a more emphatic one. I'll do my best to keep it light, and the ranting to a minimum.

The one principle I'd like to get across here isn't that of encouraging a deep scepticism of everything, irrespective of health and wellbeing. Cumulative human understanding is poor, and individual understanding is marred further by ego and tradition. People who think they know a lot don't seem to. Especially me.

Most peer-reviewed literature in bread and baking journals makes massive assumptions, is based on very flawed studies and is geared towards automating and economising industrial processes. I risk sounding like a conspiracy theorist to say we live in the dark and that you shouldn't trust anything you read, but I kind of am. Good science should be defended, and I'd encourage you to give credit to those who seem to be doing their best in the pursuit of widening our current understanding.

I've said enough in this book so that you can make great bread, I hope, but one reason to keep reading is that this stuff is really interesting. We're at the cutting edge of several subjects: bread is part of this aspirational revolution in society where we all crave not only the best but to be able to make the best ourselves. The same goes for cake, coffee, beer, bicycles... Maybe that's just me.

We're at the forefront of science – much of what I've said and all of what I'm about to say could be plain wrong. A further basic microbiological model may blow what we currently 'know' out of the water in a matter of weeks, months or even years. The way that sourdough starters and the yeasts and bacteria evolve has been studied by remarkably few people. Or rather, studied well by few people.

Then there's the debate about health, and whether making sourdough is a good idea at all. You and I might cite the strong positives for mental health, for sociability, for interest and for intrigue. There are also the positives for physical health – bread is energy. It is a basic building block of our diet. Then there are the negatives. Too much energy is stored as fat. Aren't 'carbs' and gluten bad?

I'm in the interesting position of being a doctor who lives in the public eye, runs a brewery and profits by proselytising about the excellence of carbs and gluten. I reflect on this a lot. Not just by wondering incessantly within my own head, but by checking what we know as a scientific community and as a society, and balancing the risk of what I do with any potential benefits. I'm proud to admit that I change my mind – constantly – but I also have the ability to make a decision based on what's known at any one time and be happy with it years later. You'll find direct contradictions between this book and my last on the subject, and I am fine with that.

Gluten = Bad?

If you've read my previous bread making book, you'll know my views on gluten. I haven't changed my mind on this – yet.

An inspiring surgeon of (concerningly rare) technical brilliance, who is a scientist at the top of his game, looks at the gluten argument in a different way from me and most of his other colleagues. He argues that, just as we didn't know about the effects of cow's milk protein allergy, we might not yet know about the massive fallout of gluten. Or lactose. Or wheat as a whole. So he takes the opportunity to advise patients who have so-far unexplained symptoms to try an extremely restrictive diet.

Sometimes it works – irritable bowel syndrome (IBS) and self-diagnosed non-coeliac wheat sensitivity are commonly treated diagnoses. It seems to work – often, even. But this isn't science. Sometimes things just get better. And sometimes altering your entire life and that of your family to pander to this restriction could have some additional effect.

We see the same evidence, the same sets of studies, but we've come out with differing practices. His view is that there is a host of evidence yet to be found, and this is definitely a legitimate one to hold. He might also say that you cannot apply large population studies to the individual in front of you – you treat the individual. Also a wise argument, and it's hard to ignore when it works.

Instead, I examine the consensuses by people who know better than me, again, and look at their interpretations – and I trust them. While this information might be difficult to decipher in areas of rapidly developing research, it works most of the time in medicine, and one would be subject to a lot of litigation if we only trusted the radicals. Or our own experience.

Take one example. A recent (and good) review from 2018 looking at associations between Irritable bowel syndrome and diet screened 1726 scientific papers looking for evidence. Of these, they identified nine good studies. Nine. The single very good study applicable to a gluten-free diet found no significant link between IBS and gluten intake.

This is one of many considered and scientific collations of evidence and I've hand-picked it. The truth is there's not just a 'lack of evidence' (a term used when one wants to win an argument; it means nothing). There's a repeated trend of a **lack of efficacy** of introducing a gluten-free diet as an intervention in a number of conditions.

This does not include the massive exception of coeliac disease. Coeliac affects about 1% of the population that we know about. There are probably quite a few people out there who have it, but we don't know about it. Definitely single figures, and likely not more than double the number known in the Western world. Anyone who goes to their GP with remotely linked bowel symptoms will be tested – I can say this without doubt in this litigatory medical world.

Anecdotally, there appears to be a spectrum of feelings within the coeliac community about the gluten-free bandwagon – of irritation at those who appear to demean or devalue the severity of the condition, to the joy of being able to take advantage of such a huge range of gluten-free products. I'd be interested to hear what you think.

There are also people who have allergies to certain proteins within wheat. The numbers here are uncertain, but we know they are likely smaller than the numbers for coeliac. Many studies assume its existence without actually testing for it. For patients, it can be tested for, despite not being very well understood, through blood tests and skin tests. But the tests are not good. In fact, they're terrible. They tend to throw up a lot of false positives – this means that your blood might say you're allergic to wheat, but it has no perceivable effect in practice. As a result of private allergy testing, I regularly see patients who say that they are allergic to gluten, wheat, lactose, milk protein, eggs and a combination of nuts or seeds they've eaten all their lives without incident. Yes, regularly. These tests push people into a restrictive diet that can be socially isolating, exhausting or just plain annoying.

My practice is to deal with this in a cold, scientific way – first, with appropriate investigation largely to exclude anything sinister or that we can easily treat, and then if these all come back negative, to systematically exclude and subsequently reintroduce these alleged allergens one at a time, again in a scientific way, so that we can work out what's actually having an effect, and what isn't. Sometimes we find an aggravating ingredient; sometimes none makes any difference.

Despite all the evidence, there are those who claim that wheat is somehow indigestible, ultra-refined and mass-manufactured. A lot of wheat is mass-manufactured because it needs to be to meet global calorific demand, and this is the right thing to do, otherwise disadvantaged people will starve. Much wheat is ultra-refined into white flour because it's delicious and keeps for a long time. And often wheat is indigestible, yes, if it's raw (as in the case of many mass-manufactured loaves) or if it is worked extremely hard without much water, and then fermented very quickly without care. Your sourdough will be baked extremely well following a long fermentation when much of the starch is already digested by your starter, and the gluten is barely holding itself together with the awesome crumb structure you've created. Wheat isn't the enemy – it's how you treat it that matters. Treat any grain in the same way and you'll have the same problems. A bit like people. The point is, the number of people who stand to benefit from a wheat- or gluten-free diet is in the very low percentages. Very low. Numbers following gluten-free diets have continued to surge markedly in just a few years, but the diagnoses of coeliac disease, even with this heightened awareness, have stayed stable.

Many people seem to think that avoiding, rather than excluding, gluten is in some way healthy. This is not the case as far as we know. To the best of anyone's knowledge, eating gluten doesn't have a cumulative effect on wellbeing, unlike having high blood pressure or consuming red meat. It won't cause you any negative health effects further down the line.

The most worrying thing for me is the potential this scapegoating may have. I can't cite evidence, but I can imagine a stereotypical case. Think of a man or woman, in their forties, fit and well. Then a change in bowel habit. That human stubbornness and insistence on blame: it's gluten or it's dairy, as society and social media say. An allergy test kit confirms it. Reassured. Radical change in diet. Losing weight, but no better. Then it's too late. A more serious condition has taken hold.

In summary: in those people who are suffering unexplained gut symptoms, seeing a health professional to exclude anything serious should always be your first port of call. If all the investigation comes back clear, then by all means exclude gluten. Completely, strictly and solely. Don't exclude it with anything else. People often find a change, even a complete resolution, in their symptoms. The real crux is when it's reintroduced six weeks later. The odds are in your favour – you can enjoy wheat, spelt, barley and rye in all their wondrous complexity.

Gluten Aside: Is Sourdough Healthy?
Probably not. Wait, what?

There are no magical properties of sourdough that make it inherently 'healthy'. Supplementing sourdough on top of the average diet is not going to make you live longer, cure gallstones or sort out blood pressure. The word 'health' when applied to food is stupid. Insane, even. There are almost no foods that are 'healthy' because, in excess, *any* food is unhealthy, and some 'health foods' are plain dangerous. A balanced and open mind that can appreciate the goodness in all things is healthy; restriction and anxiety or strict control aren't. There might have been a time, before the stringent food safety laws of today, when being picky gave humans an evolutionary advantage, but now, being open to consuming a wide variety of things makes living a contented, disease-light life easy.

I don't know whether replacing mass-made white bread with sourdough is going to help either. Sourdough is certainly quite a bit denser, so to maintain the same surface area for toppings you'll need higher bread calories. The key to combatting this is simple: less bread, better bread; fewer toppings, awesome toppings. Make your own sourdough and spend more on the stuff you put on it and eat less of both. The chewy texture will require more mastication and fill you up faster.

Then there's the fact that sourdough is amazing, as is making it. I don't think this can be ignored. Eating it makes you feel good; eating a loaf you've made is socially reassuring. You also must be in a comfortable place to have the time, motivation and money to do it. I'm not going to equate these with the growing public health evidence that a stressful, hard life in deprivation leads to a shorter, more unhealthy existence after adjusting for all other tangible variables, but it's food for thought.

To be clear, nothing in sourdough is particularly different from any other bread. I suggest you don't worry about such questions and enjoy any bread in moderation and with restrained toppings. I think it's nice to eat nice things and indulge in their flavour rather than their quantity. I think most people agree. Eat bread; just don't eat too much.

Low-Carb Diets

You see: I'm coming at you from every biased, bread-supporting stance.

Carbs are good. The eating-disorientated, health-food press might have jumped on the band-wagon of cutting calories by cutting carbs, but it seems like yesterday that years of research had led us to recommend that the majority of energy in your diet should be derived from complex carbohydrates.

Bread is a good source of complex carbs. In sourdough, those carbohydrates have been broken down into little sugar, some medium-length carbs called *dextrins* and the rest remains as starches of varying lengths. The acid and the cell machinery of the diversity of microflora in a sourdough starter play an important part in the breakdown of the starch – this is often said to lead to the subjective view that sourdough is more digestible. This also seems to keep moisture within the bread following baking, and it helps stabilise the starches and prevent the bread from staling.

I believe, then, that sourdough can provide a long-lasting, delicious, stomach-friendly part of your carbohydrate intake, which is part of a 'healthy' diet.

A low- or no-carbohydrate diet will cause you to become *ketotic* – that is, to have high levels of ketones. Ketones are another source of energy that some (most, including heart and brain) cells can use in the absence of glucose to create energy for normal function. Being ketotic is now such a sought-after state that you can buy meters that tell you how ketotic your breath is – technology originally developed to help those with diabetes, in which the presence of ketones can be a very bad sign.

Opting for a low-carb diet long term is a decision made in the dark. My opinion is that, if you're a healthy weight and non-diabetic, then a no-carb diet is vanity. You'll be fitter and feel healthier with a greater exercise tolerance on a decent amount of carbs. If you're overweight, then a low-carb diet short to medium term can be a good way to lose weight. Part of this is psychological, for it is also an exercise in commitment and red lines. Coming off this diet doesn't necessarily mean you'll put the weight back on. Furthermore, there's evidence that in type 2 diabetes, you can reduce your blood glucose and therefore the long-term damage associated with hyperglycaemia by going on a low-carb diet. The hope would be that you lose weight, put your diabetes into remission and largely get on with life without worry.

Not enough good long-term studies have been done. One of the few of such studies, published in *The Lancet Public Health*, 2018 (Seidelmann *et al.*), found that it mattered not only what you ate but where the carb substitutes came from. It found that a low-carbohydrate diet was associated with higher mortality than a moderate-carb diet, recommending that 50–55% of your calories come from carbs. It also found a diet heavy on plant-based carb alternatives, rather than meat, gave a better outcome.

I've hand-picked this one study of many because it's quite well done, yes, but also because it backs up my 'common-sense', utterly unscientific opinion that the solution for most is a balanced, carb-containing diet that's low in meat (but in which meat is not absent). But that's another book to write.

UNDERSTANDING STARTERS

Some people hold onto their sourdough starters with something like a weird, fetishist fascination. They feel that they must do everything possible to care for it and somehow it is their failure if it dies. Even the idea of starting a new one is abhorrent, and a slog.

For me, not so. I have lost count of the number of starters I've begun in the process of researching this book. Over fifty, at least. Each time I've been using different flours, blends of flour, water, temperatures and starter aids. Reassuringly, all except those where I was being deliberately reckless were successful.

What's been really interesting about this experience is the character that the starter provides – every one is different. I've tried to use them all as 'single origin' starters as much as possible to see how the resulting bread turns out, and each has reacted with subtle dissimilarity.

I hope the forthcoming chapter will educate, but also reassure. A starter is a fun thing to make and something you can do over and over again. You can make a new one and add it into an old one and see how it changes. Play about, experiment and, most of all, don't worry if your starter dies. It's no trouble to make a new one, and the excuse to do so should be relished.

WHAT'S GOING ON IN THERE

This is a technical bit. You don't need to know this to make great bread, so skip past it if you like.

Sourdough starters don't work like 'normal' yeast. Most starters might contain some traditional baker's yeast – also known as brewer's yeast, or *saccharomyces cerevisiae* – but this does not contribute much to the fermentation of your bread. As a result, sourdough reacts differently to the temperature and environment compared to bread made with commercial yeast.

When you make a sourdough starter the traditional way, you mix flour and water to create a fairly doughy solution. This solution is a *culture medium*, or something that provides a suitable environment for bugs to grow. It just happens that the flour, as well as providing the nutrition for the bugs, provides the bugs themselves. Loads of them.

What if it didn't? Say, for example, we baked our flour in the oven to over 120ºC (250ºF)/100ºC (210ºF) fan/Gas ½ and sterilized it, then mixed it with sterile water in a sterile container with a sterile implement: nothing might grow, ever. But practically, something probably would, since at home we're not that good at stopping bugs getting in there. In this case, it would take a very long time because the number of bacteria or yeast is so few.

In a typical sourdough starter, there are hundreds or thousands of different bacteria and yeasts all there, all viable and ready to munch through your culture medium. Which ones will depend on their numbers, their condition and the environment. As the first bugs grow, they will change the environment as they munch on flour and fart out CO_2, alcohol or acid. Then another bug might take over, and the whole thing changes again.

Competition is important. Bugs work together to optimise their growth, and as they grow they use up the energy in the flour, and this leaves less of it for other bugs. Furthermore, they produce chemicals that are either directly toxic to competing bugs or send signals slowing their growth. This results in the phenomenon of *competitive inhibition*, which will lead to certain bugs (and usually it's the same ones again and again) dominating nearly every single time.

The Uninvited Bugs

In a sourdough starter, the first bug (chronologically) you might see signs of is of the *Leuconostoc* species. This is a family of bacteria that produces gas and causes the bubbles that you see in the first day or two of your sourdough starter's growth. If you use fresh flour, or mill it yourself, this fermentation can be very vigorous indeed – doubling or tripling the size of your dough. It doesn't mind a bit of warmth, and on the starters I've made in the high 20ºCs (70ºFs) and low 30ºCs (80ºFs), I've had this fermentation kick off in a big way within 12 hours. It smells a bit like mouldy feet.

I've not used this bug for baking bread because, to be honest, it doesn't smell that nice, and I've been more focused on finding a way past it – you also can't perpetuate this culture easily, like you can a sourdough starter. That's because *Leuconostoc* tends to be inhibited in acidic conditions. As it ferments, it creates these conditions itself through its by-products. Equally, other bacteria and yeasts are churning out lactic, acetic and (less pleasant) butyric acids all the time, bringing down that pH.

You can make bread using this initial fermentation – it involves baking the entire starter at the point of high growth. This fermentation is used to make South Indian flatbreads called *idli*. These wee, light breads are made from ground rice and dried bean flour, usually *urad dal* (a black bean). These are ground into a paste that is left to ferment, and it is *Leuconostoc* that ferments it. By all means, have a go.

The Sour Bugs

In sourdough starter creation, this initial fermentation rather abruptly settles down shortly after it starts. Within a day or so, anyway. This is when a lot starts going on that you aren't really seeing: acid-producing bacteria are growing and reproducing, as well as a load of bacteria that are usually found in your gut. We'll focus on a species called *Lactobacillus*, which churns out lactic acid (hence the name), as well as acetic acid (which gives sourdough its vinegary smell). *Lactobacillus* is a ubiquitous, mostly friendly bacteria found in the human gut in modest quantities and is used to make yoghurts.

There are a few different overarching categories of *Lactobacillus* that don't matter – the main point is that none is responsible for producing the vast majority of gas that rises your bread. What *Lacto* does do, though, is give sourdough the tang after which it is named, and a good chunk of aroma. It is present in huge numbers – in healthy starters it seems to outnumber your yeast by about 100 to 1. This is a vast amount of intracellular (within the cell) machinery and a huge number of enzymes, all working to break down the starches and proteins within the flour into stuff it can use as food.

The Yeasty Bugs

And so to the yeasts. They don't mind acid much, and many thrive in the acidic conditions. Examining which yeasts thrive is interesting: many studies will detect the presence, in large numbers, of a great variety. A typical fermentation of yeast involves the breakdown of sugars into alcohol and carbon dioxide. Some yeasts will have the machinery to break down longer starches and complex medium-length carbohydrates into useable fuel. Some won't. The yeast produces loads of lovely aromatic by-product as it does this.

The yeasts that are really interesting are the odd ones out – namely, some *Candida* species (yes, they're related to *those* candida), and especially *Candida milleri*. The thing that makes this yeast interesting is that *C. milleri* can't use maltose, a sugar made up of two glucose molecules stuck together, as fuel. This is important because the primary result of starch breakdown is maltose.

The Bugs Working Together

Lots of *Lactobacillus* species can use maltose, though. Specifically, one that is found in sourdough starters all over the globe is the delightfully named *Lactobacillus sanfranciscensis.* This is named after the San Francisco sourdough cultures in which it was originally identified in the 1970s. Not only does this grow at similar temperatures and at similar rates to *C. Milleri*, but it can metabolise maltose. It does so by breaking it down into its constituent glucoses, leaving plenty left over for its yeasty buddy.

These two pals act so synergistically that they dominate the fermentation for the coming days, and this is where feeding your starter comes in. By maintaining a constant food source and, importantly, stopping the whole solution from becoming too alcoholic or too acidic, you can keep this stage of the fermentation going in perpetuity.

This is why it's important not just to feed your starter but to feed it *enough*. If you just keep adding a little bit at a time, the massive number of bacteria and yeast will munch through the available food in no time and won't have enough to grow properly. The starter will just keep getting more and more acidic, and eventually the whole machine will grind to a halt. So either pour away or use your starter in order to keep it doubling in size each time.

If you don't feed your starter, after a day or two you'll notice it split into two layers: a watery, cloudy layer and a thick, gelatinous floury layer. This separation is just a sign of the fermentation settling down. The sourdough starter will continue to become even more acidic, and the biodiversity will decrease. Some yeasts will die; many more will be inhibited. If you leave it for too long, you won't have enough yeast to do anything with and weird bugs that don't mind this environment will grow. These bugs, whether horribly smelly bacteria or brightly coloured moulds, do include the odd one that could be harmful to your health.

Don't let it get to this stage – keeping your starter in the fridge dampens down your sourdough machine (this synergy between *Lactobacillus sanfranciscensis* and *Candida milleri*), and taking it out of the fridge results in a fairly brisk jump back to life. Chilling doesn't stop the fermentation completely, but you can use this to prolong the life of your starter for a very long time indeed – in my experience, several weeks is fine.

THE NEW AGE OF SOURDOUGH STARTERS

All of the above focuses on the steps involved in a starter made with flour and water. But I recommended using juice in my guide to making a starter (see page 42). This wasn't because of the sugar in the juice – that sugar almost certainly causes inhibition of the whole process and indeed does slow it down, in my experience. We're adding juice as an easily accessible source of acid.

I have to thank Debra Wink of thefreshloaf.com for her wonderful write-up of the work she's done in identifying the stages of starting a sourdough starter, properly published in the journal *Bread Lines* in 2009. Her posts have largely popularised the '**pineapple juice method**' of creating sourdough starters – she proposed using this particularly acidic fruit juice to inhibit the growth of the initial *Leuconostoc* fermentation. She found that this accelerated the process of starting the starter, and hypothesised that this was due to competitive inhibition.

I've not had anything published in bread journals, but I've done a lot of side-by-side, real-world tests, and have found that adding juice actually slows down progress. Furthermore, the complexity of the aroma, despite the fruit, wasn't as pleasant. And yet I still advocate its use.

I mentioned I'd started about fifty or more starters while developing this book. The few I've had fail have all used water. They have all allowed bugs, not necessarily the ones that Ms Wink found, to grow and prosper, and then either dominate or use up the available food before the sourdough machine has had a chance to get going.

Every single starter to which I added a little squeeze of lemon juice, or a vitamin C tablet, or orange, apple, pineapple or mixed tropical juice, or raisins, or even diluted Coca-Cola, worked. Even the ones using the most refined and horrible white flour gave me a useable and wonderful sourdough starter. They might have taken a bit longer, but they worked.

The failed ones were as follows:

A rye starter using freshly milled grain and fermented at 30ºC (86ºF). Here, I got a very vigorous gas-producing fermentation within 12 hours. The starter split shortly afterwards, and the top became covered with a dark blue mould. I left it: it stank and never bubbled. I threw it away. A side-by-side identical attempt using tropical juice was successful within three days.

A white starter made with the cheapest possible refined plain flour at a room temperature of roughly 20ºC (68ºF). This never bubbled. Instead, it developed a horrible and extremely strong vomit-like odour. I can only assume this is one of the many gut bacteria, or a beer spoilage bug familiar to me called Clostridium butyricum. *A side-by-side, identical attempt using pineapple juice was successful, even with this cheap flour.*

A spelt starter made with wholemeal spelt flour that I found at the back of my cupboard – it was bought at least two years before. The top developed a hard crust and the middle became epically smelly, in a faecal kind of a way. I didn't do a side-by-side, unfortunately, but another I made with the juice of half a lemon following this worked fine. The right bugs were still there after more than two years; they just needed the right environment.

I know this constitutes scientific evidence of the very worst kind, but with extensive real-world studies lacking, we're forced to make best guesses. And this is my best guess: **adding acid will improve consistency in starting starters.** If 1 in 20 of you who start starters based on the rules of this book have success when otherwise you would have failed, I'm happy.

KEEPING YOUR STARTER HAPPY

There are plenty of reasons your starter can fail, but there are plenty of reasons for it to thrive, too. These are the practical things you can do to aid in keeping it healthy – and keeping you sane – and the things you can change in order to make some seriously awesome bread.

Flour

Sourdough starters can be started and maintained with almost any flour. However, because I go on about the possibilities of starting starters with any flour, in my humble experience, stoneground, wholemeal, organic flours are the ones that consistently work well. It doesn't matter whether it's rye, spelt or wholemeal, just make sure the whole meal is in it. This maximises the available bugs.

Most of the recipes in this book, though, call for a white sourdough starter. This doesn't mean your starter must have been started with white flour, but you could go down this route if you want. I hope it works. You can use posh organic white flour to maximise the possibilities of success.

I used to have several starters going at once, but it was a faff. Now, I keep whatever starter I have going, and occasionally transition it from white to wholemeal to rye and back or any which way. If I run out of a certain sort of flour, I'll feed it with whatever I've got in the cupboard.

If I've got a rye starter on the go and want to make a white bread, I have a few options. Most often, I just use my rye starter and adjust the recipe accordingly. Sometimes, I'll dilute however much starter I need with water and drain this liquid through a fine sieve or tea strainer to remove the bran. But if I really want the sinfully white nature of the bread, I'll sift out the bran in the same way, and mix the resulting startery water with white flour in a new container. By the next day, I'll have a fully active and ready-to-use white starter.

When you change your starter to a white one, the changes you notice can be quite profound – the activity will be less. Wholemeal and rye starters are very active because they have so much more available sugar for the yeast to grow, and possibly because (though I have no way of knowing for sure) you're adding so many more bugs in on top of the existing ones each time.

The acidity levels in your white starter will be higher. Some people find that their complexity is higher, too. I don't know how you'd test for this.

Starter Storage

Basically, anything. My vessel of choice when experimenting with loads of different variations of starter was a 100ml (3½fl oz) tumbler, of which I have many. They were easy to clean and I could standardise my experiments. I laid cling film (plastic wrap) on top to keep the starter moist.

I'm not suggesting you do this. I'm simply making the point that you don't need anything special, and you don't need very much flour either. All of these successful starters were kicked off with less than a tablespoon of flour. I've heard famous bakers say that the more flour you use, the better – and that's kind of true. But you don't want to be dumping more starter than you need to.

If you're making one loaf at a time, then a simple jam (jelly) jar or Kilner (Mason) jar is excellent. Washed, obviously, this holds about 200g of active starter, at a push, which is plenty. Keep 50–100g of starter back and feed with 50g each of flour and water every time. I use this for times of relative inactivity. I wouldn't screw the lid on – you can get a good seal with a jam jar, and it will explode if you do this. Just lay the lid gently on top to stop the starter drying out.

For more loaves, I'd go with a glass clip-top jar, but with the rubber seal removed. Again, this avoids the explosion or cracking risk from too much pressure. Using glass jars is handy, because you can monitor the aeration (and thus the stage following feeding) of your starter and keep an eye on its health.

Less good (but still good) is the plastic lunchbox or Tupperware. They're great for even larger volumes of dough, with an eliminated risk of glass breakages, but it also stops you seeing what's going up the sides. Unless you've got transparent plastic. That would solve the problem.

Because I'm the most indulgent hipster bread baker of them all, I keep my starter in a hand-thrown ceramic fermentation jar.

Temperature

The basic choice when it comes to temperature is whether to store your starter in the fridge or at room temperature. I would never store a starter hotter than room temperature because of how quickly you'll burn through the feeds. And if your temperature isn't controlled, you could risk going hot enough to kill your yeast.

Start your starter at whatever your room temperature is, and so long as it is somewhere between 16–28ºC (61–82ºF), it will be fine. There will be variations in how quickly it takes to get going, but your starter will get going at some point.

Storing is different. If you are storing your starter at room temperature, you have the potential to keep it very active. However, most home starters I know that are kept in this way, like mine was for many years, aren't in great health.

You should be (at least) doubling the weight of your starter every time you feed it. As an example, a starter that weighs 100g should be fed with at least 50g flour and 50g water. If you don't use it and keep it out of the fridge, you'll either have to pour away some starter or double the starter size again, this time using 100g flour and 100g water. If you let this get out of hand, it can mean a loaf's worth of starter every day is wasted.

People compensate for this by not feeding their starters properly, or less frequently. I'm guilty of this. It means you get a lot of *hooch* (that liquid that sits on the top), poor activity, unhealthy yeast and ultimately dense, slack bread made from unmanageably sloppy doughs.

So my advice is to keep your starter in the fridge. Don't convince yourself that you're going to bake sourdough every day (unless, of course, you do). If you give it a feed once the majority has been used to make dough, and you leave it out as you prove, you'll have a starter that's beginning to bubble and grow at the same time as your loaf. This can actually be really useful for tracking the progress of your loaf.

Then stick it in the fridge, after 4–6 hours or so, and it will cool down gradually. Its remaining fermentation will be very slow. As soon as you take it back out of the fridge and it's warmed up again, it's ready to use. This method works whether it's a week or two days between bakes.

Disclaimer: I doth proclaim in a lot of the recipes that you need to let your starter warm up before using. You don't, but by doing so there will be less room for mishaps. At the very least you need to give it an hour or two until the start of your first prove to help it kick back into life before it ferments your bread. This will, of course, be a case of trial and error.

Air

When starting your starter, stirring it a lot does a few things: it develops the gluten, giving you something that rises and falls with heroic stature; it redistributes your bugs, giving them easier access to more food; and it introduces air, and thus oxygen.

I've mentioned before that carbon dioxide can dissolve in dough the same way it can dissolve in liquids – in liquids it makes them fizzy, and in dough, bubbly. Oxygen can also dissolve in dough.

I do not know how starved of oxygen the bottom of a sourdough starter is, but I imagine *quite*. Nor do I know how much of an effect a lack of oxygen has on sourdough fermentation. The studies haven't been done. But stirring your starter during the early stages of cultivation and stirring plenty as you feed are probably not bad ideas.

Stiff Versus Sloppy

There's a lot of debate in the technological bread-o-sphere about whether it is best to store your sourdough starter stiff – usually about 50% hydration (1 part water to 2 parts flour) – or sloppy, at 100% hydration as I recommend (equal parts).

The truth is that it doesn't make that much difference. Stiff starters can be quite practical for big bakeries, because you can chop off pieces of them and weigh them, and you've got big machines that are able to mix it all up easily. Sloppy starters are great for the home because they are very easy to mix in, and you can store them in anything that can hold a liquid.

The differences shouldn't be much, so long as the stiff starter has been properly combined. If there are large areas within your stiff starter that contain only flour and water, and you've not got much starter mixed in here, your bugs will need to migrate into this quite solid structure, therefore negotiating a slightly more complex matrix. For this reason, stiff starters are often said to be slower growing and less acidic. Because they seemingly last longer, lots of people advocate keeping them in the fridge if you bake sourdough less frequently.

I don't see much evidence for any profound effects on the dough either way. I use sloppy because it's easy. I would go with whatever you prefer and adjust the recipes with more or less water accordingly.

STARTER STARTERS

I've briefly touched on a few of the things you might want to add to your starter in order to give you the best chance of success. For whatever reason, these help to create the environment suitable for healthy yeast and bacterial growth. This is probably because they're acidic, but it might also be that they are rich in the sorts of bacteria we're trying to culture. While I've found juice works well, you might not have juice sitting in the house. But you might have raisins.

Following starting a starter with whichever aid you decide to use, you should then go back to feeding it with flour and water. To be honest, I don't know what would happen if you kept on feeding it with fruit juice or raisin water in perpetuity – probably nothing bad. I've never tried it. But juice is expensive and water is cheap. These modifications are all based on the quantities for the sourdough starter recipe on page 41.

Fresh fruit juices I've used orange, apple, pineapple and 'tropical', in equal quantities to the flour.

Raisins A handful for 100g flour. The most-asked query from my last bread book was, 'How many raisins do I put in the sourdough starter?' – I didn't specify, because it doesn't matter.

Raisin-water Leave a handful of raisins to soak in your water overnight, then drain and mix the soaking liquid into your flour instead of water.

Vitamin C (ascorbic acid) Crush one over-the-counter Vitamin C tablet and add to the water.

Citrus I have had great success with adding the juice of a lemon or lime to the water.

Soft drinks Only use full-sugar, and dilute with an equal amount of water (Coca-Cola, for example, is extremely acidic). You can then mix it with the flour.

Fresh fruits One grated apple or pear, or a handful of crushed grapes. You name it: if it's acidic, it will work. All of these are. Add any one of these to the usual quantity of flour and water.

Adding Yeast

One technique I've previously advocated is adding commercial yeast to flour and water in order to create a starter. This was before I understood quite how dominant the sourdough machine of *Lactobacillus/Candida* really is. This method, known as the 'cheat's starter', does work. The issue with it is that you do get a lull – the first two or three feeds yield good results, and then things change. It seems that there's a gap between the inhibition of the *Saccharomyces* fermentation and the start of the proper sourdough fermentation, characterised by poor growth. Feel free to experiment.

Drying and Freezing

I often get messages on social media asking about drying or freezing a starter in order to keep it for a long period of time. Neither is perfect, nor would I really advocate either. It's pretty easy to start a new one from scratch. If you are getting good bread with a particular starter, the reality is that it probably has little to do with the starter itself.

I've seen guides for drying starters involving spreading them thinly and then putting them in the oven on a low heat. This beggars belief – temperatures over 50ºC (122ºF) will kill the vast majority of bugs in your starter. The dried flakes might add the necessary acid to get a new starter going, but there will be little left of the old.

If you would like to dry your starter, spread a few tablespoons very thinly over a sheet of non-stick greaseproof baking paper. Leave it at room temperature to dry naturally – it will take at least a day. It should then splinter and break apart quite easily. You can store this in a jar in the fridge for... I don't really know how long. Quite a few bugs will probably still be there years later.

And as for freezing, just don't. Some yeasts, in a solution of flour, do survive the freezing process. *Some*. Many will die. Seriously, don't bother freezing your starter.

STARTER TROUBLESHOOTING

If what I was saying in the previous chapter made any sense, you shouldn't need this section. Still, it's likely that some of what I say might not make much sense. If I haven't expressed it in the best way for you and your starter is in peril, these are the pages to turn to. In this coming section, I will repeat some of the things I've written about already, but I hope it has some standalone nuggets, too.

'My starter has separated into a liquid layer and a floury layer'
Try not to think of it as separation – rather, think of it as the more solid parts of your mixture settling to the bottom.

All starters settle. This is a natural process that happens as time passes. Once your yeast and bacteria have finished dissecting and then munching through your flour's starch, they slow down and relax. As they do, they stop churning up the starter, and because they've also broken down many of your proteins, the delicate structure collapses. The liquid at the top is a mixture of water, alcohol and acid, as well as plenty more bugs and some protein. Or really bad sour wheat beer, if you will. The slang name for this stuff is *hooch*.

If your starter had been bubbling plenty beforehand, take settling as a sign that the yeasts have exhausted their food source and the starter needs feeding. If you're often getting separation, it could mean a few different things – the most likely is that you aren't feeding your starter often enough to maintain good yeast activity, or that you need to feed it with more flour and water. You want to at least double the weight of your starter every time you feed it. And if you aren't going to feed it to double its weight again the next day, stick it in the fridge.

The other common cause of hooch is a starter that's been brought to the brink of death through neglect, and then an attempt has been made to revive it. In this instance, despite many feeds, it hardly bubbles and then separates. Here, your balance of yeast and bacteria is wrongly skewed towards the latter. You can either pour most of it away and try re-dosing it with rye or wholemeal flour, or you can start again.

'My starter hasn't started'
If you get no activity from your starter at all, there are a few possibilities.

If you get a separation (rather like the above) from the start without any bubbles, you've been successful in culturing lactic acid bacteria (most likely) and little else. You haven't created the wonderful synchronicity between the bugs required. The most likely issue here is that you've used the wrong flour. Use good wholemeal, preferably rye, organic flour; try adding some fruit juice.

If you get no bubbles at all, and it still smells floury after a week or more, then I'd be willing to bet that your starter is too cold. Stick it near to the heater, but not on it. It simply isn't the case that your flour is sterile – there's always something in it, and likely millions of things. Just occasionally, there are far fewer than you'd like, or the wrong organism. If in doubt, add some more flour; the dirtier and fresher flour, the better.

'My starter is black, red or blue'
Moulds are beautiful, colourful things. Their growth is relatively uncommon in a developed, active starter. They're in it, and on it, but they're stamped down by the overwhelming fermentation that dominates, and that you use in the creation of your bread.

You can start to get mould growth from as little as three days after a starter has separated (see above). The most common is a black mould, which is usually (but not always) of the *Aspergillus* species. This isn't harmful to humans, apart from those who are very unwell with diseases that attack their immune system, though I don't know what ingesting a black sourdough starter raw would do to even the healthiest of people. Probably bad things.

If you're determined to save your beloved starter (please don't be), then you can pour away the black stuff and give it a feed with some good flour. If it bubbles within a couple of days, great. If it doesn't, don't lose any sleep. Start again.

Blue or white fluffy moulds are a similar story – they grow in the presence of oxygen and are strongly inhibited by alcohol, so it normally takes quite a lengthy period of neglect for it to grow, usually on the drier bits of flour that line the sides of your starter receptacle. This is fine – just scrape them out and don't neglect your starter so much in future.

Bright pink, orange or reddish moulds tend to be the nastier ones, and might not be moulds at all, but rather bacteria. Pink examples are *T. thermophilus* (a cool, heat-tolerant organism), *E. coli* (some strains harmful, some not) and certain *Lactobacillus* strains. Starters are melting pots of interesting bugs, and you don't know what's going to happen when your fermentation settles down.

Pink moulds are more associated with producing toxins that are harmful to humans, and these toxins (called *mycotoxins*) survive the baking process. I've never heard or read of anyone becoming unwell ever, ever, ever through eating cooked sourdough. And I've checked. But I'm legally and ethically bound to suggest that if your starter has a neon mould of any such colour, then you should chuck it out and have a shower.

'My starter smells of...'

I get lots of people asking why their starter acts or smells a certain way. Often, starters have numerous unpleasant flavours mixed in with lots of nice ones. You need to decide if you like the bread that the starter makes. Don't worry about the starter itself. It should burn the inside of your nostrils a little as you sniff it, and smell alcoholic once it has passed peak volume. You might get nice banana, clove or peach notes in there. None of these makes it into the bread.

If you're worried about the smell of alcohol or nail-polish remover or vinegar (acetic acid), feed your starter more often. Or, you can try cooling it down between feeds so that it doesn't over-ferment.

Common ones are, 'My starter smells like vomit' – this is because many strains of the bugs we want in sourdough starters produce butyric acid, which gives vomit that characteristic and nose-stinging odour. Then there was the time I forgot about a spelt starter that somehow made its way to the very back of the flour drawer. Despite being contained within a supposedly sealed Tupperware, some months later I thought something must have died in the kitchen. Very few aromas make me gag, but this particular smell of rotting flesh and faeces hit the spot.

It's safe to say that if you experience either of the above, do NOT attempt sourdough starter CPR. Let it die with dignity and begin the cycle of life anew. If you consistently get off-flavours that you think are affecting your bread or you're just not that comfortable with, change the flour you feed it with and (as always) feed it more often.

'My starter doesn't rise and fall – it's lethargic'

You want your starter, following feeding and mixing, to rise dramatically. Quite what volume it reaches will depend on the dimensions of your container, but it should double or triple in size following a feed and be filled with loads of tiny bubbles.

If your bubbles are numerous but not evenly distributed, and your starter seems to take ages to get going, you needn't worry. It's perfectly healthy, but it's just not mixed in well enough. You should incorporate your new flour and water until you've got a smooth, consistent dough.

Despite this, if you're still not getting the rise, then try a period of keeping the starter out of the fridge and being really strict with feeding it every day. If, even then, you're still not getting a rise, consider the temperature as a factor. You should warm it up to see whether that helps.

Finally, if your starter is white, try adding some stoneground wholemeal or rye into the mix, as well as increasing the ratio of new flour and water to old starter. A few daily feeds and it will likely get going.

'My starter exploded everywhere and it broke my expensive jar'

This is, for the most part, a good thing. It means that you've got a very active starter indeed.

Sometimes, though, bread with broken glass isn't great. And some people think that a starter that is too active isn't necessarily all that. When making breads like a San Francisco-style sourdough, you might not want such a bubbly starter. You want one that's a little sluggish, makes your dough tangier and more complex, and takes longer to prove at working temperatures.

If you're looking for this, you should actually change to a more refined, whiter flour. This reduction in nutrients will increase the fermentation time and decrease its health. You'll get more vomitty, nail-polishy flavours, and you'll have a more extensible dough that you can do more with.

'My starter is full of flies'

This isn't a problem I've had a huge amount of experience with because I'm usually pretty good at covering my starters.

Don't worry, though. I have had an infestation problem once, while testing starter methods for this book. I had a line of starters of mildly different moisture contents, covered with a sheet of cling film (plastic wrap) that subsequently blew off. Flies landed in a couple. They hadn't even got going then, but I decided to run with it. I swear they were the best-smelling, most active starters of the bunch.

I did fish the flies out prior to using them, but I can't guarantee there weren't any decomposing legs in there. Flies are great carriers of all kinds of bacteria and yeast – some of these could cause spoilage, but some will add interesting and possibly awesome flavours. Embrace the fly.

'My starter isn't working after drying or freezing'

I've a simple policy on drying and freezing starters – don't do it (see page 99). There's no point. If you want to gift starters to other people, hand them some cold starter in a jar. If you're worried about going on holiday for a couple of weeks, don't be. Stick your starter in the fridge. If it's months, just start a new one when you're back. Or bring it with you and feed it from time to time.

Drying a sourdough starter, usually by spreading your starter very thin on a sheet of non-stick greaseproof baking paper and leaving it, gives you a lot of yeast and bacteria that returns to the dormant state it was in the flour. Then they start to die. Yes, some bugs will remain, but your flour already has plenty to get you going. There's no need for these extra ones. The acid, though, might help things get going a little more reliably.

Freezing, on the other hand, causes ice crystals to form within the cells of your yeast and bacteria. This causes some, and likely the vast majority, to die (see page 99). Not all, and some of your starter will survive. But it will be in desperate health and require at least four or five days before it is back to normal. Why not just start a new one, and delight in its individuality? You can even give it a new name, if you are that way inclined.

BREAD TROUBLE-SHOOTING

These are all relative terms. Your bread is probably awesome and you're nit-picking. If your bread really, really isn't awesome, don't despair. Let's fix it for next time. I'm sorry if your particular quandary doesn't appear: this list isn't exhaustive, but it covers most of the common 'flaws'.

If you are of the mindset that bread doesn't have flaws and instead each loaf is a manifestation of the baker's individual creative freedom, regardless of their results, good for you. Skip past this chapter.
I am envious.

'My bread is dense'

Denseness is a sign of insufficient yeast activity. This can mean your bread is underproved, or hasn't been given enough time to prove. Very commonly, it can mean that the temperature of your dough was too low. Try using warmer water and proving somewhere warm using an active sourdough starter, especially during the first prove. This will also aid the structure of your dough – your gas-filled, acidic dough will have very good strength.

Conversely, an overproved dough can be dense. Time and *Lactobacillus* bacteria will break down protein, and that causes your dough to slop and its air-capturing ability to be diminished. Otherwise, overproving can cause your gluten to be overstretched and the delicate matrix to collapse when the dough is moved to the oven. This is more common in doughs that are a little underdeveloped and need a bit more stretching and folding for the amount of moisture they have.

Dense doughs can be caused by starter woes. Most likely, your starter could be in a poor condition. If in doubt, take it out of the fridge and feed it daily, pouring away the excess starter. It could be that you've just added too little, or your recipe calls for too little.

'My dough hasn't risen at all'

Don't worry if it looks like this – often sourdough can rise very slowly and changes can be hard to notice. It's difficult to know whether it's doubled in size, let alone risen by half, especially if you're intermittently knocking air out by stretching and folding. One option for dealing with this is to take a picture on your phone of your bowl just after mixing, and then again after the time that should have elapsed. Compare the two.

If it genuinely appears that your dough hasn't risen, then I'd encourage you still to shape it and bake it, then see what happens. I feel a lot of these complaints are made about doughs that are subsequently thrown away. You just don't know – your second prove might take off, especially with a bit of heat. Following baking, you might find a massive expansion and perfectly adequate aeration. If not, examine the crumb structure. If it's dense, see the previous point about dense loaves. If it's utterly solid, your starter's probably the issue.

'My sourdough is too sour'

This is usually an issue with the starter. Some starters, especially those fed infrequently and kept at room temperature, can be very sour. This causes a slow or delayed rise, a flat, floppy dough and a very tangy, chewy crumb. If this is you, work on your starter activity levels, and keep it in the fridge when not in use.

It can be that you've got a very active starter, and it's being used too late in the cycle of feeding – if you leave it for more than 24 hours since the last feed, or more than a week in the fridge, often the acid will dominate. Try to use your active starter at peak volume, 8–14 hours after feeding. If you have a penchant for a very sour loaf, you could try leaving your starter for longer than 24 hours before using it.

While rye flour is a little more sour than wheat flour, a wholemeal or rye starter tends to produce much less tangy loaves. Yeast populations and sugar availability are much higher in these starters, so they tend to ferment faster and cleaner.

'My dough flops or spreads before baking'

This is the big one – I get more questions about this than any other flaw. If your dough doesn't have enough strength, the solutions are numerous.

The simplest way to increase strength is to reduce the amount of liquid in your dough. This is fine when you're starting off, but it will give you a slightly denser bread with a crumb that isn't so soft.

Assuming the recipe is good, the most common reason for a lack of strength in colder-climate countries is a less-than-vigorous fermentation. You want your yeast to produce carbon dioxide at a high enough rate to keep inflating your bubbles. This gives the dough lots of strength.

Therefore, a poor starter is commonly to blame – follow the entire section on starter trouble-shooting, pages 101–3. If you're sure it isn't that, try increasing the temperature of your water and proving in a warm place – aim for the dough to be about 25ºC (77ºF).

At this point, if your fermentation is fine and you're still getting sloppy dough, it's either to do with the development of your gluten, or a lack of tightness when shaping. The first often leads to the second.

Gluten could be developed further by kneading longer at the beginning, but if you overdevelop at this stage, your gluten can become too tight. Compromise and add some stretches and folds during the first prove. Two or three, spaced out, following an initial (but modest) mix is usually enough to sort out your dough strength.

If you're not in the habit of dividing and pre-shaping your wet doughs, get into it. It's pretty much essential for maintaining enough strength to get a decent shape. If you're having any trouble with my guide on page 58, you can pre-shape just as you normally would do your final shape. Just give it a bench rest, then do it again.

Finally, a sloppy dough could be the shaping itself – make sure you've got light fingers, work quickly and use floured hands to stop them sticking. You don't want to bash and squeeze the gas out of the dough as many traditional French or English bakers might – it's a delicate process.

'The dough's too wet to work with'
First, check the recipe. Make sure that you weighed all the correct ingredients with accuracy. Check your scales. Does a pack of butter weigh the amount stated, or a 1kg bag of sugar actually weigh exactly that?

If so, it's probably a situation that's similar to my last point on sloppy doughs. Wetness is usually a result of poor dough strength. If you're starting out, the easiest way to increase dough strength is to add flour, and that's fine. Just add a little and feel how the dough develops – but try not to add quite as much the next time.

A dough that is stretched and folded during its first prove following a decent knead will feel completely different to a dough that's left without fondling. Temperature is also an important factor. Doughs that rise quickly will maintain more strength, whereas the bacteria that prosper in the cold will break down the proteins in the dough to give you an even floppier, wetter-feeling dough.

If you are concerted in your efforts not to add flour, good on you. Try adding some spaced-out episodes of stretching and folding during your first prove. Each time you'll feel the dough becoming a bit bouncier, then flop back again over the next hour or so. Repeat, and it will come together. Make sure you don't miss out your pre-shape and bench rest prior to the final shaping.

'My dough deflates before baking'
Deflation happens when the dough has been overproved. The gluten structure is overly stretched to precarious levels, and so it will collapse with the slightest provocation. You'll say goodbye to all that aeration you've been waiting for. I'd still bake your loaf, because many of these burst bubbles will fill back up again during the time in the oven. You'll just notice your crumb is a little close, with lots of middling, thick-walled bubbles.

Rest for less time following shaping, or reduce the temperature. The cold helps with the gluten's stability, so a cold and overproved loaf is more stable than a warm one, which tends to splat. That's partly why proving in the fridge is a relatively safe thing to do.

If your shaped dough is already overproved and you've forgotten to preheat your oven, get it in the fridge as soon as you realise. If the dough looks particularly swollen and unstable, I wouldn't bother scoring, as the cuts won't open up and you'll just end up deflating things further.

'My crust is pale, thick and tough'

A thick crust may be because your bread has been baked for a quite a long time. I don't mind this, and from time to time that's what I'm after. But a thick, tough, tooth-breaking crust isn't a good thing. There are quite a few causes.

The first is poor or non-existent shaping – this appears in loaves baked in tins or if made in bread makers, as some people assume you don't need to shape. Not only does the dough weld itself to the sides, but the top is thick and dense. What makes a good crust are the layered sheets of gluten, aligned parallel to the crust. Fail to achieve this and the crust becomes craggy, bubbly and altogether poor.

The other reason for a thick, unpleasant crust is inadequate caramelisation. This could be because it has been underproved, but it is usually because there's not enough moisture: either your proving dough has been left open to the elements and developed a dry, leathery skin on it, or you've not added enough steam at the beginning of your bake. A fan oven can really dry out loaves, so you need to be careful to add extra steam. To test whether it's this, bake your loaf in a pot with the lid on for the first 20 minutes and see what happens.

'My loaves burn easily'

This is an interesting one. The first thing to check is your oven temperature – obviously, this means making sure you're setting it to the right temperature. If necessary, buy an oven thermometer. All ovens have cold and warm spots, even efficient fan ovens. But you should put it roughly in the centre of your oven, and ensure that it is what it says it should be in that spot. Adjust as necessary.

If it's not that, it could be your loaves. Overproving during the first prove, especially a cold and very long one, can cause an overabundance of sugars. These are more likely to burn. I like that burnt sugar look and taste, though – it might be that you need to adjust what you define as 'burnt' and what you see as 'caramelised'.

'My crumb is raw or doughy in the centre'

If I've made a mistake with any recipe timings, please write to me. But I don't think I have, and lots of people are paid to check this stuff.

A raw crumb happens when there's a mismatch between your loaf looking cooked but still not being baked in the middle. The solution is to turn down your oven and bake for a bit longer. It helps to check the true temperature of your oven using an oven thermometer, as above.

Sometimes doughiness can be caused by other things: often too much sugar added to your dough will cause your crumb to be overly wet and dense. I've seen this if I've gone a wee bit overboard in how much honey I'm adding to a walnut loaf. The same has happened in brioches, where I've experimented by adding lots of sugar. This gives the texture of a sweaty insole.

'My bread stales too quickly'

There's no great secret to storing bread. In my view, the best place is on the chopping board, crumb side down. Sourdough is awesome in that, despite a lack of any additional preservatives, it keeps and keeps and keeps. I'd be highly surprised if your bread is stale within the first few days, at least.

It might have dried out slightly, and people often confuse this with staleness. Sliced sourdough makes excellent toast, and you'll find a lot of the moisture returns if you toast your bread. For breads designed to be torn rather than sliced, sticking them back in the oven with a little steam can work wonders – you just have to be happy with a slightly thicker crust.

For a bread that has even greater longevity, you can try proving for longer (creating more acid) or using a starter that's a little more acidic to begin with; one that's not been fed so regularly. It also helps to check your salt levels: if you've been scrimping on the salt for noble health reasons, don't. Two per cent of your flour weight should be enough salt for decent longevity.

'The flavour is lacking'
Did you remember to add the salt after the autolyse? Did you really? Fine.

When making bread using commercial yeast, it's easy to make a flavourless bread. When making sourdough, it's quite hard. The fermentation is inherently interesting and diverse. But if you prove your dough warm and fast, you can sometimes get a sourdough that doesn't have the deep complexity or the tang that you want.

Proving warm can be helpful – the yeast activity keeps the dough strong. To add flavour, try using a proportion of wholemeal flours. Wheat, rye or spelt will give you something extra. The alternative is to retard one of your proves in the fridge – preferably the second one. This allows you to develop the dough before chilling it to maximise flavour, creating an irregular structure and letting you bake it at the time that suits you.

'I don't have lots of huge bubbles'
You've done well. You're making sourdough, it's working out. But the crumb doesn't have that huge, open structure that you've seen from the very best.

There's no one answer to this question. Big, irregular bubbles are things that commercial bakers have been trying to eliminate for hundreds of years because it isn't particularly practical to spread and butter. But now they're a sign of good sourdough, for stupid reasons, and people want to emulate them. Follow the steps in this book and you should achieve them. The key points are summarised below:

- An active starter, above all
- A high-hydration dough
- An autolyse, without salt
- Modest initial mix
- Warm, active first prove with two or three stretches and folds
- Gentle pre-shaping and shaping
- A very steamy bake, such as inside a lidded pot or a Dutch oven

'What are the small bubbles on the crust?'
These are called 'bird's-eye' bubbles. If you've got an active starter, you'll notice them a little less often – check the bottom of your loaves and you might find a few. In France, they're not encouraged and some bakers will go to great lengths to reduce their formation.

They're formed when you've got a fairly acidic environment – usually when using a starter that's been fed less often or with less flour. This causes the gluten to break down over a long, retarded prove, and so the carbon dioxide dissolves in the dough – think of it as slightly fizzy.

During this protracted prove, a dry skin on the outside of your dough will form, keeping the whole thing contained. When you finally bake the bread, it will cause the gas to come out, breaking through the dry skin and creating lots of little bubbles.

If you want more of these bubbles, as found on San Francisco-style loaves, feed your starter less often (or store it warm) and retard your second prove. If you want fewer bubbles, make sure you've got a very refreshed, active starter.

'My loaf has irregular oven spring or random growths'

Oven spring is largely due to the carbon dioxide in your dough filling the bubbles and then expanding them rapidly. If this is going on while the crust has already formed, it tends to expand along the lines of your scores. The bubbles expand along the path of least resistance. Therefore, if the majority of your crust has formed but a cold spot means that one bit hasn't quite yet, your bubbles will expand this way. This can lead to 'growths' on the side of your bread where the dough has broken through.

You can stop this by scoring as per my guide on page 65 – shallow but decisive and along the lines of the dough's shaping. Plenty of steam will delay crust formation and allow the loaf to expand properly. Finally, don't bake your loaves too close together, or you'll create uneven crust formation and consequently irregularity will be inevitable.

'The sides are rounded and oven spring was poor'

This is a common problem found when good yeasted bread makers switch to sourdough. This is usually a combination of overdevelopment and underproving.

This means that the dough has been kneaded to pass the windowpane test (see page 49), usually without any kind of an autolyse. This leads to a dough that's fairly elastic, but not extensible, in which case quite a lot of force is required to stretch out the gluten and your sourdough. Even during the most active of warm fermentations, your dough will struggle.

You could try using a flour with a lower gluten content, or increasing your dough's hydration. But if you've started already and you can see that you've got a nice, smooth dough that isn't rising, just give it a little time and the bugs will begin to break down your gluten. It'll be fine, but will take a bit longer. Then, bake it in a lidded pot or Dutch oven to maximise oven spring.

In future, if using the same recipe, reduce your initial kneading and give the dough a few stretches and folds to compensate. The section on dough rheology (page 76) will be especially useful, I think.

'My scores don't open up'

Like any of these problems, there's no single solution.

The most common reason for this is shaping that is not quite adequate, which in itself is often caused by a dough that isn't strong enough to begin with. If you haven't created adequate tension in the dough, it won't burst open. Practise your shaping, and give it a pre-shape.

It goes without saying that you need to have proved your bread properly for it to burst open – those bubbles have to be contained within the dough in order for them to expand. If there aren't any bubbles, you'll have a dense brick of a loaf.

Conversely, if your dough has too much gluten development and not enough yeast activity to expand your bubbles (for example, during a long, cold first prove), you'll have a solid dough with very thick-walled bubbles. The pressure required to overcome the force of the gluten is quite huge, and so you won't reach your potential expansion in the oven.

If your dough is a little overproved during the second prove and your bubbles have reached the maximum size they possibly can, your scores won't open. A relatively lightly proved dough, following an adequate or extended first prove, has the potential for massive expansion in the oven if scored properly. This is why baguettes are have such impressive 'ears' (see page 142).

'I've got a line of dense dough at the bottom (or at the side) of tins'

Inherently there's a risk that proving in tins (or even proving the loaf the same way up as it's going to bake) is going to cause an irregularity in your crumb, with dense dough and smaller bubbles towards the bottom, and big bubbles that open up at the top.

Usually, and as is the case with many problems, this is made more likely by inadequate dough strength or shaping that needs a bit more tightness. If you dump your loaf in the tin without shaping, it's going to have a flat, dense bottom because you've not developed a structure that can support it. When stretching and folding, make sure the dough is shaped a little tighter.

Then, the only thing you've got to do is make sure not to overprove it; once the gluten is stretched to that extent, the structure will fail and you'll end up with a line of stodge in whichever place that it was surrounded by tin.

'There's massive bubbles or tunnels through the loaf, or under the crust'

There are a few reasons for this. I've often seen it in a loaf that's had a too-cold or underactive first prove – you might notice this happening to loaves as you move into the winter months. Get the prove a little warmer, or pitch a more active starter.

I've also seen it in loaves that have been well developed but then overproved during the second prove. If your loaf was impressively swollen before baking, then it's a sign it was overproved. As you move it about and score it, fragile bubbles might burst and consolidate into one large hole.

Another possible reason for this is that it has very poor strength. Add some stretches and folds during the first prove, pre-shape and then shape.

RELAXED RECIPES

If the *pain au levain* chapter (page 39) felt like a bit of an onslaught, this one will hopefully be a little more tranquil. Each recipe is one that doesn't require quite the dedication encouraged thus far – either they don't bother with the traditional shaping process, or they're just a little bit more forgiving.

These are good opportunities to get used to the handling of really wet, sticky and very stretchy sourdough doughs. By all means jump in and make the recipe for *pain au levain* from start to finish, but you can get used to a few of the processes using the following. They are still utterly flavourful loaves with amazing aeration. They're just, by their nature, a bit more zen, and not likely to induce stress if it's your first attempt.

These recipes are designed for single home batches, but you can split them into smaller batches or double or triple them accordingly.

PAVÉ RUSTIQUE

While you can shape this bread as per the guides on pages 60–3, one of the ways that you can get used to wet doughs that require shaping is to make them into squares. It isn't a cop-out, as square breads can look cool. It's called a *pavé* because it looks like a cobblestone. Since you aren't handling them so much, you maintain a lot of the initial aeration. These big bubbles expand to create an amazing crumb structure. You should apply this principle of gentle dough-handling to all of your sourdoughs.

Any *pain rustique* dough in the English-language bread world is probably based, loosely, on that by Jeffrey Hamelman in his book *Bread*. It's a soft, wet dough with a very creamy crumb, and is especially suited to shorter, warmer proves. Like this one.

I've added wholemeal (wholewheat) into the final dough – and you can make this with a rye starter or a white one. If you're new to bread making, a rye starter will mean the dough is drier and more manageable. If you've got a wholemeal starter, use this and add a little rye to the dough instead.

For 2 small loaves:
100g rye (or white) sourdough starter
400g strong white flour, plus extra for dusting
50g wholemeal (wholewheat) flour
330g tepid-warm water
10g table salt
semolina, for dusting

Start by taking your sourdough starter out of the fridge about 8–14 hours before you want to bake. If it hasn't been fed recently or its activity has waned, give it a feed when you take it out.

In a large bowl, weigh your flours. Add in your sourdough starter. Mix warm and cool water in a jug to get approximately 25ºC (77ºF) (colder than a swimming pool, warmer than tepid), and pour this in. Mix everything together very roughly until you have a lumpy dough – use a wooden spoon, your hands or a dough hook.

Let the dough rest for about 20–30 minutes – this short autolyse will help it come together much better. Ideally, cover the bowl with a damp tea towel or a plate to stop it drying out.

Add your salt, and then mix your dough – I'd recommend trying it by hand. The slap and fold method works very well – see pages 50–1. You want to develop the gluten well here – at least 10 minutes of mixing. It might pass the windowpane test (page 49). Alternatively, you can stretch and fold the dough (page 55) and then repeat this at least every hour of the prove until it seems strong.

Wrap your bowl in a couple of large tea towels to keep it warm and stop the dough from drying out. Leave in a relatively warm place for about 4 hours or so. If you aren't stretching and folding every hour, a single stretch and fold about 2 hours in would be beneficial for the dough's strength.

Once your dough is looking larger and quite aerated, it's ready to shape. Don't worry about pre-shaping. Flour a work surface, and a couche or heavy tea towel at the same time (you can use a square proving basket if you have one). Turn your dough gently out onto the surface – use a dough scraper to cleanly separate it from the side of the bowl so as not to stretch the dough too much. Divide the dough by cutting in half using your dough scraper. Dust your hands lightly in flour to stop them from sticking to it.

With floury hands, gently stretch out each dough into a large square. Be careful not to tear it. You want each to be about 20cm (8in) square. Then fold the dough in half so that it makes a rectangle and it has floury sides on the top and bottom. If it has stuck, use your scraper and add more flour. Brush off any excess flour from the top, and fold it in half again, gently pressing and holding to make the surfaces stick together. You've now got a lightly shaped, wet, aerated square loaf.

Use a scraper, or your hands if it hasn't stuck, to lift the dough onto your floured couche. You can use anything hefty and square-edged (this book will do) on each side to keep it supported as it proves for 1–2 more hours. You want it to grow by about half again.

Preheat your oven 30–40 minutes before you think it will be ready if it has a stone or heavy baking surface inside. You can bake these loaves inside a pot or cloche – just make sure it's going to fit. Alternatively, use a baking tray. Go for 250ºC (480ºF)/230ºC (450ºF) fan/Gas 9.

Dust a tray or board with semolina when you're ready to bake, and then dust some more semolina onto your proven dough. Get your hands under your couche and flip the dough onto the tray, keeping all the bubbles inside. Score gently – I like to use one diagonal line.

Transfer to the oven and add steam using your chosen method – I'd pour some water into a cast-iron pan that's sitting in the bottom of the oven, or bake under a lid or cloche. Turn the oven down to 230ºC (450ºF)/210ºC (410ºF) fan/Gas 8. Bake for 20 minutes and then either vent the oven by opening the door and allowing the steam to escape, or remove the lid or cloche, and bake for another 30 minutes, or until a deep golden. Cool for at least 30 minutes before eating.

FOCACCIA INTEGRALE

To those who feel that the principle of this recipe is an abomination, I implore you to try it.

Integrale means wholemeal. My version of this Italian flatbread is made with good British flour and a decent portion of wholewheat or rye flour – for ease, we'll use whichever makes up your starter. While the focaccia is indeed an ancient bread, the idea that it must only be made with white flour is modern – flours have never been as refined as they are today, and we are hopefully beginning to revolt against this.

This is a recipe for you to play with. The dough is soft and forgiving, and you can incorporate loads of things into it: nuts, chopped olives, onions, garlic or sundried tomatoes all work well. The high oil content helps give it a crumb structure that is rather eccentric and uneven, as it interrupts your gluten – that's why we add it after the mixing. Further oil doused over the top is essential.

Some would say use cheap oil for inside and expensive oil on top. Instead, just use the best oil, all the time. Buy it in bulk if you can, directly from the producers in France, Italy, Spain or Greece. Each country has its own varieties and *terroirs*, and each will make a different focaccia – this is also part of the fun.

Makes 1 large focaccia:

150g rye or wholemeal (wholewheat)
   sourdough starter
425g strong white flour
8g table salt
350g tepid-warm water
100g good-quality extra virgin olive oil,
   plus extra for oiling and drizzling
2–3 tsp good-quality sea salt flakes
herbs or toppings as you see fit – I like a handful
   of olives, a few tomatoes on the vine, a sliced
   red onion or a sprig or two of rosemary

Ideally, take your starter out of the fridge at least 8–14 hours before you want to bake. If it hasn't been fed recently, give it a feed when you take it out. You can use it straight from the fridge, but your first prove will take quite a bit longer.

In a large bowl, weigh your flour. Add the table salt, then mix this in using your fingers. Add in your sourdough starter. Mix warm and cool water in a jug to 25ºC (77ºF) (colder than a swimming pool, warmer than tepid), and pour this in. Mix everything roughly until you have a very wet dough.

Let the dough rest for about 20–30 minutes – even allowing for a short autolyse of 10 minutes makes a difference. Cover the bowl with a damp tea towel or a plate to stop it drying out during this time.

Knead your dough – for this dough (which is very wet), stretching and folding intermittently works very well (see page 55), but I'd still give it a little bit of working before adding the oil. The slap and fold method – see pages 50–1 – also works well. Give it 5 minutes of mixing, and as soon as it feels smooth, add your oil. Mix this until completely combined and you've got a very soft, shiny dough.

Wrap your bowl in a couple of large tea towels to keep it warm and stop the dough drying out. Leave in a relatively warm place for about 4 hours. Alternatively, you could retard this prove overnight in a cool place, covering the dough with a plastic bag. I would do a stretch and fold following this, if so, then leave it in a warm place for 1 hour before shaping.

This dough should appear large and slightly terrifying, with loads of big bubbles. If it isn't, leave it a little longer. Once it is, oil a roasting tin and then add a little oil on top of your proven dough. Your hands should be very oily, too. Use your hands or a dough scraper to scrape your dough out of the bowl and into the tin. If it sticks, don't worry – you can lift it off with your scraper and then add more oil.

Flatten your dough slightly, being careful to maintain its delicate air bubbles. Fold your dough in half, and then fold your new, longer dough in half again. I think of this like folding an A4 (US letter) piece of paper twice so that you've got a smaller piece of paper. Add more oil if it's sticking, and gently push your dough out into the corners of a 30 x 40cm (12 x 16in) roasting tin.

Stick your tin inside a plastic bag and leave to prove for 2–3 more hours at room temperature. Alternatively, you can retard this prove overnight or for up to 24 hours until your bread is ready to bake. You want it to grow further by about half.

Preheat your oven to 250ºC (480ºF)/230ºC (450ºF) fan/Gas 9 at least 30–40 minutes before you expect to bake your bread. If you have a stone, place in the oven to heat up. Just before it's ready to bake, remove the focaccia from the plastic bag and poke indentations using oiled fingers in the dough, giving the focaccia its characteristic holes. Top with some flaked sea salt, at least, and any olives, vegetables or herbs you like. Drench the whole thing with generous drizzles of oil.

Place in the oven and add steam using your chosen method – for example, adding some water into a cast-iron pan that's sitting in the bottom of the oven. Turn the oven down to 220ºC (430ºF)/200ºC (400ºF) fan/Gas 7. Bake for 20 minutes, and then vent the oven by opening the door and allowing the steam to escape. Bake for another 15–20 minutes, or until a good golden brown.

Leave to cool for at least 15 minutes. Then add more oil on top. Slice and serve hot if you like, but it does also keep extremely well. Just add more oil when you serve it.

UNBLEACHED BAPS

These sourdough buns are so soft and sticky, they hardly need adornment with butter or oil. They're simple to make, without being complicated by tricky shaping techniques. In fact, they're an excellent demonstration of how you can shape breads without any flour whatsoever. This is all down to the magic of the dough scraper.

This is a high-hydration dough – meaning it is very wet and tacky. If you couple this with unbleached white flour as I recommend, you'll have a fairly light crust with a very soft centre. I bake these on trays using baking paper for ease, but you could prove them on a couche and slide them individually onto a stone for a more rustic, crusty roll.

The addition of seeds – here, a mixture of sunflower and poppy – suits rolls or buns particularly well. In larger loaves where you're hoping to take the crusts to near-burnt levels of darkness, the seeds carbonise to the extent that they are almost unpleasant. But in this recipe, you retain nearly all their flavour. Feel free to use any combination of seeds that you like.

For a dozen baps:
150g rye or wholemeal (wholewheat)
* sourdough starter*
425g strong white flour
10g table salt
300g tepid-warm water
25g sunflower seeds
25g poppy seeds

Take your sourdough starter out of the fridge about 8–14 hours before you want to bake. If it hasn't been fed within the last week, or you can't see noticeable bubbles, give it a feed. If you do have to feed it, use white flour.

In a large bowl, weigh your flour. Add the salt, and then mix this in using your fingers. Mix warm and cool water in a jug to about 25ºC (77ºF) (colder than a swimming pool, warmer than tepid), and pour this in. Add in your sourdough starter. Using a spoon or a dough hook, mix everything until you have a lumpy dough.

Optionally, autolyse: let the dough rest for about 20–30 minutes. Ideally, cover the bowl with a plate or a damp tea towel to stop the dough drying out.

Mix your dough – the slap and fold method works well (see pages 50–1). Or not, if you'd rather. You can get

away with murder when making these rolls – I'd think about just a couple of stretches and folds (see page 55), one now, and one again after a couple of hours. Your dough will need 4 hours' total proving time at a warm room temperature, covered with a plate or damp tea towel, but 6 hours at a cool room temperature, or overnight if it's even colder than that.

Once your dough is looking large and aerated, it's time to divide and shape. First, find a baking tray and line it with a sheet of non-stick greaseproof baking paper – the additional non-stickability is important here. Turn your dough gently out onto an unfloured surface and use a dough scraper to separate it from the side of the bowl so as not to stretch it too much. If you want all your rolls to be the same size, you can weigh them: they should each be about 73g. Otherwise, you can guess – chop with your dough scraper into 12 roughly even sticky piles of gloop.

If your dough is sticking to everything, wet your hands and dough scraper. Keep everything wet; don't add more flour. Just as when pre-shaping (see page 58), drive an angled dough scraper sideways, scooping the dough underneath. Keep pushing your scraper along the surface to tighten the dough. Next, scoop the dough the same way towards you and repeat until you've got a vaguely smooth ball of dough. Scoop this onto your prepared, lined tray. Repeat this for all your buns, keeping them spaced a little apart.

While they are still sticky, sprinkle with the seeds: first the sunflower seeds, then the poppy seeds. If you have too many seeds, you can add more just before they go in the oven. Leave to prove for 2 more hours – you want them to grow further by about half and be nearly touching each other. I'd put the entire tray inside a large plastic bag; alternatively, you can spread or spray some oil on some cling film (plastic wrap) to lay over the top of the rolls to stop them drying out.

About 20 minutes before you think they will be ready, preheat your oven to 250ºC (480ºF)/230ºC (450ºF) fan/Gas 9. Preheat for longer if you're using a baking stone or heavy surface underneath your tray.

Remove your tray from its plastic bag (or remove the cling film), place in the oven and add some steam: some water poured into a cast-iron pan that's sitting in the bottom will be fine. Turn the oven down to 220ºC (430ºF)/200ºC (400ºF) fan/Gas 7. Bake for 10 minutes, and then vent the oven by opening the door and allowing the steam to escape. Bake for another 20 minutes, or until light and golden. Cool for at least 20 minutes before enjoying.

EPIC BUNS

My wife has, in the past, complained at the relative infrequency of my cake baking: "It's just been bread, bread, bread." My answer? More bread.

To combine a sweet dough with wholewheat or rye flour might seem like a strange concept, but it fits in situations of light spice, like this one. It contributes a certain earthiness and texture that works well with cinnamon. It turns out that using just the amount you've got within your sourdough starter addition is perfect for adding flavour without being overbearing.

This recipe is basically my favourite in the world. Imagine a cinnamon bun, but altogether more bready and flavourful, then topped with the best icing (frosting) that exists: cream cheese buttercream. The sweetness is balanced by the savouriness of the bread, the tang of the starter and the richness of the buttercream. It's just epic.

I often use plain white flour here for a softer, tighter crumb. Strong flour is fine, though; it will just make it a little more chewy. If you combine this with some unbleached white, I'd imagine you'd get a pretty nice, sticky bun. I've never not had good aeration using plain, aided by baking under the cover of foil, which prevents crusts from forming, thus allowing the buns to rise unrestrained.

For a dozen large buns:
150g wholemeal (wholewheat)
  or rye sourdough starter
400g plain (all-purpose) white flour, plus extra
  for dusting
6g table salt
50g caster (superfine) sugar
190g milk, warmed until tepid in
  the microwave
1 medium egg, at room temperature
50g unsalted butter

For the filling:
50g unsalted butter, melted
150g light brown soft sugar
14g ground cinnamon

For the toppings:
2½ tbsp golden syrup (optional)
150g full-fat, I repeat, full-fat, cream cheese
250g icing (confectioners') sugar

Start by checking on your sourdough starter and taking it out of the fridge the night before you bake. If it wasn't fed before being put in there and it's been more than a week, give it a good feed and leave it to rise for 8–14 hours.

Make the dough. Sorry for the numerous ingredients – just weigh all of them except the butter into a large bowl and mix together. This dough will feel fairly stiff compared to most in this book – that's OK. Cover your bowl and let it sit for 30–40 minutes to autolyse.

If your butter is coming straight from the fridge, heat it gently (I use a microwave) until soft, then add this to your rested dough. Use your hand or a dough hook to mix in the butter until completely combined. Hopefully, this will be enough mixing to have developed your gluten – the dryness of this dough gives it plenty of strength.

Leave your dough for about 4 hours at a warm room temperature. You should see it swell, but not quite double in size. Just when you're about done, flour a surface lightly with plain (all-purpose) white flour.

Continued on page 126

Turn the dough out onto your floured surface and dust with more flour. Stretch and then roll it out into a large rectangle about 50cm (20in) wide by at least 30cm (12in) long; the bigger your rectangle, the better. Use more flour to stop it sticking.

For the filling, brush the melted butter thinly over your rolled-out slab. Next, sprinkle over the brown sugar and then dust with an even, light coating of cinnamon.

Roll up your dough along its long edge, like you're rolling a Swiss (jelly) roll – so that it turns into a 50cm (20in) sausage. This creates the spiral. Slice your dough sausage into 12 roughly equal pieces using a dough scraper. Line a large roasting tin with a piece of non-stick greaseproof baking paper and arrange your buns with the spirals facing upwards – leave a little space between each one. Don't worry if the spirals seem compressed. They'll open up.

Cover the tin with foil. Leave your buns to rise for another 1½ hours at room temperature, or until swollen nicely, before placing them in the fridge to prove until you're ready to bake (up to 12 hours).

About 20–30 minutes before you're going to bake them, preheat your oven to 200ºC (400ºF)/180ºC (350ºF) fan/Gas 6.

Bake for about 30 minutes, keeping the foil on the entire time. The lack of crust might seem unnerving, but trust me, it's worth it. You know they're done when they bounce back when pressed with reassuring doneness. While they're baking, you can optionally mix the golden syrup with 2–3 tsp just-boiled water – this should be brushed on top of the buns as soon as they're baked, adding further sweetness and moisture.

Don't start making the icing until your buns are well on their way to cooling. Use a whisk (preferably electric) to beat together your cream cheese and icing (confectioners') sugar in a large bowl; no sifting is required. You need to beat for at least 5 minutes, and eventually you'll have stiff-ish peaks. Don't relent by adding more icing sugar to make it stiffer – you just need to keep going. Use a flat knife to spread this across your cooled buns. Be happy.

NEAPOLITAN-STYLE PIZZA

I'm not Italian. I've never even been to Naples. And because of that, I don't buy that this can't therefore be the best pizza recipe you'll ever try. It might *not* be, but it doesn't mean it *can't* be.

I'm very fortunate to have a truly excellent Neapolitan pizza place just a few minutes' walk from my house. They utilise a very hot wood-fired oven to bake pizzas in 90 seconds or less, and you're often served their smoking, speckle-crusted pies with slightly soggy centres before the drinks have even come, with a side order of nonchalance.

I've tried lots of ways of re-creating the intense, dry heat of a wood-fired oven at home. I even built a wood-fired oven out of a barrel that I chopped in two using an angle grinder. If you want to try it, just sit a cut barrel on some slabs of granite and build an arc of bricks around the entrance using fire cement, *et voilà*. Pizza oven.

While the outdoor pizza is good for parties and summer, Glasgow doesn't have much summer, and in truth, I don't throw many parties. Step forwards, then, the 'skillet-broiler' method, and its variations. This is basically when you use your hob to get a cast-iron frying pan very hot, build your pizza on top of this and then finish it off under the grill to melt the cheese and char the crust. The issue with this is that it doesn't heat the bottom and top together, reducing oven spring potential. It doesn't give you much time to add toppings before burning the base either.

I compromise by getting a cast-iron surface really, really hot over my largest gas burner, while I build up my pizza on a semolina-dusted peel. The thick cast iron holds plenty of heat to cook the pizza. When the pizza is ready to go, I slide it onto the pan and stick it straight under the grill, which has been preheating equally hot. After you've cooked the first pizza, you'll see whether or not you need to spend a bit of time on the hob to crisp the base a little more.

For 4 pizzas:
100g white sourdough starter
400g strong white flour (preferably Italian
  '00' pizza flour), plus extra for dusting
7g table salt
260g tepid water
plenty of semolina, for dusting
  (flour will do, though)

For the topping:
3 garlic cloves
1 tbsp good olive oil
400g tomato passata (sauce)
salt and freshly ground black pepper
2 x 125g balls of mozzarella
cured meat or salami (optional)
a handful of fresh basil leaves (optional)

It's best to make your dough at least 24 hours before you plan to make pizza. The dough keeps for 3–4 days, at least, and I know those who always have a supply of sourdough pizza dough in the fridge, just in case. Make sure your starter is nice and healthy, and that the majority of it consists of white flour.

Make the dough. In a large bowl, weigh out your flour and add the table salt. Mix these together to combine, then add the tepid water and starter. Use a wooden spoon to combine everything into a wet and sticky dough. Cover the bowl, then leave it for at least 1 hour at room temperature.

While you could mix this dough vigorously, we don't want to overdevelop the gluten. It should remain soft and sticky. I'd do a couple of stretches and folds (see page 55), and watch it rise over about 6–8 hours at room temperature. It should be very bubbly and sticky. At this point, cover with a plastic bag, put it in the fridge and leave it. It can be left for up to 3–4 days, albeit becoming slightly tangier each day. It's best used between 24 and 48 hours.

Before it's time to bake, get organised. Make your pizza sauce – peel and finely chop your garlic and place this in a pan with the oil. Gently infuse over the lowest heat for 5 minutes (don't burn it). Add your passata (tomato sauce), stir and turn up the heat to simmer. Add salt and pepper to taste. This can be prepared in advance and chilled, if you like. Chop your mozzarella into slices and place this in some kitchen paper (paper towels), or wrap in a cloth, to dry.

While some people like to pre-shape their pizza dough to make a very round disc, I'm a bit more rustic. Dust the work surface with plenty of semolina and a little flour, or just flour if you don't have any. Turn your dough out on top, and then add more semolina and flour again. Divide your dough using a scraper into four equal lumps, and coat each of these with semolina, too. It's not possible to use too much. Once your doughs are divided and your toppings are prepared, you can preheat your grill (broiler) as hot as it goes with the door as close to closed as possible, and then get a cast-iron pan or surface onto your hob (stovetop) to heat as hot as you dare.

Work quickly. Dust some semolina on a tray or peel. Take a piece of dough and stretch it flat. Don't use a rolling pin. Throwing the dough in the air and spinning it really does help. You want the centre of the dough almost translucent, and you should leave a 1-cm (½-in) thick rim around the edge to give a good puff and stop the sauce leaking. Place this on your peel. Give the peel a good shake to make sure the dough isn't sticking. Add more semolina if it does. Spread some sauce on top, no more than 3–4 tbsp, and then a quarter of your mozzarella and some slices of cured meat or salami, if using. Add a few fresh basil leaves, if you like. Give it another shake to make sure it isn't stuck.

Gently slide this onto your smoking hot pan. Use thick, thick oven gloves to move this under your grill, and shut the door (or close it as much as possible if your grill turns off when you shut it). Cook for 2 minutes, then check it. You want the edges of the crust to be just about blackening, and the cheese melted and bubbling but not browning. Keep going if it isn't. Lift up the edge to check underneath. If it's still soggy on the bottom but done on top, put it back on the hob for a minute or two. For the next pizza, if it wasn't quite cooked underneath, you can leave it on the hob for up to a minute before placing under the grill.

Enjoy hot, as fresh as humanly possible. It takes the sacrifice of one person to make the family's pizza, but it's so worth it. Between each pizza, get your surface back on the hob to heat up to frightening levels again before you slide your next pizza on top. The dream is to have two surfaces, for back-to-back pizzas, for ever.

WHITE BREADS FOR SHARING

This is an indulgent chapter. All of the following are institutions that I'll be in trouble for somehow defacing.

But playing around with the classics is both fun and important, in order not to struggle towards perfection but to see what works for every one of us. Your definition of a San Francisco sourdough might not match the fluffy-haired Scotsman's, and my baguette recipe certainly doesn't comply with stuffy French laws on the subject.

These recipes, though, will provide you with a certain standard, and I believe it is very high indeed. Have a go, and have a play, and let me know how you get on. These smooth white doughs are a joy to handle.

PAIN DE MIE AU LEVAIN

I am including this recipe for my editor, Sarah, because it is the bread that she has raved about more than any from my first book. I've also had plenty of people on Twitter and Instagram sending me pictures of their magnificent yeasted *pains*, and this makes me happy.

This recipe works to fill a notable void. The bread is complex in flavour and long-lasting, but soft-crumbed and light. Your sourdough doesn't have to be chewy and crusty. *Pain de mie* is a derogatory term in some French bakeries, describing a soft supermarket-style loaf that comes ready-wrapped in plastic. Some artisans never lost the wonderful art of making a good one, and a few others have reclaimed its virtue. It's the everyday bread: *mie* means crumb, and so this bread is about maximising your soft crumb.

For 1 large or 2 small pains de mie:
150g white sourdough starter
425g strong white flour, plus extra for dusting
10g table salt
225g tepid-warm water
50g slightly warmed milk
40g unsalted butter, softened, plus extra
*   for greasing*

Start by making sure your starter is active. If in doubt, keep it out of the fridge, double the starter in weight and wait 8–12 hours before beginning.

In a large bowl, weigh your flour and then weigh your salt on top. Rub this in so that it is mostly combined. Then, add your water, starter and warm milk on top and mix everything together until roughly combined. Leave to rest for 20–30 minutes before continuing.

Add your butter, and then knead your bread properly until it's just about passing the windowpane test (see page 49). Any method will do, including in a mixer.

Cover your bowl and leave your dough somewhere warm – close to (but not on) a radiator will do. You want it warmer than room temperature, about 25ºC (77ºF) if possible. Wrap it in a couple of tea towels to insulate it.

After 3–4 hours, it should have risen quite substantially. You should now scrape it from its bowl, being careful to maintain its delicate structure, and onto your unfloured work surface. Use a dough scraper to pre-shape (see page 58) your dough into rough boules and leave them for 20–30 minutes. Meanwhile, grease as many loaf tins (either one 900g/2lb tin or two 450g/1lb tins) as you need with plenty of butter.

After your bench rest, lightly flour your surface and flip your dough onto the dusting. Shape it gently into a batard shape (see pages 62–3) and then gently transfer it to your tin. Place your tin inside a plastic bag and leave it at room temperature for about 2–2½ hours, or until notably huge. Alternatively, you can retard your bread in the fridge from about an hour into this prove.

I like to stone bake my loaves, so I preheat my oven to 250ºC (480ºF)/230ºC (450ºF) fan/Gas 9 at least 30–40 minutes before I'm expecting my loaf to be ready. If you're not using a stone, 10 minutes will do. When your dough has risen by at least one and a half times, remove it from the plastic bag and stick it in the oven. Add plenty of steam, and turn your oven down to 220ºC (430ºF) /200ºC (400ºF) fan/Gas 7. Bake for 35–40 minutes for one large loaf, or until golden brown on top.

Remove your tin from the oven and bash out your loaf onto your work surface – it should come out easily. Place the bread back in the oven for 5–10 minutes for slightly crustier sides. If you'd prefer not, leave it where it is and enjoy the thin, delicate crust. Cool for at least an hour before slicing, however hard that may be.

SAN FRANCISCO WHITE SOURDOUGH

Like the beer scene, the bread scene in San Francisco has evolved rapidly in recent years. The teachings of Tartine and others in the original new wave of bakeries have spread rapidly, and the popularity of sourdough and the reputation of bread styles from the city have grown hugely.

This has led to a general heightening of the bread standard worldwide, which is good. And although it has been a couple of years since I've been in San Francisco, even then you could see those who were taking advantage of its reputation to flog poorly made white loaves. It cheapened the whole movement – especially if your bad loaf was hollowed out and filled with even worse clam chowder.

It is therefore hard to define 'San Francisco sourdough' – but I'll try. The classic breads have similar properties: they're made with refined and very strong white American and Canadian flours. The starters are refreshed without quite the same regularity or volume of those across the Atlantic, and as a result, they're more acidic. This acidity is then accentuated with a long and cool prove.

This results in a well-fermented bread with a rich golden crust. The tang is very apparent. The crumb is soft and custardy, and it has the characteristic irregular and large bubbles. It's what people think of when they think 'sourdough'. And here's how to make a loaf.

For 1 large loaf:
425g very strong white flour, plus extra for dusting
150g white sourdough starter, 18–30 hours
* following its last feed*
300g tepid water
10g table salt
semolina, for dusting

In a large bowl, weigh your flour, starter and tepid water. Mix these together with a dough hook or wooden spoon and let them sit for 30–60 minutes – otherwise known as the autolyse.

Following this, add your salt (don't forget!) and hand knead for about 5 minutes or so, or until it feels smooth and supple in your hands. I'd use the slap and fold method (see pages 50–1), as this gives the dough some strength. Alternatively, you could mix in a stand mixer at low-medium speed (speed '2' usually) for about 5 minutes.

Cover your bowl with a plate or tea towel and let it sit in a relatively warm place – near a heater is fine. You want to leave it for 4 hours or so. During this time, I'd give it

at least two or three stretches and folds (see page 55) to imbue strength.

Once your dough is suitably airy and maintaining its shape between folds, scrape your dough out onto an unfloured work surface. Use a scraper to pre-shape the loaf by driving your scraper underneath to tighten it (see page 58). Bench rest for 30 minutes.

If your loaf has spread out significantly (into a flat, pancake-like mound), it's not going to survive the long, retarded prove I'm recommending. In this case, pre-shape it again, or shape once using flour and then shape again following a 30-minute bench rest.

When ready, dust your proving basket with plenty of white flour. Then shape the loaf as you prefer – I like my San Francisco sourdoughs to be round (see pages 60–1) because that's what I've always made, but they can be any shape or size you want. Stick the loaf in its proving basket and then place inside a plastic bag to keep it hydrated.

Rest for 1 hour at warm room temperature – about 25ºC (77ºF), if you can. Then, stick the loaf in the fridge, covered with a plastic bag, and leave it for 12–18 hours, or until you can't wait any longer. Don't go longer than 24 hours or so if you want the loaf to maintain any sort of shape. If you are looking for even more tang than this loaf provides, use an older or less well-fed starter, or retard the first prove.

About 30 minutes before you plan to bake, turn your oven on, or even slightly earlier if you're using a baking stone. Preheat it to at least 250ºC (480ºF)/230ºC (450ºF) fan/Gas 9. If you're baking in a pot or Dutch oven, you can preheat this, too. I think it gives a slightly better rise and flavour; some like to use cold pots and this certainly has a lower chance of your getting burnt.

Dust a peel or tray with semolina and a little flour. Turn out your loaf and give it a score – I like a simple, single score if it's a batard shape (see page 180), or a square pattern if we're talking about a boule (see page 65). Slide your loaf onto your baking surface and add steam either by spraying the loaf and stone or putting a cast-iron pan filled with water in the bottom of the oven and closing the door. If using a pot, just put the lid on.

Bake for 20 minutes and then vent the oven by opening the door, or remove the lid from your pot. Keep baking for another 20–30 minutes; I wouldn't take the crust too dark. Just enough. Once done, leave to cool for at least 30 minutes before touching.

CIABATTA

You bought this book, or had it bought for you. That means that you're probably not the most compromising person, I would guesstimate. That also means that you probably don't want a recipe for a half-arsed ciabatta.

The *ciabatta* (meaning slipper) is defined by its extremely light and open crumb structure. As a consequence, the dough is pretty difficult to handle. This is because it just about hits the magic 100% hydration: equal parts flour and water. If you imagine what it's like to handle your white sourdough starter as dough, then handling this dough is similar to that. To increase the difficulty, we're not using particularly strong flour either; instead, it's authentic Italian '00' pizza or ciabatta flour.

In order to get this right, you should develop the gluten well, prior to building strength. Yes, there's a place for stretches and folds, but this is so wet that they don't do much without a knead to start with. To keep the strength up, it also helps to prove this dough on the warm side of room temperature and your starter should be very active.

This is one of the few situations where I recommend the 'double hydration' method of mixing. In fact, I don't think I mention it anywhere else. This dough is so wet that it would take an unreasonable amount of mixing to develop the dough as it is. Therefore, knead or mix with about 70–80% of the water until the dough is just about windowpaning, and then add the rest. It will still need quite a bit of work after this, but it's worth it. In the end, you'll have a fantastically light dough.

A note: ciabatta, as opposed to focaccia, doesn't contain olive oil. It should never contain olive oil. But have oil for drizzling on after baking.

For 2 large ciabattas:
150g white sourdough starter
425g strong white flour (preferably Italian '00' pizza
   or ciabatta flour), plus lots for dusting
25g fine semolina, plus extra for dusting
425g tepid-warm water
10g table salt

Start the night before you plan on making your ciabattas – check your starter and feed it if necessary. It should be very active. If in doubt, take it out of the fridge and feed 8–14 hours before starting.

In a large bowl, weigh your flour and semolina. In a jug, weigh your tepid-warm water, and add about four fifths of this. Next, add your sourdough starter, and mix everything together until roughly combined. A short autolyse of 30 minutes will help your dough come together much better when mixing.

Add your salt and mix your dough – it will already feel pretty wet, but it is joyful to slap it about using whichever technique you prefer (see pages 50–2). Do this for about 10–15 minutes. Alternatively, use an electric mixer. When the dough is just about able to windowpane (see page 49), place it back in its bowl and add the rest of your water. Work using your hand or a mixer to combine until it is not just homogeneous but you feel it has some hope of maintaining a structure. This will take another 5 minutes.

Cover your bowl and leave your dough somewhere warm. You want to ferment it between 25–30ºC (77–86ºF), for about 3 hours. Despite your kneading efforts, this dough will flop. You want to stretch and fold (see page 55) every 45 minutes or so.

When your dough is quite aerated and holding a little bit of structure between stretches and folds, flour a work surface with plenty of flour. Also prepare a couche or tea towel by dusting it with plenty more flour. And I mean plenty. Scrape your dough out onto your surface. Your dough will instantly weep and spread. Quickly, as if you were laminating (see page 56), fold it in three, like a letter. Then do the same thing to your new long rectangle. Dust off any excess flour as you fold it.

Hopefully you've got a square-ish dough that's holding its sides. Cut your dough into two rectangles. Using floured hands, gently stretch out each rectangle and place it on your floured couche. Add the other rectangle next to it, creating a fold of couche between them to stop them sticking together.

Fold your floured couche over the top of the dough rectangles to cover and leave to prove for another 1½–2 hours. When you can, remember to preheat your oven to 250ºC (480ºF)/230ºC (450ºF) fan/Gas 9. Ideally,

bake these as hot as possible on a baking stone or on a cast-iron slab. They should be preheated for at least 40 minutes.

Your ciabattas will be very delicate. The important bit here is not to disturb their fragile structure. Dust some flour and some semolina onto a tray or peel, and gently use your couche to flip your ciabattas one at a time onto your peel. Give it a shoogle to make sure they don't stick.

Your ciabattas don't need to be scored. Just slide them onto your hot surface and add lots of steam to the oven by putting a cast-iron pan in the bottom of the oven and filling with water. Turn the oven down to 220ºC (430ºF)/200ºC (400ºF) fan/Gas 7 and bake for 30–35 minutes, or until they are a deep golden brown. Vent the oven halfway through to release any remaining steam. Let cool until barely warm before serving.

TIGER BREAD

A tiger bread is a wonderful sourdough, and baked according to the guidelines below, it becomes a lustfully structured and epically crusted bread; a grand centrepiece that can fight it out with the best of them. This recipe stays true to its roots: no wholemeal (wholewheat) or rye or spelt in sight. I recommend this as a well-developed, quick-proved dough that's baked without retardation. Keep the fermentation going, keep the strength up, and watch the awe-inspiring growth.

For 1 large tiger loaf:
150g white sourdough starter
425g strong white flour, plus extra for dusting
275g warm water
10g table salt

For the paste:
4g (half a sachet) fast-action dried yeast
100g warm water
100g rice flour
20g sesame oil
20g caster (superfine) sugar
3g salt

Start by taking your sourdough starter out of the fridge about 8–14 hours before you want to bake and giving it a feed. Feel free to use your starter straight from the fridge if you're confident in its activity.

In a large bowl, weigh your flour. Add in your sourdough starter. Mix in water that's at a tepid-warm temperature, until you've got a rough dough. Let the dough rest for about 20–30 minutes – this short autolyse will help it come together much better.

Meanwhile, make your tiger paste. Simply mix together all the ingredients in a small bowl until combined. Cover your bowl with a plate to stop it drying out, and then set aside at room temperature. Forget about this for a while.

Add the salt and mix your dough – an electric mixer or any hand-kneading method (see pages 50–2) will work very well. You do want to really develop the gluten – at least 10 minutes of mixing. It should pass the window-pane test (see page 49). While this might be surprising to some sourdough makers, it helps it achieve that supermarket-light crumb.

Wrap your bowl in a couple of tea towels to keep it warm and stop the dough drying out. Leave in a warm place for about 3 hours. A single stretch and fold (see page 55) about 2 hours in will be very good for the dough's strength – but with a good knead and a warm prove, it won't need much help. Once your dough is looking larger and quite aerated, pre-shape (see page 58): turn your loaf out onto an unfloured surface, and use your dough scraper to drive under it, tucking in the sides and tightening the top. Leave it to bench rest for 30 minutes.

Next, dust a round, cloth-lined proving basket with flour. Flour another part of your surface and scoop your prepared loaf onto it, smooth side down. Shape as you would for a boule (see pages 60–1). Transfer to your proving basket and leave it somewhere warm for 1½–2 more hours. You want it to grow by about half. Preheat your oven to 250ºC (480ºF)/230ºC (450ºF) fan/Gas 9 30–40 minutes before you think the dough will be ready to bake, with a stone or heavy baking surface inside. Don't bake inside a pot or cloche.

Turn your proving basket out onto a semolina-lined peel or tray. Dust the dough a little with a pastry brush to remove any excess flour. Next, take the paste that has been sitting all day and brush it over the top of the dough. Leave it to dry for another 10 minutes, and then slide onto your baking surface.

Turn the oven down to 230ºC (450ºF) /210ºC (410ºF) fan/Gas 8. Bake for 20 minutes and then vent the oven by opening the door, and then bake again for another 30 minutes, or until the edges of the paste crust are turning a dark golden brown. Cool for at least half an hour before slicing.

DEMI-BAGUETTES À L'ANCIENNE

I was going to call this recipe 'baguettes', but I didn't want to upset more people than I had to. Truly, it is difficult to make an authentic baguette at home simply because of the size of domestic ovens. These half-baguettes, made wholly with sourdough, are awesome things.

They are perfect for par-baking and throwing in the freezer – just cut the bake short by 10 minutes. That way, you can get all the hard work out of the way and always have bread available within 15 minutes, cooked straight from frozen.

Your choice of flour for baguettes is important. Don't use stronger Canadian or American flour (usually called 'very strong' flour). This is quite a dry dough in comparison to most in the book – a very strong flour will make the dough too elastic, and you won't get the classic 'ear' forming on each cut as they expand. Any standard strong flour will do, but ideally you want good British flour from a local mill. Yes, British: I've had the best results with local unbleached varieties.

You can get French baguette flour online or from a load of specialist shops. The French flour system is a little confusing – but if you go for T65 flour, then this is about the right level of extraction and milling for baguettes. The '65' refers to the mineral content in the flour (usually about 0.65%) and equates to its level of refinement.

You'll want a couche to complete this recipe – this is a stiff linen cloth you dust with flour and then use to line up all the baguettes. This allows the baguettes to survive their long, flavour-inducing second prove without spreading too much. If you don't have a couche, you can use a heavy tea towel.

For 4 demi-baguettes:
100g white sourdough starter
400g strong white flour, plus extra for dusting
8g table salt
280g tepid-warm water
semolina, for dusting

The night before you bake, take your starter out of the fridge. If it hasn't been fed recently, feed it by mixing in equal weights of flour and water, to double the size of the starter.

In a large bowl, weigh your flour. Add in your salt and mix these roughly to combine. Mix together some warm and cold water in a jug until it feels just warmer than tepid, about 25ºC (77ºF), then add this and your sourdough starter. Mix using a wooden spoon, a dough hook or your hands until you've got a lumpy, messy dough.

Let your dough rest – autolyse – for approximately 30 minutes. You'll want to cover the bowl with a wet tea towel or a plate to stop the dough drying out.

Knead your dough for 5–8 minutes, or until it is starting to become smooth and supple; see the kneading guides on pages 50–2. Baguettes are made with quite a dry dough traditionally, so they have strength by default. You do not need to knead it as much as you do a wet dough – indeed, if you overdevelop the gluten, you'll have tight baguettes that don't rise.

Leave your dough, covered, for 4–5 hours. This will vary depending on temperature. The dough should become very bubbly in this time.

Use a dough scraper to scrape your dough out onto a clean, unfloured surface. Use the scraper to chop the dough into four equal pieces – you can weigh them if you're feeling finicky. To get a real burst of oven spring, baguettes benefit from a pre-shape (see page 58). Rest for 30 minutes following this.

Shape your baguettes. Start by flouring a couche or tea towel, and placing this on a baking tray. Then, following the shaping guide on pages 146–7, create tight, sausage-shaped pieces of dough. After shaping, place your baguette on your couche using a fold in the material to stop neighbouring doughs touching.

Prove for 30 minutes at room temperature, and then move your tray into the fridge. You should cover your baguettes if possible – dusting the tops with a little flour and then laying some cling film (plastic wrap) over the top will be adequate. Prove in the fridge for 8–14 hours, or until you are ready to bake.

Ideally baguettes should be stone baked. If you have baking stones, make sure to preheat your oven at least 40 minutes before you plan to bake. Regardless of what you're using, preheat your oven to 250ºC (480ºF)/230ºC (450ºF) fan/Gas 9. If you are using a baguette tray or a baking tray, don't worry too much about it – you'll still have good results. Dust a tray or board with semolina.

One by one, turn each baguette from your floured couche onto your semolina-covered peel. Each one should now be upside down compared to how it was proved. Score each one down its length, either with one, two or three slashes. Each score should overlap the last by one third, and each one should be almost parallel to the side of the dough – that's how straight. Your blade should be held at an angle, just to break the skin.

Slide your baguettes onto the hot baking stone and add steam – either by pouring water into a cast-iron pan sitting in the bottom of the oven, or by spraying the baguettes and stones with water. Turn down your oven to 230ºC (450ºF)/210ºC (410ºF) fan/Gas 8. If you have a fan oven and can turn the fan off, then do so.

Bake for 15 minutes, and then open the oven door to let any excess steam out (remove your cast-iron pan if it still has any water in it). Bake for a further 20–25 minutes, or until the baguettes are a deep chestnut brown. Cool on a rack before enjoying.

SHAPING AND SCORING BAGUETTES

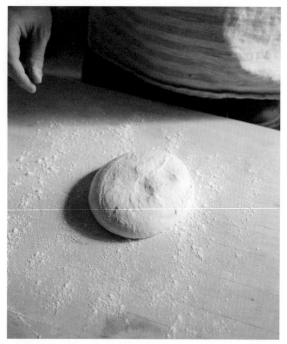

1. SCOOP YOUR PRE-SHAPED DOUGH ONTO A FLOURED SURFACE, SMOOTH SIDE DOWN

2. FOLD THE BOTTOM THIRD OF THE DOUGH OVER, PRESSING TO SEAL

3. FOLD THE TOP THIRD OVER AND SEAL

4. KEEP ROLLING THE TOP OF THE DOUGH TOWARDS YOU UNTIL IT FEELS TIGHT

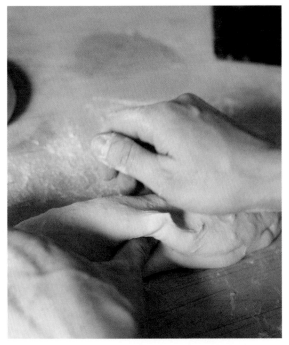

5. FOR EXTRA TIGHTNESS, FOLD OVER YOUR SEAM, SEALING WITH THE HEEL OF YOUR HAND

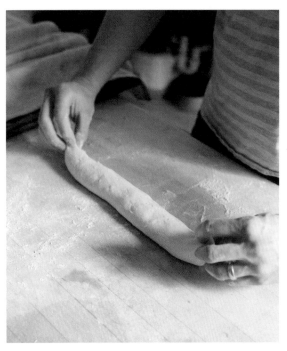

6. GENTLY ROLL THE DOUGH BACK AND FORWARDS UNDERNEATH YOUR OPEN HANDS TO MAKE IT LONGER

7. TRANSFER TO YOUR FLOURED COUCHE TO PROVE, SEAM SIDE UP

8. TURN ONTO A DUSTED PEEL. SCORE DOWN THEIR LENGTH TO THE TIPS, ALMOST PARALLEL TO THEIR EDGES

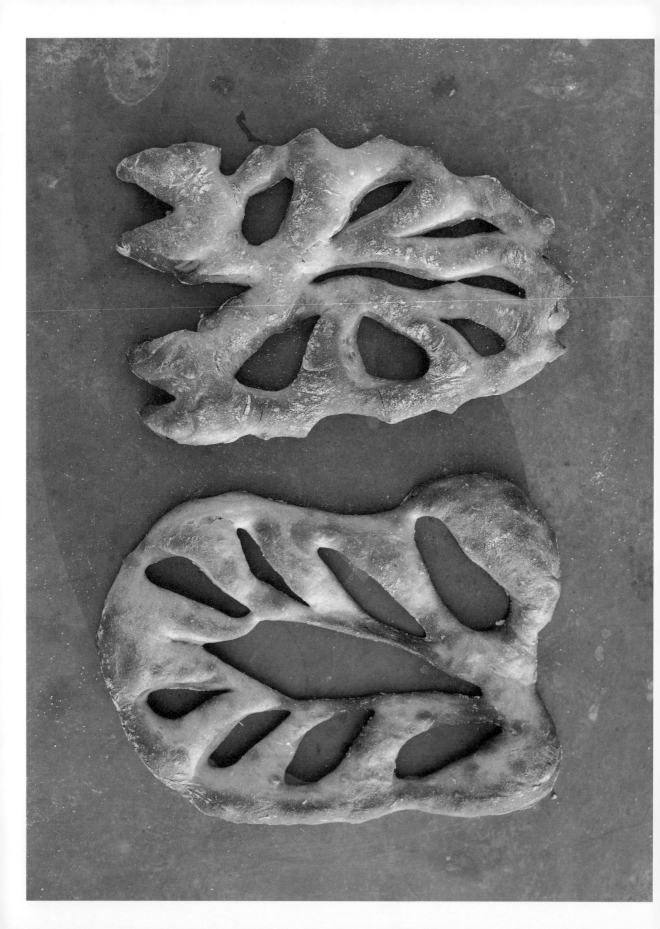

FOUGASSE AND VARIATIONS

Fougasse is a French version of focaccia. The words even have the same derivation – they come from the Latin *focus*, presumably referring to the intense heat in the hearths of the great stone ovens that were once used to bake them.

Like pizza, fougasse doesn't require much of a second prove. The intense heat causes the bubbles to expand rapidly and you get a light structure contained within tunnels of a truly epic crust. For crust lovers, this is *the* bread, and sourdough suits it so well.

I've had and made fougasse of all shapes and sorts. I like the simplest variations, such as these, made from a largely white, quite wet dough, and either shaped into a wheat sheaf-like shape using a dough scraper and baked for maximum crust, or topped with olives, anchovies, tomatoes or herbs. Smothered with Gruyère, ham and mushrooms is nice, too.

This dough is pretty wet, which in a home oven helps with the lightness and the magnificent rise. Transferring them to the oven can thus be a little precarious, but use plenty of flour and semolina and you'll be fine. You might be able to fit two on a tray or stone, but I'd take your time and bake them one at a time.

For 4 fougasses:
150g white sourdough starter
425g strong white flour, plus extra for dusting
10g table salt
280g tepid-warm water
semolina, for dusting
a small handful of cherry tomatoes, a few anchovies,
  small handful of chopped olives, dried or fresh
  herbs or grated cheese, if/as desired

Start the night before – check your starter and feed it if necessary. It should be room temperature before you use it, and be very active. If in doubt, keep it out of the fridge, feed it to double its size and wait 8–14 hours before starting.

In a large bowl, weigh your flour and then weigh your salt on top. Rub this in so that it is mostly combined. Then add your tepid-warm water and sourdough starter on top. Mix everything together until roughly combined. Leave to rest for 20–30 minutes before continuing – in other words, the autolyse.

Mix your dough – this is a very forgiving, wet, all-white dough. It's an absolute joy to knead. Get it out

and 'show the dough who's boss' (thank you for that, Richard). See pages 50–1 for slapping guides. Once it's done or you've gotten bored, stick it back in the bowl.

Cover your bowl and leave your dough somewhere warm. You're talking 4–6 hours at 18–20ºC (64–68ºF), but you could do it in as little as 2 hours in the high 20ºCs (high 70ºFs), if you're desperate for bread. I'd do a couple of stretches and folds during this time to help it keep its strength (see page 55). Remember to preheat your oven to 250ºC (480ºF)/230ºC (450ºF) fan/Gas 9. Ideally, you should bake these as hot as possible on a baking stone or on a cast-iron slab. It should be preheated for 30–40 minutes.

Because the dough isn't proving again, you need to be careful to maintain its delicate structure. Add a mixture of flour and semolina to your work surface, and use a dough scraper to scrape the dough out of the bowl and on top. Fold your dough in two, like closing a book, so that now you've got flour and semolina on both sides of it. Move it around to make sure it isn't sticking.

Cut your dough into four equal flattish slabs. Pat the sticky sides with a bit more flour, and use floured hands to work on one at a time: flatten it into a rough disc, and use your dough scraper to make a cut down the middle. Then, make three or four angled cuts on each side in the same way – these should be at quite a severe angle, maybe 10–20 degrees off parallel with your central cut. Spread your dough to open these cuts. Use plenty of semolina to stop any sticking.

Slide your peel underneath your dough and make sure you're happy with the arrangement. This is the point at which you can add any toppings, if you want to use them. Open your oven and slide your prepared dough in. You need to be quick, like pulling the tablecloth out from under a fully laid table. If you aren't, feel free to rearrange your fougasse on the stone without burning yourself. Add steam either by spraying the dough and stones or putting a cast-iron pan filled with water in the bottom of the oven and closing the door.

Bake for 12–15 minutes while you shape the next dough. It's OK to open the oven as the bread is baking and add another. Re-steam after each new fougasse goes in.

These breads should be a deep golden – if you prefer them even crustier, you can bake them for an extra 5 minutes or so. Leave them to cool, but if there was ever a bread I'd advocate enjoying hot from the oven, this is it.

LITTLE BREADS

This is probably my favourite chapter: it is one for honing your skills. Professional bakers get good by doing the same thing over and over again, all day and every day. It's hard to hit that same level of mastery at home, and especially to maintain that same level of consistency.

Try, when shaping your pretzels, bagels or your *bolillos*, first not to make them all the same, but to see what feels right from one to the other. Strive to improve every one, and if you make a mistake, there are plenty of others that will be absolutely fine. When you're happy with however you are choosing to shape them, then go for consistency. There are fewer things more satisfying than a tray of absolutely identical buns.

SALTY BOLILLOS

Every culture seems to have its own imitation of the French baguette; some of these likenesses are flattering, some are not. Formerly under French occupation, you might think first of the truly remarkable baguettes you can get in parts of northern Vietnam. You might also consider, with stereotypical British politeness, why we continue to abide the quite awful supermarket baguettes here. Before I stray further down the road of cultural misconceptions, Mexico's answer is the *bolillo*.

In order to maintain a very shiny, soft crust, I don't flip these like I would baguettes, and thus don't prove them within a couche. Just leave them on non-stick greaseproof baking paper on a tray, and then bake straight from there. If you've got a stone, stick the tray on the stone.

For a dozen bolillos:
500g strong white flour
8g table salt
150g white sourdough starter
300g tepid-warm water
sea salt flakes, for sprinkling

In a large bowl, weigh your flour. Add in your salt and mix these roughly to combine. Mix together some warm and cold water in a jug until it feels just warmer than tepid, about 25ºC (77ºC), then add this and your active sourdough starter. Mix using a wooden spoon, a dough hook or your hands until you've got a lumpy, messy dough. Let your dough rest – autolyse – for approximately 30 minutes. You'll want to cover the bowl with a damp tea towel or a plate to stop the dough drying out.

Knead the dough for 8 minutes, or until it is getting quite smooth and supple. This is a medium-wet dough; it works well if you start out with the slap and fold (see pages 50–1) and then switch to the English knead (see page 52). These loaves have quite a lot of extra water compared to baguettes, so will need a little extra care and a little extra working.

Leave your dough, covered, for 2–3 hours. Personally, I'd stick the bowl in the fridge, covered, and leave it overnight, or up to a day. If you'd rather not do this, leave it an extra couple of hours at room temperature.

Remove your bowl from the fridge and use a dough scraper to tip it out onto a clean, unfloured surface.

Use the scraper to create a rough sausage shape, and then chop the dough into 12 pieces – you can weigh them, if you like. If they feel slack, rather than tight and responsive, use your scraper to pre-shape each one (see page 58).

Shape your bolillos just like you would tiny little batards – this is great practice and good for consistency (see pages 62–3). Make sure to taper the ends into points. Once shaped, place them side by side on a baking tray – if you can't fit them all on one with room to expand, use two. Leave them to prove for an hour or so. If you have baking stones, make sure to preheat your oven at least 40 minutes before you plan to bake. Regardless of what you're using, preheat your oven to 250ºC (480ºF)/230ºC (450ºF) fan/Gas 9.

Score each bolillo with a single slash from tip to tip. Then, sprinkle with a small pinch of sea salt per bolillo and place your tray into the hot oven. Add steam – either by pouring a cup of water into a cast-iron pan sitting in the bottom of the oven or by spraying the dough and stones with water, or both. Turn down your oven to 220ºC (430ºF) /200ºC (400ºF) fan/Gas 7. If you have a fan oven and can turn the fan off, do so.

Bake for 10 minutes, and then open the oven door to let any excess steam out, removing your cast-iron pan if it still has any water in it. Bake for a further 20 minutes, or until the bolillos are a light golden brown. Remove and let cool for at least 10 minutes before serving.

BURGER BUNS

The bun is an oft-underrated test of a baker's – and a burger-builder's – skill. It must be a pedestal on which the patty sits, and its crown. It shouldn't be chewy or showy. It should soak up any juices from the meat while maintaining enough integrity to be squeezed without disintegration. No small task.

There is no greater sin than the burger served within a small ciabatta, for example. The big, firm holes let juices drip down your fingers. It's the wrong shape, often with the burger sticking out of the sides. It's chewy and distracting.

The brioche, or rather a brioche-like hybrid, is good, and now a standard at higher-end burger joints across the world, but it is prone to a certain sogginess. This is where sourdough comes in: your levain will give you the firmness required for perfect pick-up-ability, and an awesome flavour to boot. It also keeps very well for several days (or freezes); so long as the brioche bun is toasted before serving, it will be as good as fresh.

This is a bread book, and so I'm not going to spend too much time on the burger itself. Or any time, in fact. I'll only say I'm a fan of the Heston method of plastic-wrapping your high-fat minced (ground) beef into a sausage and slicing into patties with a sharp knife. This gives you the ultimate in tenderness, especially when cooked rare.

For half a dozen medium burger buns:
100g white sourdough starter
220g strong white flour
5g table salt
50g milk
2 medium eggs, at room temperature
100g unsalted butter, softened
1 egg, beaten with a pinch of salt, for brushing
sea salt flakes, for sprinkling

Take your sourdough starter out of the fridge about 8–14 hours before you want to bake. It should be very active. If it isn't, give it a feed. If it doesn't rise impressively, leave it out and feed it again the next day.

In a large bowl, weigh your flour. Add your table salt, and then mix this in using your fingers. Add in your sourdough starter and your milk, and then break in your eggs. Mix everything together. I wouldn't bother autolysing here – you won't have any trouble with extensibility.

Mix your dough – this is one dough that works very well in an electric mixer, if you have one. Knead until

your dough is supremely stretchy. It must come close to the windowpane test (see page 49). Once it has, you can think about adding your butter. If your butter isn't properly soft, give it a buzz in the microwave. It doesn't matter if it's a bit melted. Mix your butter in and keep working until the dough is shiny, smooth and consistent.

Get the dough somewhere warm; warmth is essential if you want a good prove here. Cover your bowl with a plate or tea towel and give it a good 4 hours near a heater. If it's cold, the fat will set it fairly solid and it won't rise. You can do a stretch and fold (see page 55) depending on how wet it feels; if it's gloopy, go for it. If it's holding its shape, don't worry.

Once your dough is looking rather big and quite aerated, you can divide and shape. Find a baking tray, and line it with a sheet of non-stick greaseproof baking paper. Turn your dough gently out onto an unfloured surface – use a dough scraper to separate it from the side of the bowl so as not to stretch the dough too much. Divide your lump into six, or if you're making a big batch, you can weigh each bun depending on how much you increased the quantities by.

Just like when pre-shaping (see page 58), drive an angled dough scraper sideways, scooping the dough from underneath. Keep pushing your scraper along the surface to tighten the dough. Then, scoop the dough the same way towards you and repeat, until you've got a smooth ball of dough. Scoop this onto your prepared, lined tray. Repeat this process for each bun, keeping them well spaced.

Cover your buns, either in a plastic bag or by laying a sheet of oiled cling film (plastic wrap) on top. Leave to prove back in their warm place for 2 more hours – you want them to grow quite significantly, without becoming unstable. About 20 minutes before you think they will be ready, preheat your oven to 250ºC (480ºF)/230ºC (450ºF) fan/Gas 9. Preheat for longer if you're using a baking stone or heavy surface underneath your tray.

Remove the buns from their plastic bag (or remove the cling film), and brush the egg wash over the tops. Stick your tray in the oven and turn it down to 220ºC (430ºF)/200ºC (400ºF) fan/Gas 7. Bake for about 25 minutes or until just turning a rich, dark caramelly brown. Leave to cool on the tray, then store. They'll keep for 3–4 days in an airtight container.

HOT DOG BUNS

There's an article to be written about the amazing time we have putting these books together. You might imagine that a studio photoshoot is a precise and potentially stressful situation, calculated, timed and run with a rod of iron by hired home economists.

Many are. Not so ours. The book's team – author, editor, photographer, designer, host – and often our families get together to create the photographs and the feel of the book collaboratively. Occasionally, we'll create recipes on the fly depending on what ingredients we have to hand, or just what takes our fancy. This time we had hot dogs. Massive American hot dogs, and sauerkraut and sauces and all the awesome things that can make a hot dog even better. The only thing we didn't have was a vessel to transport a hot dog to each person's mouth. I gladly stepped up.

This is an adaptation of my *pain de mie* recipe on page 133: basically, we're after soft rolls with a relatively high fat content for a light and airy structure. Bake them fast and hard and you won't get much in the way of a crust. Serving suggestion included.

For 8 large hot dog buns:
150g white sourdough starter
425g strong white flour, plus extra for dusting
10g table salt
275g tepid-warm water
50g unsalted butter, softened, plus
*   a little extra for greasing*

Start by making sure your starter is properly active. If it isn't, don't bake. If in doubt, keep it out of the fridge, double the starter in weight and wait 8–12 hours before beginning.

In a large bowl, weigh your flour and then weigh your salt on top. Rub this in so that it is mostly combined. Then add your tepid water and sourdough starter and mix everything together until roughly combined. Leave to rest for 20–30 minutes before continuing.

Add your butter, and then give your dough a good knead until smooth and uniform. This is quite a dry dough, so it suits the English Knead method (see page 52), but you could use an electric mixer to good effect.

Cover your bowl and leave your dough somewhere warm – close to (but not on) a radiator will do. You want it warmer than room temperature, about 25–27ºC

(77–80ºF) if possible. Wrap it in a couple of tea towels to insulate it.

Meanwhile, line a large 30 x 40cm (12 x 16in) roasting tin with non-stick greaseproof baking paper. After 3–4 hours, your dough should have risen substantially. Scrape it from its bowl onto a floured surface. Use floured hands to form into a long sausage shape, and then use a dough scraper to chop this into eight roughly equal portions.

Shape each wee piece of dough as if you were starting to do so for baguettes (see pages 146–7), but don't stretch them out too far. Place each lined up inside your roasting tin, leaving about 1cm (½in) between each. Cover the tin with cling film (plastic wrap) or a plastic bag to stop them drying out. Leave at room temperature for about 2–2½ hours.

I preheat my oven to 250ºC (480ºF)/230ºC (450ºF) fan/Gas 9 at least 30–40 minutes before I'm expecting my buns to be ready. When they have risen by at least one and a half times, stick them in the oven. Add plenty of steam, and turn your oven down to 220ºC (430ºF)/200ºC (400ºF) fan/Gas 7. Bake for 20–25 minutes, or until a pale golden brown on top. Leave to cool before slicing and stuffing with hot dogs.

PRETZELS

Pretzels are my second-favourite bar snack. Sprinkled with good sea salt, they are the perfect accompaniment to a pint of lager – I'm right into the maltiness of *helles*, a robust lager from Munich, but they would equally work well with a crisp, dry *pilsner*. In fact, any lager will do, so long as it abides by the *Reinheitsgebot* (German beer purity law).

In order to obtain the beautiful dark brown shine required of a pretzel, you soak your dough in an alkaline substance prior to baking: this vastly increases the speed of the Maillard reaction (browning reaction between proteins and sugars). You should then bake fast and hard for a deep-brown crust that remains flimsily thin.

Your choice of alkaline substance is difficult. Please be careful if you use the traditional chemical: lye (caustic soda, or sodium hydroxide). Wear rubber gloves and goggles – this stuff is truly life-ruining if mishandled. It will blind you if it gets in your eyes. It will burn your skin. It will kill you, and kill you quite horrifically, if you or someone else accidentally ingests it. But if you want the best pretzels, then you'll need to use this. It is also the best drain cleaner imaginable in its pure form.

If that scares you, then you can make a less dangerous alternative by baking some bicarbonate of soda (baking soda) in the oven: the heat causes the conversion of sodium bicarbonate to sodium carbonate. This releases some CO_2, which can help make cakes or scones rise. Unfortunately, when there is too much sodium carbonate, cakes, scones or soda bread taste too 'bicarby'; that's why we use baking powder, which contains a combination of sodium bicarbonate and tartaric acid. The reaction between the two creates CO_2 without soapiness.

Baked bicarb (I should call it carb, really) is also quite alkaline; much more so than plain bicarb. It should still be handled carefully, but isn't quite so scary as lye. For the chemists: a 5% solution of caustic soda has a pH of >14. A solution of 5% sodium carbonate has a pH of 11.5. Because pH is a logarithmic scale, that means the caustic soda is at least 316 times more alkaline than the sodium carbonate. And therefore 316 times more burn-y. Practically, this means you'll need much longer exposure to the latter for anything close to a half-decent crust.

For a dozen large pretzels:
400g strong white flour, plus extra for dusting
220g tepid water
150g white sourdough starter
7g table salt

For the bath:
1 litre cold water
20g lye (caustic soda) (or 50g
  bicarbonate of soda/baking soda)
sea salt flakes, for sprinkling

In a large bowl, weigh your flour. Mix together some warm and cold water in a jug until it feels just warmer than tepid, about 25ºC (77ºF), then add this and your sourdough starter. This is a very dry dough. Mix using a wooden spoon, a dough hook or your hands until you've got one solid lump.

Let your dough rest for approximately 30 minutes – this autolyse, without salt, really helps when managing such tenacity. Cover the bowl with a damp tea towel or a plate to stop the dough drying out.

Add your table salt, then knead your dough for 10–15 minutes, or until it is properly shiny and smooth. The best way to do this is in a stand mixer, to be honest, but otherwise the English knead (see page 52) will work well. Like with bagels (see page 166), the pretzel is aided by a good lot of kneading.

Leave your dough, covered, for 3 hours or so at room temperature. Your proving time will vary depending on temperature. Don't worry about any stretching and folding – it doesn't need it. The dough should be plenty strong enough.

Lightly flour a work surface. Use a dough scraper to move your dough out onto it and then use floured hands to gently roll it out into a big doughy sausage. Use your scraper to chop this into 12 equal pieces – you can weigh them if you want to be conscientious. Prepare two trays by coating them with a tea towel or cloth and flouring it, or by lining with non-stick grease-proof baking paper.

You should start like you would with a baguette (see pages 146–7). Sprinkle a little flour onto the surface and place your first piece of dough on top. Fold each piece like an A4 (US) letter going into a windowed envelope: first the side towards you, and then the side away from you. Tighten it further into a very tight sausage, then use the open palms of your hands to roll this dough backwards and forwards. Keep a chunky bit in the middle about 2.5cm (1in) thick, but then taper it each side into thin spindles. The total length should be about 40cm (16in), ideally.

Shape the dough into an upside-down 'U', with the swollen bit in the middle at the curve of the 'U'. Twist the two ends around each other two or three times, leaving at least a few centimetres of each strand free at the end. Then invert your 'knot', and press each free end onto the edge of the main body of your bagel. Place on your cloth- or paper-covered trays and repeat.

Leave your pretzels to prove for an hour or so – no more. This gives you time to clear some space in the freezer. Freezing is an optional step that helps them hold their shape much better in their caustic bath. Slide a tray under your tray or cloth and place in the freezer. Leave them in there for 30 minutes.

Before you start your bath, preheat your oven to 220ºC (430ºF)/200ºC (400ºF) fan/Gas 7. Pretzels are fine just baked on baking trays, as we're not after a supremely crisp base. About 20 minutes of preheating will be plenty.

Prepare your bath. Don rubber gloves (NOT nitrile or latex) and goggles, and fill a bowl (stainless steel, glass or hard plastic) with the cold water. Add your lye and stir gently until it has completely dissolved – **always add lye (caustic soda) to water, never add water to caustic**, otherwise the exothermic reaction as it dissolves will cause dangerous spluttering. If you're using bicarb (baking soda), weigh it out and stick it on a baking tray, and bake during your 30 minutes of pretzel freezing in your preheating oven. Stir to dissolve this in your water.

Using a gloved hand or a stainless-steel slotted spoon, dip each frozen pretzel into your lye. Hold it here for 5 seconds, and then remove it, letting any excess drip away. If using baked bicarb, leave it in the bath for roughly 20–30 seconds before draining. Place each nearly-dry pretzel on a new baking tray, preferably lined with some non-stick greaseproof baking paper.

Use a lame or razor to score the thick part of all your pretzels, and then sprinkle with plenty of sea salt. Place your trays in the oven to bake for about 15–20 minutes. They should be a deep and shiny golden brown, almost like they're dipped in plastic, with a magnificent pale 'ear'. Cool for at least 10 minutes before eating.

BAGELS GALORE

Tight-crumbed, weak-crusted and cooked twice: first boiled and then baked. The bagel's archetypal chew is so suited to sourdough that I'm amazed anyone makes these any other way.

On telly shows such as *Bake Off*, contestants are encouraged to personalise. You can't just make a bagel – you must make *your* bagel. And this causes me endless annoyance, because sometimes the classic or the simple is the best version of a thing. Bagels are probably the only exception.

While the simple, white bagel has its place in my toaster, other kinds of bagel will suit themselves to different fillings and different moods. Its low-hydration dough can cope with additions of plenty of flours and whole wheats, and seeds and nuts of any sort can be stuck on top. And if you've got a variety of seeds handy, then you can easily make 12 different sorts of bagels in a batch by mixing and matching them. Go on, have fun. Just remember that nothing toasts quite like a plain white one. For any whole-cereal bagels, replace the white starter with your desired wholemeal (wholewheat), spelt or rye starter.

For a dozen bagels:
450g plain (all-purpose) white flour,
  plus extra for dusting
100g white sourdough starter
10g table salt
250g tepid water
a little oil of any sort, for greasing
6g bicarbonate of soda (baking soda)
poppy seeds, sesame seeds, sunflower seeds,
  pumpkin seeds, for topping
semolina, for dusting (optional)

In a large bowl, weigh your flour. Add in your starter and salt and combine these together. Mix together some warm and cold water in a jug until it feels just warmer than tepid, about 25ºC (77ºF), then add this and your sourdough starter – you'll find that this is quite a dry dough. Mix together using a wooden spoon, a dough hook or your hands until you've got a solid lump of a thing.

Let your dough rest for approximately 30 minutes – this autolyse really helps you manage such a dry dough. Cover the bowl with a damp tea towel or a plate to stop the dough drying out further.

Once rested, knead your dough for 10–15 minutes, or until the dough is properly shiny and smooth. The best way to do this is in a stand mixer, to be honest, but otherwise the English knead (see page 52) will work well. The dense, chewiness of bagels requires quite a lot of dough development; just know that eventually it will get there.

Leave your dough, covered, for 3–4 hours near a source of heat, such as a radiator. Your proving time will vary depending on temperature. This dough swells – you do indeed want it to nearly double in size. There's no need to stretch and fold this one.

Lightly flour a work surface. Use a dough scraper to move your dough out onto it and then use floured hands to gently roll it out into a big doughy sausage. Use your scraper to chop this into 12 equal pieces – you can weigh them if you want to be conscientious. You don't need to pre-shape bagels.

You want to start shaping your bagels almost like you're making them into baguettes (see pages 146–7). You shouldn't need any flour as your dough is so dry. Fold each piece like an A4 (US) letter going into a windowed envelope: first the side towards you, and then the side away from you. Next, use flat hands to roll this dough backwards and forwards until it's a sausage shape about 20cm (8in) long. Taper the edges slightly, and then curl your dough into a ring shape, overlapping your tapered edges. Place a flat palm over this overlap with your fingers through the ring of the bagel and rock back and forth to seal. Repeat.

You can leave your bagels to prove for the second time on a floured couche (or tea towel), or just a tray covered with non-stick greaseproof baking paper, knowing that you might need to unstick them using a scraper later. I cover them with a sheet of cling film (plastic wrap) wiped or sprayed with a little oil to stop them drying out. Prove for 1–2 hours at a warm room temperature: near a heater or a sunny window. If well covered, bagels prove in the fridge extremely well after an hour or so.

Before you start boiling, preheat your oven to 250ºC (480ºF)/230ºC (450ºF) fan/Gas 9. Bagels are best stone-baked, but you'll need two stones to fit all twelve bagels on. If you are using stones, preheat the oven for at least 40 minutes.

Bring a pan of water – ideally a pan wide enough to fit four bagels at a time – to a rolling boil. Add in your bicarbonate of soda (baking soda). Scoop or scrape each bagel into the water, as many as you can fit floating side by side. Boil the bagels for 1 minute before using a slotted spoon to turn over and boil for a further minute.

Remove the bagels and pop them on a sheet of non-stick greaseproof baking paper to sit and steam. They're sticky, so now's a good time to add toppings. Seeds can be spread out on a tray or board and you can plonk the bagel on top, coating it.

Traditionally, bagels are baked on wooden boards, seed side down, for a few minutes, before being flipped and the boards removed (before they catch fire). Don't worry about this. You can use semolina to coat the bottom of your bagels and slide them onto your stone, or you can bake on a baking tray on the stone. Stick them in the oven any which way and turn it down to 220ºC (430ºF)/200ºC (400ºF) fan/Gas 7. Bake for 20–25 minutes, or until as golden as you like.

CROOKED ENGLISH MUFFINS

I had a recipe similar to this in my first book and it is so good I had to include it again, with a few changes. This one is designed to be started the night before, producing a big sheet of dough that's proved overnight so that they're ready to griddle for breakfast. Of course, these should be cut out into circles, but that can be a bit wasteful. Instead, if you make them square, you waste almost none, and they're more practical for layering eggs, bacon and avocado on top. If you're doubling or tripling this batch, you can stack up to three layers of dough on top of each other, with your couche or tea towel folded over to stop them sticking together.

For 8 large muffins:
425g strong white flour, plus extra for dusting
150g white sourdough starter
300g tepid-warm water
10g table salt
polenta (cornmeal), for dusting

Start in the late afternoon, the day before your planned muffin morning. For me, this is after work on a Friday, or Saturday early evening. Weigh the flour, starter and water together into a large bowl. Mix until you've got a rough dough. Leave this to autolyse for 30 minutes.

Add your salt and mix the dough until smooth – about 10 minutes. I like to use the English knead (see page 52) for this dough because it's fairly dry. Or, realistically, a stand mixer. That's fine. I'd recommend keeping kneading until it's very smooth; it might even pass the windowpane test (see page 49). If it doesn't, though, don't worry.

Leave for 3–4 hours at a warm room temperature. This dough has plenty of strength because it is quite dry – there's no need to stretch and fold unless you're worried that it looks too wet to handle. You want your dough to not-quite double in size: increasing by half will be fine.

Dust a couche or heavy tea towel (dish towel) with plenty of white flour. Rub it in so that the flour is engrained, and then sprinkle more flour on. You really don't want them to stick. Then, if you've got some, sprinkle polenta (cornmeal) lightly on top. Place this on a tray that fits in your fridge, covered with a plastic bag.

Flour a work surface and turn your muffin dough out onto it. Gently fold your dough in two, like closing a book, meaning that both the top and bottom of your dough are now covered in flour. Lift this dough and place it on your floured couche. Gently stretch and press down on your dough with your hands to create a large rectangle that's about 2.5cm (1in) thick. Then, if your couche or tea towel is big enough, fold it over the top of the rectangle so that it's covered. If it isn't big enough, flour a tea towel and place this on top.

Leave to prove at room temperature for an hour or so if you have the time, making sure your tea towels haven't stuck; if they haven't, place your tray in the fridge and leave overnight. If they have stuck, flour another tea towel with far more flour than you used the first time. Gently prise away your muffins and leave to prove overnight on your fresh one (in the fridge).

In the morning, preheat a heavy pan (preferably cast iron) over a low-medium heat for about 5 minutes. Don't add any butter. While that's heating, remove your dough from the fridge. Use a scraper to cut into squares: it's important that each edge has been cut, so even if you're right at the edge of your large rectangle, cut off a sliver. Place a few at a time in your pan and heat for 3–4 minutes. They will rise quite impressively, but don't worry if they do so unevenly. Once a deep golden, turn over and cook for another 3–4 minutes on the other side.

Leave to cool for at least 10 minutes before slicing. In an airtight container, they will keep for 2–3 days. They freeze particularly well: slice in two before freezing, and that way they can be toasted straight from the freezer.

DARKER BREADS

Making breads with wholemeal, spelt or rye flours isn't any more difficult than making them with only white, and indeed I chose a fairly rye-heavy bread as the base for my opening, explanatory recipe: my *pain au levain* (see page 46). Making dark doughs is a little bit different to those made solely with white flour. The dough is rougher, and has a tendency to tear rather than stretch (it's more *tenacious*). You need more water, and with that and all the bits that get in the way of your gluten matrix, your doughs have lower strength.

Don't be put off, though. This is where the flavour is and where most people fall truly in love with bread baking. I forget that these breads have fibre and are supposedly better for us; for me, that is so far down the list of why I'd bake them.

MICHE D'ECOSSE

This bread is all about flavour. Sod the huge open bubbles of your ultra-aerated loaves; here we go back to basics and make the best loaf in the world.

This is your *pain de campagne* but amplified. Denser, yes, and that's OK. This loaf uses a combination of good flours – wholemeal rye, wholewheat and unbleached, stoneground white – and is fairly epic in size to warrant excessively long baking, resulting in a truly wonderful loaf.

Ultra-crusted with a tangy, flavourful crumb, it's one to take your time over and savour.

Some argue that to create a proper *miche* you need a wood-fired oven, as they use in the world-famous Poilâne in Paris. This is nonsense – a wood-fired oven imparts almost no flavour (likely no flavour at all) to your final loaf. You can get the same effect at home with good heat and a baking stone.

There are a few technical aspects to making this bread that I'd bear in mind – it helps not to worry too much about oven spring. Your dough should be almost (but not quite) overproved. You don't particularly want massive rise in the oven, as this will ruin your artistic scoring and provide you with that very irregular crumb that we aren't particularly after.

So it's important to keep an eye on this one during the second prove – you want good development to hold it together and, after 3 hours of proving, when you think it's about ready, that's the time to fridge it. Leaving it 6–10 hours will give you a good level of tang. Much longer than half a day and it can become too much.

For 1 huge loaf:
200g active rye sourdough starter
700g strong white flour, unbleached and, stoneground, plus extra for dusting
150g wholemeal (wholewheat) flour
50g rye flour
20g table salt
700g tepid-warm water
semolina, for dusting

Because we're using quite a small amount of starter to make a big loaf, it needs to be active and established. If it hasn't been fed recently, feed it. Mix in equal weights of rye flour and water in order to at least double its size. Leave for 14 hours before using.

In a large bowl, weigh your three flours. Add your salt and mix everything together. Combine some warm and cold water in a jug until it feels just warmer than tepid,

about 25ºC (77ºF), then add this, too, followed by your active sourdough starter. Mix using a wooden spoon, a dough hook or your hands until you've got a lumpy, messy dough.

Let your dough rest – autolyse – for about 30–60 minutes. You'll want to cover the bowl with a damp tea towel or a plate to stop the dough drying out.

Knead your dough for 10–15 minutes, or until it is starting to become smooth and supple. This dough is unruly, and you'll find it very wet to begin with. But it will come together. The slap-and-fold method tends to work well (see pages 50–1), as does using a mixer. If you choose the latter, give it a stretch and fold (see page 55) immediately following mixing.

Leave your dough, covered, for 4–5 hours. This will vary depending on temperature. The dough should swell and you might notice a few bubbles, but the top of the dough tends to look pretty smooth.

Use a dough scraper to scrape your dough out onto a clean, unfloured surface. Pre-shape (see page 58) by driving a solid scraper underneath the dough, tucking the sides in as you do. Repeat this until you've got a smooth-ish ball. Try to keep as much of the aeration as possible. Leave it for 30 minutes.

Flour a very large proving basket, or if you don't have one (most don't), make one using a floured tea towel and a mixing bowl or wok. Then shape your miche. Which shape doesn't really matter; I like to go round because I can make a proving basket big enough. Therefore, I shape as if a boule (see pages 60–1) and place it in my make-do basket.

Place your proving basket inside a plastic bag to stop it drying out and then prove for 3 hours at room temperature. After this, you can either preheat your oven or move it into the fridge for even more flavour. Prove in there for 8–10 hours.

Ideally, your miche should be stone baked, or baked on a flat piece of cast iron. Make sure to preheat your oven at least 40 minutes before you plan to bake. Regardless, the temperature should be 240ºC (460ºF)/220ºC (430ºF) fan/Gas 9.

Once proved, dust a peel or tray with some flour and semolina. Very gently turn your loaf out on top. It will spread slightly, and that's OK. Give it a shoogle to make sure it isn't sticking. Use a lame to flamboyantly score your initials or first initial in the top – if it is correctly (over)proved, this should open minimally.

Slide your loaf onto your preheated baking stone or tray and turn your oven down to 220ºC (430ºF) /200ºC (400ºF) fan/Gas 7. Bake for 1 hour, at least, or until the crust almost looks burnt and the flour on top has a yellowish hue. Let it cool down completely before slicing. This loaf makes the best toast, especially 3–4 days down the line.

PANE RIMACINATO

This bread is yellow-crusted, rich and chewy. There's the crack of the toasted seeds on top and the crunch of the crust beneath. Rubbed with garlic and drizzled in oil, there's only one thing better. The same bread, this time toasted, buttered and chopped into soldiers for dipping into a soft-boiled egg sprinkled with sea salt.

This bread is made largely from durum wheat, the very hard variety of wheat used to make semolina. This is in the form of *farina di semola rimacinata*, which translates as 're-milled semolina flour', and therefore the title for this recipe is literally 'Re-milled Bread'. Don't be tempted to substitute standard semolina in this recipe: it will work if you leave it to autolyse for a very, very long time, but to proceed as below, you do need to use semolina flour. See the photograph on page 14.

For one large loaf:
150g strong white flour, plus extra for dusting
300g semolina flour
100g white sourdough starter
325g tepid water
10g table salt
sesame seeds, for sprinkling (optional)
semolina, for dusting

In a large bowl, weigh your flours, starter and tepid water. Mix these together with a dough hook or wooden spoon and let them sit for 30–60 minutes. The autolyse is very important for your semolina flour, in order for it to hydrate fully.

Add your salt and knead the dough for about 5 minutes or so, or until it feels smooth and supple and any graininess is gone. It will feel quite wet initially, so I'd use the slap and fold method (see pages 50–1). Return it to your bowl.

Cover your bowl with a plate or tea towel and let it sit in a relatively warm place – near a heater is fine. You want your fermentation to be about 25ºC (77ºF), for about 4 hours or so. During this time, I'd give it at least two stretches and folds (see page 55) in order to give your dough some extra strength.

Once your dough is maintaining its strength between folds, scrape it out onto an unfloured work surface. Use a scraper to divide into your desired number of loaves, and pre-shape by driving your scraper under-

neath to tighten your loaves (see page 58). Bench rest, uncovered, for 30 minutes.

When ready, dust your proving basket with plenty of white flour. Then, shape your loaf as you prefer – I've gone for a boule (see pages 60–1). Once shaped, work quickly to press some sesame seeds into the sticky skin of your dough, and then place it, seed side down, in your basket. Keep the basket in a plastic bag to prevent it drying out.

Rest for 2 further hours at warm room temperature. If you like, you can retard your loaves in the fridge, covered, after an hour or so. About half an hour before you plan to bake, stick your oven on, or even slightly earlier if you're using stones. Preheat it to at least 250ºC (480ºF)/230ºC (450ºF) fan/Gas 9. If you're baking in a pot or Dutch oven, preheat this, too.

When ready to bake, dust a peel or tray with semolina and a little flour. Turn out your loaves and give them a score – I like a square-shaped score here to minimise 'ears' and accentuate the effect of the sesame seeds. Slide your loaves onto your baking surface and add steam by pouring water into a cast-iron pan sitting in the bottom of the oven, or cover your pot with its lid.

Bake for 20 minutes, then vent the oven by opening the door, or remove the lid from your pot. Bake for another 20–30 minutes; take it so that the edges of the tears in your crust are just the right side of burnt. Once done, leave to cool for at least 30 minutes before touching.

ALL WHOLE WHEAT

This is the holy grail of breads for bread makers: a 100% wholemeal (wholewheat) bread with an open crumb and lightness that means it's not just a concentration of epic earthy flavour, but actually pleasant to eat. It shouldn't be stodgy, but rather firm and sliceable.

Especially in softer wheats, you want to maintain as much of the viability of gluten as possible: let prove too long and it will break down and you'll end up with stodge. If you don't give your flour and water adequate time to hydrate, then you'll have an unworkably grainy and tearable (tenacious) dough because the gluten cannot properly connect, and that will end up as a dense loaf.

This problem is solved by a good, long autolyse without the starter. This allows the moisture levels in the bran and the rest of the dough to equalise, as well as to begin in the makings of an extensible gluten network. Over the same autolyse, you can get a levain going from your sourdough starter so that it is fresh, active and not too sour.

For 1 large loaf:
For the autolyse:
350g wholemeal (wholewheat) flour, plus extra,
for dusting
350g tepid water

For the levain:
50g wholemeal (wholewheat) sourdough starter
125g wholemeal (wholewheat) flour
125g tepid water
10g table salt

To start, you'll need two bowls. In your larger (main mixing) bowl, weigh your flour and water for the autolyse, which is very important here, as it lets the wholemeal grain properly absorb the water.

In your other bowl, make your levain. Mix together your starter, flour and water. Leave both bowls to sit for 8–10 hours – ideally, overnight at room temperature.

Add your levain to your autolyse along with the salt, and start to work into a dough. It will benefit from 10 minutes of kneading: you should start to feel the strands of gluten forming around your fine bran. It is fragile, and if you overstretch it, it will tear.

Cover your bowl and leave the dough somewhere at room temperature for 3–4 hours. This will be plenty, because we've guaranteed ourselves a very active

levain. I'd do a couple of stretches and folds (see page 55). Be gentle, keeping as many gas bubbles as you can; don't overstretch to the point you can see strands breaking.

You might not notice much of a rise, and that's OK. I wouldn't pre-shape here, because the risk of over-tightening it and destroying a very delicate structure is too great. Simply flour a work surface, and either flour your proving basket or grease your tin. Turn your dough out onto your floured surface and shape for a batard (see pages 62–3).

Prove in the tin or basket for another 2 hours at room temperature, or you could retard this prove after an hour or so for anything from 8–12 hours. I would preheat my oven to 250ºC (480ºF)/230ºC (450ºF) fan/ Gas 9 at least 30–40 minutes before I'm expecting my loaf to be ready, especially if you're stone baking, which I would recommend here.

I wouldn't score this loaf. A little flour dusted on top prior to baking can be effective visually. Place your tins in the oven, or use a peel to slide your loaf in, and turn it down to 220ºC (410ºF)/200ºC (400ºF) fan/Gas 7. Add some steam: I pour water into a cast-iron pan on the floor of the oven. Vent the oven after 20 minutes, and bake for another 20–30 minutes after that. Cool for at least 1 hour before attempting to slice.

FRESH SPELT BATONS

The more I get into milling my own flour, the more I find myself appreciating the difference in the taste and the quality of freshly ground grain – it's another level. The closest equivalent I can think of is coffee. For years, we used packaged ground coffee. Then some of us switched to whole beans with a home grinder, and the flavour markedly improved. And some more of us now roast our own, or only source coffee from the local roastery mere days after it was fired. Maybe growing and drying my own wheat is the next step.

Of course, the joy of the all-bleached-white, silky sourdough is quite real. There's a place, and indeed several cookbooks, for the packaged white. This recipe is a compromise between the two: half freshly ground organic spelt (or good wholemeal spelt flour if you don't have a mill) and half unbleached white flour. This allows you easy access to all the gluten of the white flour, and all the texture and flavour of the spelt. If you're milling your own, you can even set the grind to extra rough for even more texture.

These are chunky batons because it's probably my favourite compromise between crust and crumb: its tight shaping allows for great 'ears' in the crust, but it isn't so thin that you can't use it for a slice of toast.

For 3 batons:
100g white sourdough starter
200g wholemeal spelt flour
200g unbleached strong white flour, plus extra,
  for dusting
275g tepid water
8g table salt
semolina, for dusting

The night before you bake, decide whether your starter needs to be fed. If it hasn't been fed within a week or you're in doubt about its activity, take it out of the fridge and feed it by mixing in equal weights of flour and water, to double the size of the starter. If you're happy with yours, leave it in the fridge, covered, until up to a few hours before baking.

On the day of baking, or at least the day of proving, start by milling your spelt. It's going to get a good autolyse, and because of all the support it's going to have from the white flour, you can afford to mill it quite coarsely for a more interesting texture.

Into a large bowl, weigh your freshly ground spelt and the white flour. Mix together some warm and cold water in a jug until it feels warmer than tepid, about

25ºC (77ºF), then add this and your active sourdough starter. Mix using a wooden spoon, a dough hook or your hands, until you've got a lumpy, messy dough.

Let your dough rest – autolyse – for about an hour. You'll want to cover the bowl with a damp tea towel or a plate to stop the dough drying out. This is an essential step for properly rehydrating your fresh whole meals.

Add the salt, and then knead your dough for 5–8 minutes, or until the dough is starting to become smooth and supple. See the kneading guides on pages 50–2. After the autolyse, you'll find this a manageable, fairly dry dough. It shouldn't be too sticky, and you don't need to knead it forever. Return it to the bowl.

Cover with a plate or tea towel and leave it for 4–5 hours to prove. This will vary depending on temperature. The dough should become nice and bubbly. I'd try to stretch and fold it once or twice (see page 55) – if it seems to hold its shape and doesn't spring back into a gloopy mess after the first, don't bother the second time.

Use a dough scraper to scrape your dough out onto a clean, unfloured surface. Use the scraper to chop the dough into three roughly equal pieces. Then use it to pre-shape (see page 58) into smooth oblong lumps and leave them on your surface to rest for 30 minutes or so.

Shape. Start by flouring a couche or tea towel, and place this on a tray. You can then proceed in two ways, and both are legitimate. You can shape them as for batards (see pages 62–3) and then gently roll the dough backwards and forwards until you've got elongated versions. I've had best results, though, shaping really tightly as you would for baguettes (see pages 146–7), but without spending too long rolling them back and forth to lengthen. Transfer your batons onto your couche, seam side up, creating folds in the material to act as barriers between the loaves.

Cover with a floured tea towel and prove for an hour at room temperature. Alternatively, after 30 minutes, you can move your tray into the fridge to retard this prove. Leave it in the fridge, covered, for 8–14 hours, or until you are ready to bake. This is particularly useful if you want to bake first thing in the morning.

I would stone bake these, or use a cast-iron surface. In either case, preheat your oven at least 30–40 minutes before you plan to bake, to 240ºC (460ºF)/220ºC (430ºF) fan/Gas 9.

Dust a peel or tray with some semolina and, in turn, invert each baton from your floured couche onto it. Each one should now be seam side down. Score down their lengths, either with one large score or with two that overlap slightly.

Slide your batons onto the hot baking stone and add steam by pouring water into a cast-iron pan sitting in the bottom of the oven, or spraying the batons with water. Turn down your oven to 220ºC (430ºF)/200ºC (400ºF) fan/Gas 7. If you have a fan oven and can turn the fan off, do so.

Bake for 15 minutes, and then open the oven door to let any excess steam out. Bake for a further 20–25 minutes, or until the batons are a deep golden brown. Cool on a rack before enjoying. They should be warm, not hot, before you break or slice them open.

OVERNIGHT OAT SOURDOUGH

This bread offers something that many don't: stickiness. This is soft and moist, and stays so for days. It toasts quickly, giving you a crisp film of golden brown crust, but the centre remains soft and tender. It might seem like a faff to make, but it isn't: because of the protracted autolyse, it doesn't take you any more time than any other bread. You just need to start making this bread when you've still got some of your last loaf left. Let's get something out the way: don't use posh oats. Cheap porridge oats, the ones where you struggle to find an entire whole flaked oat in the packet, are perfect. If you go for posh oats, they won't absorb the required water, your dough will be hopelessly sloppy, and then the baked bread will be filled with dry flakes.

For 2 small loaves:

150g rye or wholemeal (wholewheat)
  sourdough starter
10g table salt
butter, for greasing
posh porridge oats, for topping (optional)

For the oat soaker:

100g cheap porridge oats
180g tepid water

For the autolyse:

400g unbleached strong white flour, plus extra
  for dusting
275g tepid water

Start the night before. Make your oat soaker – mix together your porridge oats and tepid water in a bowl, cover with a plate or some cling film (plastic wrap) and leave in the fridge for at least 12 hours. At the same time, make your autolyse – weigh together the flour and water in a large bowl and mix until you've got a lumpy dough. Cover and leave to autolyse for a similar time: 12 or so hours.

The next day, bung the oat soaker, starter and salt into the bowl with the autolyse ingredients. Mix everything together until completely combined in a near-homogeneous dough. If it feels a bit wet, don't worry. Your oats probably need a bit more soaking.

Knead for a couple of minutes or so, just so that your dough is starting to feel a little more supple and your oats are unquestionably distributed. Stick it back in the

bowl, cover and prove for 4 hours, or a little longer. It will take a wee while to warm up to room temperature, as your oat soaker would have been cold prior to being incorporated. Carry out two or three stretches and folds (see page 55) when you remember to, in order to strengthen the dough as much as possible.

When notably risen and aerated-looking, scrape your dough out onto an unfloured surface. Use your scraper to split it into two and pre-shape it (see page 58) into balls, then leave it to rest on the bench for about half an hour. Meanwhile, grease some tins with some soft butter or dust proving baskets with plenty of flour. You can even add some posh porridge oats to aid in the non-stickiness.

Flour your work surface and flip your dough onto it, smooth-side down. Shape as a batard (see pages 62–3). Place in the tin, and then put your tin inside a plastic bag. Leave your loaf to prove for another 2–3 hours, or stick it in the fridge, covered, after an hour or two to retard the prove.

At least 40 minutes before baking, preheat your oven to 250ºC (480ºF)/230ºC (450ºF) fan/Gas 9.

Score deftly and deeply into your loaves: you might need a couple of swipes at it, as the oats can cause trouble here. Chopping lightly into it with scissors works well. Place your tins on your surface, and add steam by filling a cast-iron pan with water and placing on the oven floor. Bake for another 20–30 minutes, or until deep brown, then remove from the tins and bake for a final 10 minutes. Cool for at least half an hour before slicing.

LEFTOVER-BREAD BREAD

I had to include a new recipe for this loaf, following such amazing feedback and viral spread thanks to my previous version. Dubbed *Revival Bread*, the idea was to use up any stale bread left over from previous batches, in a zero-waste sort of ideal. This is not just thrifty, but gives great flavour and massive oven spring to your new loaf.

Well, now it's back, and this time it's sourdough-specific. And as such, it's become a strangely involuted bread: the sourdough starter is used to make a bread, which subsequently becomes stale. Then the same starter is used, with the stale bread, to make a new bread. This bread then becomes stale and is used to make another bread with the original, refreshed sourdough. You could then go on and on and on in two endlessly overlapping cycles.

For 1 large loaf:
150g rye sourdough starter
300g strong white flour, plus extra for dusting
6g table salt
leftover breadcrumbs, for dusting (optional)
semolina, for dusting

Bread soaker:
150g old bread
320g water

Any time the day before you're planning on baking, make your bread soaker. Tear up your stale old bread, crusts and all, into chunks. Add your water and stir together. Cover with a plate or some cling film (plastic wrap) and stick it in the fridge.

Also the day before, take your starter out of the fridge and feed it. I use a rye starter, but you could use any sort.

Weigh your flour in a new bowl, and then the salt. Distribute the salt roughly, and then add in the soaker and active starter. Mix everything together until roughly combined and set aside to autolyse for half an hour or so.

Kneading this dough can be a bit of a pain, but you must do so to break up any big chunks of old bread. Otherwise, stretch and fold in order to develop things (see page 55). Over the next 5–6 hours, I'd stretch and fold at least four times so that you've got a strong and tight dough. It should be proving, covered, at room temperature.

Turn your dough out onto an unfloured surface. Pre-shape (see page 58) using your dough scraper, and then leave it to rest for about 30 minutes. In the mean time, dust a round proving basket with flour, or a mixture of flour and leftover breadcrumbs.

Lightly flour a work surface and scoop your dough onto it, smooth-side down. Shape as a boule (see pages 60–1) using floured hands and place in your proving basket. Leave to prove for about 2–3 hours, depending on temperature.

If you're using a stone, then at least 40 minutes before you're ready to bake, you should preheat your oven to 250ºC (480ºF)/230ºC (450ºF) fan/Gas 9. I bake this in a preheated pot, which I warm up for 20–30 minutes.

Dust the dough and a peel or tray with semolina. Turn your dough out onto it and then score. I like a single cross, because it allows for quite massive oven spring upwards. Slide your loaf onto your surface or into your pot, and either add steam by pouring water into a cast-iron pan in the bottom of the oven, or replacing the lid of the pot.

Bake for 20 minutes before venting the oven or removing the lid. Bask in the glory of that oven spring. Bake for a final 20–30 minutes, or until it's a speckled dark golden, chestnut brown on top.

ANCIENT EINKORN BATARD

I've mentioned before that a few people are taking wheat farming and its effect on the environment seriously, in a really geeky way. These men and women have brought back ancient grains from the edge of extinction and earned them worldwide acclaim, and they've helped to create limitless new strains by cultivating fields full of wheats of all sorts, which live harmoniously together without the need for crop rotation.

Fields like these are now cropping up (sorry) all over the world and you no longer need to know a farmer or own a mill to get to experience the awesome flavour of these grains. Any Einkorn or ancient wheat blend can be used in this recipe.

The single issue with using these flours is that, in the traditional sense, they're crap for bread baking. While the flavour may be fantastic, they've got a terrible quality of gluten. This means you're likely to have a very difficult-to-handle dough. Which I've made even worse by including lots of water.

The result, if you're careful to stretch and fold and stretch and fold, is a deliciously open, custardy crumb structure and beautiful, dark brown crust. The flavour, sweet and nutty and complex, makes this one of the best loaves I've made and now a solid part of my repertoire.

For each large batard:
150g white sourdough starter
150g wholemeal Einkorn flour
225g unbleached strong white flour,
  plus extra for dusting
275g tepid-warm water
8g table salt
semolina, for dusting

The night before you bake, decide whether or not your starter needs to be fed. If it hasn't been fed within a week or you're in doubt about its activity, take it out of the fridge and feed it by mixing in equal weights of flour and water, to double the size of the starter. If not, leave it in the fridge until a few hours before baking.

In a large bowl, weigh your Einkorn and your white flour. Mix together some warm and cold water in a jug until it feels warmer than tepid, about 25ºC (77ºF), then add this and your active sourdough starter. Mix using a wooden spoon, a dough hook or your hands until you've got a lumpy, messy dough.

Let your dough rest – autolyse – for about an hour. You'll want to cover the bowl with a damp tea towel or a plate to stop the dough drying out. Like when working with freshly milled grain, ancient blends benefit from an autolyse for proper rehydration.

Add the salt and then knead your dough for 5–8 minutes, or until it is starting to become smooth and supple. See the kneading guides on pages 50–2. After the autolyse, you'll find this a manageable, fairly dry dough. It shouldn't be too sticky, and you don't need to knead it forever. Return it to the bowl.

Cover with a plate or tea towel and leave it for 4–5 hours to prove. This will vary depending on temperature. The dough should become nice and bubbly. I'd still try to stretch and fold it (see page 55) two or three times during this period, as it can be quite tricky otherwise.

Use a dough scraper to scrape your dough out onto a clean, unfloured surface. Use a hard dough scraper to pre-shape (see page 58) into a smooth oblong lump and leave it on your surface to rest for 30 minutes or so.

Shape. Start by flouring a proving basket, and then flour a work surface. Turn your dough, smooth side down, onto the flour, and shape them as for batards (see pages 62–3). Transfer into your proving basket.

Prove for an hour at room temperature. Alternatively, after 30 minutes, you can move your basket into the fridge to retard this prove. Here, leave it in the fridge, covered, for 8–14 hours, or until you are ready to bake. This is particularly useful if you want to bake first thing in the morning.

I would stone bake these, or use a cast-iron surface. In either case, preheat your oven at least 30–40 minutes before you plan to bake, to 240ºC (460ºF)/220ºC (430ºF) fan/Gas 9.

Dust a peel or tray with some semolina and, in turn, invert your batard from your floured proving basket onto it. Each one should now be seam side down. Score down their lengths, either with one large score or with two that overlap slightly.

Slide your batard onto the hot baking stone and add steam by pouring water into a cast-iron pan sitting in the bottom of the oven, or spraying it with water. Turn down your oven to 220ºC (430ºF) /200ºC (400ºF) fan/Gas 7. If you have a fan oven and can turn the fan off, do so.

Bake for 15 minutes, and then open the oven door to let any excess steam out. Bake for a further 25–30 minutes, or until your loaf is a deep, dark golden brown. Cool on a rack before enjoying.

BITTY BREADS

You'll find some bread books filled with '120 recipes' – each so subtly different from the last and pristinely photographed with differently coloured backdrops to make them look more individual.

There aren't any contrived loaves in this book. There are no more recipes than there needs to be, and hopefully as few words as I could get away with without leaving things unexplained.

This chapter contains a selection of the many doughs I've played around with, both in terms of component flour and lumpy additions. These really work, they're really loved and I beg you to try them all.

SANDWICH SEEDED

The sandwich is of ancient origin and British nomenclature. In my experience, this simple but joyous thing is quite often decimated in the United States; prevailing still are plastic cheese and soggy lettuce within sweet breads that taste of cardboard and are soaked in high-fructose corn syrup and set with gelatine.

Having said that, the best sandwiches I've ever had have also come out of the States. I believe the bread revolution has been instrumental in this – awesome artisanal meats, cheeses and vegetables need equally excellent artisanal bread. That's what I tell myself; the cynic in me says that the prevalence of cheap, sad meat leads to an imbalance between the bread-to-filling ratio, of which I've had no experience in other countries.

Certainly, the best seeded and multigrain breads I've had have been on the West Coast of the USA. They're probably so popular (and thus so developed) partially for questionable mooted health benefits. Of those I've tried, many are dominated by caraway or fennel. While these are legitimate choices if you like that sort of thing, I like my bread to be pleasing to as many people as possible and to keep my friends. As a result, I don't add caraway or fennel.

As for what else to add, I'd suggest using whatever you have lying around. A search through the back of the dry store-cupboard will usually yield something. I bought a lot of sesame seeds and sunflower seeds from the cash-and-carry some years ago, and I'm still trying to get through them.

For 1 large loaf:

30g sesame seeds, plus extra for topping
15g flax seeds
20g sunflower seeds
450g plain (all-purpose) white flour
100g rye or wholemeal (wholewheat)
*   sourdough starter*
300g tepid-warm water
10g table salt
wholemeal (wholewheat) flour and semolina,
*   for dusting*

Start by toasting your seeds, if they aren't already pre-roasted. You're not using that many, so you can do this in a couple of minutes by sticking them in a clean, dry frying pan (skillet) and placing them over a low-medium heat. Keep them moving; as soon as you notice the odd bit of golden-brown scorch (or can smell it), then remove the pan from the heat. Set aside to cool while you do everything else.

In a large bowl, weigh your flour, active starter and tepid-warm water. Mix these together using a wooden spoon or a dough hook, and let them sit for 30 minutes. This is your autolyse – don't forget that you've not added the salt, so place it next to the bowl ready.

This is a dough of standard wetness. Add your salt, and knead for 5 minutes or so, or until it feels smooth and tight, though it doesn't need to come close to passing the windowpane test. Either of the kneading methods (see pages 50–2) would do. Return the dough to your bowl.

Cover the bowl with a damp tea towel or an upturned plate, and prove for about an hour or so. After this time, add your seeds. Then, you want to stretch and fold (seee page 55) your dough on at least three separate occasions over the next 3–4 hours. This incorporates your seeds, but also increases the strength of the dough. Following the second time you do this, your dough should feel a lot bouncier (tenacious) and far less gloopy.

Scrape your dough out onto an unfloured work surface. Use a dough scraper to pre-shape by driving it underneath the sides, following the guide on page 58. Bench rest your loaf for 30 minutes.

Dust your proving basket with enough wholemeal (wholewheat) flour so that you're comfortable there's going to be no sticking, then sprinkle some spare, untoasted sesame seeds on top. Shape your loaf as per your basket (see pages 60–3) and then place it in a plastic bag to prove.

Rest for 2–3 hours at room temperature, or retard your loaf in the fridge after an hour or two. About half an hour before you plan to bake, preheat your oven to at least 250ºC (480ºF)/230ºC (450ºF) fan/Gas 9. If you're baking in a pot or Dutch oven, you should preheat this too. If you're using a baking stone, you might need to preheat for longer.

Dust a peel or tray with semolina, or a little flour if you don't have any. Turn out your loaf and score – you want good bursts to give contrasts with the seeded skin, so make it decisive and simple. You might need a little force to pierce through the skin of seeds. Slide your loaves onto your baking surface and, if not using a pot, add steam either by spraying the dough and baking stone, or putting a cast-iron pan filled with water in the bottom of the oven and closing the door.

Bake for 20 minutes and then vent the oven by opening the door, or remove the lid from your pot, if using. Keep baking for another 25–35 minutes, or until the seeds have become golden but not blackened. Leave the loaf to cool for at least 30 minutes before even thinking about slicing.

ROME-STYLE PIZZA

Technically, the difference between Roman and Neapolitan pizza is simple: the former contains olive oil, the latter doesn't. Otherwise, Rome-style pizza is far less policed by pizza enforcers the world over. There's massive variation.

This particular strain was introduced to me by a relatively new pizza place, just down from the Glasgow Royal Infirmary in the city's East End. The restaurant creates massive trays of ultra-high-hydration, very well-fermented dough, baked once with a sparse topping of simple tomato sauce, or of thinly sliced potato or a little cheese.

Each tray is cooled and then dressed with fresh ingredients: cherry tomatoes, ricotta, mozzarella and herbs, to name but a few. When you order, your pizza is baked again, to just relax your chosen toppings and further crisp the dough. The resulting crust is monumentally crisp and sweet, in a really good way. The middle of the dough is soft and light, and the toppings are extremely fresh.

It was a revelation, so much so that I now do the same at home. Having the dough pre-prepared means you can sort it out well in advance and then have fresh pizza ready to order within 10 minutes.

You can ferment this dough for up to a couple of days. Ideally, you want it fermented for about 24 hours; after this, I feel that (though still good) the resulting dough isn't quite as light and becomes quite a bit chewier. That's fine if you like that sort of thing.

For 2 large trays of pizza, serving 4:
100g white sourdough starter
450g strong white flour (preferably Italian '00' pizza or ciabatta flour)
10g table salt
350g tepid water
50g good extra virgin olive oil
olive oil, for greasing

For the sauce:
15g olive oil
3 garlic cloves
400g passata or canned whole tomatoes
sea salt

For the toppings:
a punnet of cherry tomatoes
250g good mozzarella or ricotta
lots of fresh basil
good olive oil, for drizzling
black pepper

Ideally, take your starter out of the fridge at least 8–14 hours before you want to bake, and give it a feed when you take it out. If you're happy with its activity, you can use it without adulteration. Take it out a few hours before you're going to start.

Weigh your flour and salt into a mixing bowl. Add in your sourdough starter, and then your water. You want your water to be tepid – from a mixer tap is fine. Mix everything very roughly until you have a very wet dough. Let the dough rest, or autolyse, for about 20–30 minutes – as it's so wet, this will help it become more manageable. Cover the bowl with a damp tea towel or a plate to stop it drying out.

Work your dough – I'd intermittently stretch and fold (see page 55), but only after working it for a few minutes. The slap and fold method (see pages 50–1) works well. After you've gotten tired of working it – for me that's usually 3–4 minutes – add your oil. Mix this until completely combined and you've got a very soft, shiny dough.

Leave your dough for about 3–4 hours at room temperature. You want to stretch and fold it every hour or so, resulting in at least three stretches and folds through this prove. When you stretch it, make sure to really stretch it. Then stick the dough in the fridge, covered. Leave it there for 12–36 hours.

At any point, make your tomato sauce. Add the oil to a saucepan and place over a medium heat. Thinly chop your garlic, and add this to your pan. Fry for a minute or so, or until the edges are blushing golden. Add your passata or tomatoes, and then season with sea salt. Turn down the heat when it begins to bubble, and then simmer for about half an hour or so. Taste and season again if it needs it, and then blend to a smooth paste. Leave to cool, cover and then chill until ready to use.

A couple of hours before you want to bake, oil two large roasting tins, at least 30cm (12in) square, and then add a little oil on top of your proven dough. Your hands should be very oily, too. Use a dough scraper to scrape your dough out of the bowl and onto one of the tins.

Chop your dough into two using your scraper. Carefully lift one half onto the other oiled tin. Press each half down gently, trying to maintain its delicate structure, to fill each tin.

Pop each tray inside a plastic bag and leave to prove for another 1½ hours at room temperature. Preheat your oven to 250ºC (480ºF)/230ºC (450ºF) fan/Gas 9, at least 30–40 minutes before you expect to bake. This works so much better if you've got stones: just pop the tins on top of them.

Just before you want to bake, spread your tomato sauce over each pizza, leaving 2cm (¾in) of crusty edge. Pop the pizza in the oven: don't worry about adding steam. Turn the oven down to 220ºC (430ºF)/200ºC (400ºF) fan/Gas 7. Bake for 30 minutes, or until the tomato is dry and really getting a few speckled bits of deep chestnut around the edge. Remove from the oven and let cool for anything from a few minutes to a few hours. This gives you a chance to sort out the toppings.

Be adventurous here, more so than me. I slice the cherry tomatoes and sprinkle these on top, then layer over the cheese and tear fresh basil everywhere. I turn the oven right up to 250ºC (480ºF)/230ºC (450ºF) fan/Gas 9, then stick it back in to bake for a final 5–6 minutes. Stop when the edges are just the right side of burnt. Serve immediately, drizzled with good olive oil and sprinkled with black pepper.

WALNUT LEVAIN

Who am I kidding? This bread isn't American, it's French (like pretty much everything good and tasty). But I had it first from Acme Bread in San Fran, and I liked it. A lot. Enough to steal it while just about crediting its creators. That makes it not stealing, right?

I've a funny relationship with walnuts. I actively dislike a raw walnut. But roasted or even cooked within dough or cake they have an awesome, aromatic flavour. Walnut loaves are a favourite – I used to make a honey and walnut hybrid yeasted dough that worked very well with butter and even better with blue cheese.

This bread doesn't need honey. The sourdough will make it more than sweet enough during the long proves. Another fortunate (depending on your view) side effect of the long prove is the purple hue this loaf turns – tannins seep out from the skins and colour the dough quite uniformly if the nuts are added early, or give a mottled effect if added late.

For 1 large loaf:
150g wholemeal (wholewheat) or rye starter
425g strong white flour
300g tepid-warm water
10g table salt
100g whole, untoasted walnuts
wholemeal (wholewheat) flour
  and semolina, for dusting

Start by taking your sourdough starter out of the fridge anything from 8–14 hours before you intend to bake and give it a feed to double its weight. Alternatively, if you're confident in its activity, you can take it out of the fridge a couple of hours prior to using.

In a large bowl, weigh your flour. Add the sourdough starter. Mix warm and cool water in a jug to get approximately 25ºC (77ºF), slightly warmer than tepid, and pour this in. Mix everything together very roughly until you have a lumpy dough – you can use a wooden spoon, your hands or a dough hook.

Let the dough rest for 20–30 minutes – a short autolyse will help it come together. Ideally, cover the bowl with a damp tea towel or a plate to stop it drying out.

Add your salt into the dough. I'd knead it well until it's very stretchy and supple. When it's almost there, add the walnuts and continue kneading. Mixing in the walnuts reduces our dough strength, so you need to compensate for this. Alternatively, you could stretch and fold the dough (see page 55) and then add the walnuts, and repeat the stretch and fold every hour or two.

Wrap your bowl in a couple of large tea towels to keep it warm and stop the dough drying out. Leave in a relatively warm place for about 4 hours or so. If you aren't stretching and folding, then make sure you do one or two stretches and folds to help your dough's strength.

Once your dough is looking big and puffy, it's ready to pre-shape. Turn your dough gently out onto an unfloured surface – use a dough scraper to cleanly separate it from the side of the bowl. Using the dough scraper again, drive underneath the dough to create some tension (see page 58), then let your dough rest on the surface for 30 minutes, or until you're ready to shape. There's no need to cover it.

Dust a proving basket, your hands and the work surface with wholemeal (wholewheat) flour, and then use a scraper to flip your dough into it. Shape your dough for a batard (see pages 62–3), or however you like, creating good tension. Don't worry if some of the walnuts burst from it. Place your dough in your basket and place inside a plastic bag. Prove for a couple of hours at room temperature, before sticking in the fridge for 8–12 hours. If you want it quickly, prove for 3 hours at room temperature.

Preheat your oven 30–40 minutes before you think your dough will be ready, especially if it has a stone or heavy baking surface inside. You can bake inside a pot or cloche, preheated or not. Your oven temperature should be 250ºC (480ºF)/230ºC (450ºF) fan/Gas 9.

When you're ready to bake, dust a tray or peel with semolina and then sprinkle some more onto your proven dough. Flip the dough onto your tray and score – I tend to go for a cross or a chevron cut.

Slide onto your prepared surface and into the oven. Add steam using your chosen method – I'd pour some water into a cast-iron pan that's sitting in the bottom of the oven, or bake under a lid or cloche. Turn the oven down to 220ºC (430ºF)/200ºC (400ºF) fan/ Gas 7. Bake for 20 minutes and then either vent the oven by opening the door and allowing all the steam to escape or remove your lid. Bake again for another 30 minutes or until deep golden. Cool for at least 30 minutes before enjoying.

DANISH RYE
(RUGBRØD, OR SEEDED PUMPERNICKEL)

This is a loaf I don't make nearly enough – then when I do, I'm reminded of its awesomeness and immediately bake it again in a big batch, slice it, wrap it and freeze it. It withstands the freezing process particularly well, maintaining moisture forever. You can then just stick one slice at a time straight into the toaster and always have access to posh toast or Danish open sandwiches: smørrebrød.

The Americans call this style of loaf a pumpernickel – if you want the truly dense American version of this Germanic classic, you can omit the seeds. I'd definitely keep the whole rye flakes, though: they provide much-needed texture to the loaf. Some recipes will go crazy, adding all sorts of extra grains, nuts and seeds. If you have anything you want to add, go for it. I do like walnuts in this bread. But otherwise, I find that keeping it simple is best.

The rye flakes mentioned above, also known as cracked rye kernels, can be difficult to find: these are the rye equivalent of porridge oats. On the high street, you can get them in most health-food and organic shops. Big supermarkets might also have them, but admittedly, the easiest place to find them is online.

For 1 shallow loaf in a 900g (2lb) tin:
350g wholemeal (wholewheat) rye flour,
* plus extra for dusting*
150g rye flakes (cracked rye kernels)
100g rye sourdough starter
350g tepid water
100g sunflower seeds
50g flax or sesame seeds
7g table salt
butter, for greasing
seeds, porridge oats or rye flakes, for topping

In a large bowl, weigh your rye flour and your rye flakes. Then add your starter and your tepid water, and mix everything together until roughly combined. An autolyse is extremely important here, as it lets the wholemeal grain properly absorb the water. Leave it a couple of hours at room temperature.

During the autolyse, weigh your sunflower and flax or sesame seeds. Stick them on a tray and place in a non-preheated oven. Set it to 200ºC (400ºF)/180ºC (350ºF) fan/Gas 6, and cook the seeds for just 5 minutes or so.

They should smell aromatic without being roasted. Leave them to cool.

After your autolyse, add the salt to your dough and give it a knead for 3–4 minutes (see pages 50–3) – this isn't always done traditionally, but I find it really helps with the lightness of your final loaf. You'll find the gluten developing and the dough holding its shape far better. At this point, add your cooled seeds and mix until they are evenly combined.

Cover your bowl and leave your dough somewhere at room temperature. I'd prove for 3–4 hours; not too long, as your starter will have got stuck into the fermentation already. I'd do at least one stretch and fold (see page 55), more for the purposes of redistributing moisture, as water can leach out of this dough and sit on top.

You might not notice much of a rise, but there should be something. Use a dough scraper to turn the dough out onto an unfloured surface and pre-shape (see page 58) into a single lump. Leave it to rest for 20–30 minutes. Meanwhile, grease your loaf tin with plenty of butter.

After your bench rest, lightly flour your surface with rye flour and flip your dough onto it. Shape it very gently into a baton shape (see pages 62–3) – if you press too hard you'll simply tear the structure. Gently transfer it to your tin, seam side down. Place your tin inside a plastic bag and leave it at room temperature for about 2 hours, or until notably bigger again. Alternatively, for epic and earthy flavour, you can retard this loaf in the fridge, covered, to bake the next day.

Despite this being in a tin, I still like to stone bake my loaf, so I preheat my oven to 250ºC (480ºF)/230ºC (450ºF) fan/Gas 9 at least 30–40 minutes before I'm expecting it to be ready. If you're not using a stone, 10–15 minutes will do.

Sprinkle with seeds, oats or rye flakes. Usually there's no need to score. Place your tin in the oven and turn it down to 220ºC (430ºF)/200ºC (400ºF) fan/Gas 7. Add some steam: I pour water into a cast-iron pan on the floor of the oven. Vent the steam from the oven after 20 minutes, and bake for another 25–30 minutes after that for one large 950g (2lb) loaf tin (or another 10 minutes for half-size 450g (1lb) loaves).

Following this, remove from the oven, bash the loaf out of the tin and place back in the oven for 5–10 minutes, for slightly crustier sides. Cool for at least an hour before slicing.

LEMON AND POPPY SEED LOAF

I'm not a fan, as you'll have read repeatedly by now, of adding things to breads for the sake of it. When it comes to personalising and pimping – as encouraged by televised baking competitions – 99 times out of 100, the addition serves to distract or detract from the quality of the bread or cake. If you're thinking about adding strawberries to your bread, for example, take my advice – just don't do it. The best way of working strawberries into bread is in the form of strawberry jam. Maybe with clotted cream, and few sliced fresh strawberries on top. Mmmm.

However, this bread is one of the few exceptions to my rule. The flavour is awesome – the lemons add neither sweetness nor sourness because only the zest is used, creating a delicate aroma that marries well with complex white sourdough. The poppy seed gives an equally delicate, nutty flavour – both have a bitterness and astringency that balances the sweetness of the bread. And it still maintains a little gastronomic humour, paying tribute to its otherwise very cakey namesake.

The resulting bread is something that's very versatile: it could be served with anything that goes well with lemons (most things), but it could be used as your daily bread and toasted. My favourite accompaniment so far is smoked salmon.

This isn't one you'll bake once and that will sit on the side, going stale between slices: it will become a new staple.

For 2 sizeable batards:
700g strong white flour, plus extra for dusting
200g white sourdough starter
500g tepid-warm water
14g table salt
50g poppy seeds, plus extra for sprinkling
3 lemons, zested
semolina, for dusting

Into a large bowl, weigh your flour, starter and tepid-warm water. Mix these together with a dough hook or wooden spoon and let them sit for 30–60 minutes. This is your autolyse.

Following this, add your salt (don't forget!) and hand knead for about 5 minutes or so, or until it feels smooth and supple in your hands. I'd use the slap and fold (see pages 50-1), as this gives the dough some strength. Alternatively, you could mix in a stand mixer at low-medium speed (speed '2') for about 5 minutes. Towards the end of mixing, add your poppy seeds and lemon zest, and continue mixing to incorporate them evenly.

Cover your bowl with a plate or tea towel and let it sit in a warm place. You want to leave it for 3–4 hours, depending on temperature. During this time, I'd give it at least two stretches and folds (see page 55) in order to give your dough more strength.

Once your dough is bubbly and maintaining its strength between folds, tip it out onto an unfloured work surface. Use a scraper to divide your dough into two, and pre-shape by driving your scraper underneath to tighten your loaves (see page 58). Bench rest for 30 minutes.

Dust your proving baskets or a heavy couche with plenty of white flour, and sprinkle with a few more poppy seeds, if you have them. Then, shape each loaf as you prefer – I like these to be squat batards. Stick each loaf in a proving basket and place the proving baskets inside plastic bags to stop the dough from drying out.

Rest the loaves at room temperature for another 2 hours. You want each to increase in size again by about half. Alternatively, for greater flavour and a deeper acidity that works well with the lemon, you can retard this prove in the fridge, covered, after an hour or so.

About half an hour before you plan to bake, stick your oven on, or 10 minutes earlier if you're using baking stones. Preheat it to at least 250ºC (480ºF)/230ºC (450ºF) fan/Gas 9. If you're baking in a pot or Dutch oven, you can preheat this, too.

Dust a peel or tray with semolina and a little flour. Turn out your loaves and give them a score – I like to have a little bit of fun with this loaf, slicing three or four times at least, and possibly adding some lemony patterns on top. Anyway, you can do what you like. Slide your loaves onto your baking surface and add steam, either by pouring water into a cast-iron pan sitting in the bottom of the oven or by spraying the loaves with water.

Bake for 20 minutes and then vent the oven by opening the door, or remove the lid from your pot. Continue baking for another 20–30 minutes, or until your crust is golden but not getting too dark. Once done enough for you, leave to cool for at least half an hour before slicing.

CRISPBREAD

These are sourdough crackers – extra-thin versions of *knäckebröd* or crispbreads. In Scandinavia, they were considered a very humble food for generations past. Now, they're about a fiver for a wee box at the supermarket.

You can top these crackers with anything you like. I particularly like germ (wheatgerm) – the fatty, yolk-equivalent of the wheat seed. Because of its moisture and its fat content, it doesn't stay fresh long. Keep it in the fridge, and try to order it directly from your supplier. You can use anything: seeds are especially nice, pressed in just before baking.

But back to the dough. Any sourdough can be used to create crispbread, so long as it is rolled thinly enough and pricked to prevent puffing. Having a good portion of the flour as wholemeal (wholewheat) or rye helps the eventual cracker crumble and crack. In this case, getting the dough thin enough can be tricky: you can stretch, rest and roll using a rolling pin.

I don't knead this dough – instead, I do a very long autolyse to increase extensibility. Then, rather than stretch and fold, I leave the dough to bulk ferment for as long as possible at as low a temperature as possible. This creates a sticky dough, but one that can be stretched very thin. Use plenty of flour and you'll be fine.

For 6–8 large crispbreads:
150g wholemeal (wholewheat) rye flour,
  plus extra for rolling and stretching
150g unbleached strong white flour
175g tepid water
150g white sourdough starter
5g table salt
2–3 tbsp crushed wheatgerm, or nuts
  or seeds, for topping

In a bowl, weigh your two flours. Add in your water, and mix this together until you've got a stiff dough. Cover the bowl and leave this for about 8–12 hours. At the same time, take your sourdough starter out of the fridge and feed it.

After this time, add the sourdough starter to your dough, as well as the salt. Mix everything together until you've got something that's consistent. You don't need to work it really hard. You don't even have to knead it, but using something like the English knead (see page 52) might help in bringing the ingredients together. Once the dough is uniform, stop. Stick it back in the bowl and cover.

Prove for 6–8 hours at a cool room temperature. Don't chill it in the fridge so that it is cold – this will make stretching a little harder, and it won't ferment quite so well. Your crackers would be leathery rather than crisp.

Preheat your oven to as hot as it goes – usually 250ºC (480ºF)/230ºC (450ºF) fan/Gas 9. You want to do this at least 40 minutes before you aim to bake if you've got a baking stone. If not, 10 minutes will do.

Generously flour a work surface using rye flour, and tip your dough out onto it. Move it around to coat with flour and add more if necessary. Do add some more flour on top. Chop your dough into six or eight roughly equal chunks - don't be sticking wee bits of chopped floury dough together to make it more even; whatever size the chunks come out at is fine.

Use floured hands to stretch each chunk of dough until it is as thin as you can make it. We're talking really thin – if possible, almost translucent. Use flour to stop it sticking. Then use a rolling pin to get them even thinner. If you're struggling, you can place the tough sheet in the fridge for a few minutes as you start the next one. Once rolled, you bake them in whatever shape they come out at, or you can cut them into large circles using a plate and a knife, and cut small holes in the centres to facilitate breaking into portions.

Slide a peel or baking tray under your crispbread and use a fork to prick all over: this stops it forming one massive air pocket. Gently brush the top of the crispbread with some water, and then sprinkle with some crushed wheatgerm or press your seeds into the top. Slide your crispbreads into your oven or bake on a tray and bake for 6–8 minutes, or they are turning a dark golden brown. They might take a bit longer if the thinness isn't quite there. Repeat until you've got none left. Note that they won't be 100% crisp until they've cooled – this will take approximately 10 minutes.

FICELLE WITH OLIVES

Ficelle's literal translation is string, but it has become known within the English language (or rather, my English language) as an especially long, thin baguette. The many overlapping cuts burst open and give the appearance of a frayed piece of string stretched straight.

Because of their relative length, they're great for practising scoring. Like a baguette but even more so, their small size requires even more precision, and even more delicacy. If you can manage these, then you can master the baguette. I've made these when stressed for dinner parties and have often found it easier to lazily slice them down their entire length. It does give quite a rustic (read: rough) opening.

The olives within this recipe, made into a tapenade with the traditional dried *herbes de Provence*, can get in the way of your gluten structure if mixed in too early – that's why I'd really recommend leaving them until shaping. If you do this, you see the difference in the way the loaves hold their shape; it gives a smooth glistening crust and a far more pronounced oven spring.

For 4 ficelles:
70g white sourdough starter
300g strong white flour
5g table salt
190g tepid-warm water
semolina, for dusting

For the tapenade:
100g black olives, pitted and drained
1 tsp capers
1 tsp olive oil
½ tsp herbes de Provence

The night before you plan to bake, check your starter. If it isn't in great health, feed it by mixing in equal weights of flour and water to double the weight. Leave it out of the fridge. If you're confident in its activity, leave it in the fridge for now, but take it out a few hours before you're going to start.

In a large bowl, weigh your flour. Add in your salt and mix these roughly to combine. Mix together some warm and cold water in a jug until it feels just warmer than tepid, about 25°C (77°F), then add this and your active sourdough starter. Mix using a wooden spoon, a dough hook or your hands. It should be just combined.

Let your dough rest for approximately 30 minutes – autolyse. You'll want to cover the bowl with a damp tea towel or a dinner plate to stop the dough from drying out.

Knead your dough for 5–8 minutes, or until the dough is just starting to become smooth and supple (see pages 50–2). Alternatively, you could stretch and fold your dough a couple of times during the first prove (see page 55). Like the baguette, this is quite a dry dough, giving it strength. You don't need to knead it as much as you do a wet dough – indeed, if you overdevelop the gluten, you'll have tight loaves that don't rise.

Leave your dough, covered, for 4–5 hours. This will vary depending on temperature. The dough should become large and bubbly, and have risen by at least half. Alternatively, you can retard this prove in the fridge with the bowl covered in a plastic bag after a couple of hours, and reduce the length of the second prove to 1–1½ hours at room temperature.

Use a dough scraper to scrape your dough out onto a clean, unfloured surface. Use the scraper to chop the dough into four equal pieces. I would weigh these, as little differences go a long way when your doughs are this tiny. Pre-shape – I'd just use an angled dough scraper driven across a work surface to tighten them – see page 58. Rest for 30 minutes following this.

During this time, make your tapenade. Don't use a blender – very finely chop your olives and capers using a sharp knife. Be conscientious to make your pieces nice and small. Then add these to a small bowl and add in your olive oil and herbs. Mix to make a paste.

Lightly flour a work surface and flour a couche at the same time. Take one piece of dough and place it, smooth side down, on your surface. Flatten gently with the heel of your hand, and spoon a quarter of your tapenade on top, spreading it over the centre of the dough. Fold the dough over the top of the tapenade to cover it, first from the side towards you and then the side away from you. At this point, you can continue to follow the shaping guide for baguettes (see pages 146–7), tightening the dough towards you and then elongating before placing them neighbourly on your couche. Don't worry if the olives burst out of the dough a little.

Prove for 30 minutes at room temperature, and then move your couche into the fridge. You should dust the ficelles with flour and then lay some cling film (plastic wrap) over the top to keep them from drying out. Prove in the fridge for 8–14 hours, or until you are ready to bake.

Like baguettes, these should be baked on a stone or a heavy steel tray. If you've got this facility, make sure to preheat your oven at least 30 minutes before you plan to bake. Regardless, preheat your oven to 240ºC (460ºF)/220ºC (430ºF) fan/Gas 9.

Dust a peel with semolina. One by one, turn each ficelle onto your semolina peel, seam-side down. Score each one down its length, either with one slash or multiple slashes. Score at a sharp angle, very lightly and quickly, just to break the skin.

Slide your ficelle onto the hot baking stone; I like to do this sideways so that they slide onto your stone all at once. Add steam – either by pouring water into a cast-iron pan sitting in the bottom of the oven or spraying the ficelle with water. If you have a fan oven and can turn the fan off, do so.

Bake for 15 minutes, and then open the oven door to let any excess steam out (remove your pan if it still has any water in it). Admire their magnificent rise. Bake for a further 15 minutes, or until the breads are to your liking – for me, that's a deep golden brown. Cool on a rack properly.

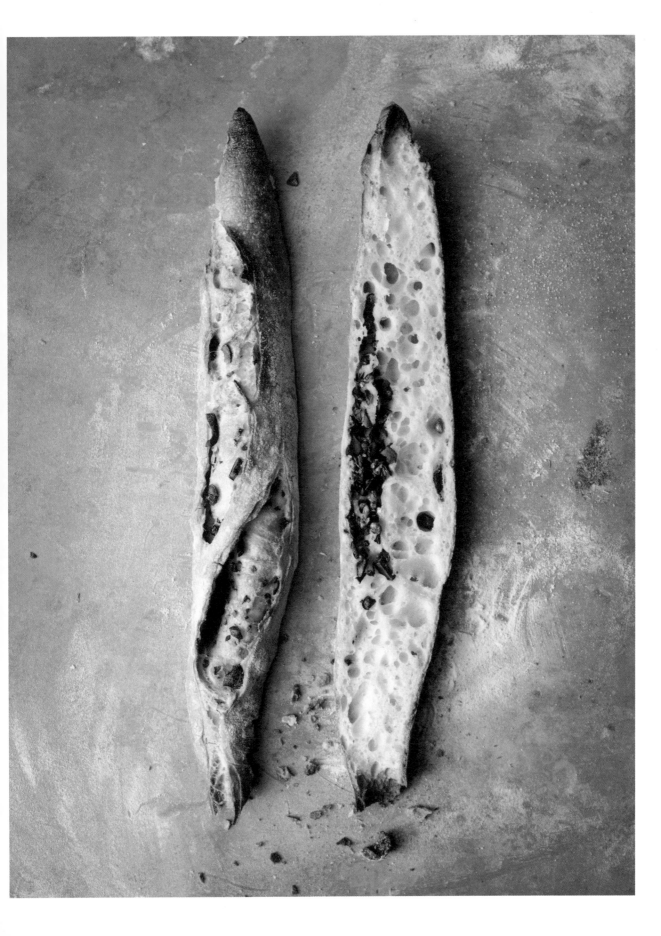

ENRICHED

This is a chapter devoted to enriched breads. There's been the odd example dotted about already – Burger Buns (page 157) and Pain de Mie (page 133), for instance – but this chapter contains only those breads that are defined by their soft, pillowy sweetness rather than with ulterior savoury intent. Most are designed to be enjoyed as sweet treats, with the exception of the infinitely versatile Brioche (page 221).

Enriched usually means that the dough contains additional butter, eggs and sugar. There's a tendency to generalise these fluffy doughs as 'brioche' – but they aren't. Brioche is altogether special. Doughnuts made with a brioche dough, for example, are bad. It's important to have the right dough for the right situation. Don't be doughist.

THE WORLD'S BEST DOUGHNUTS

I think I only wrote this book so that I could include this recipe. These naturally leavened doughnuts are quite simply the best things I've ever eaten. Even better than the Bread Ahead doughnuts from Borough Market – a bold claim, but I stand by it.

One can go on about health and the implications of eating unhealthy things, and I do. Daily. Hourly, I promote a wholesome life to my patients. And I believe, more strongly than you can quite imagine, that making and eating a doughnut like this is probably one of the healthiest things you can do. Why? Because the happiness you feel by going through this process from start to finish is as close to pure joy as I know.

While they are awesome simply fried and dusted with cinnamon sugar – and even more amazing stuffed with good raspberry jam – I couldn't give you this recipe without also including a stand-out *crème pâtissière* (set custard) recipe. This should be piped in so that it is bursting out of each doughnut at the top.

As with all enriched sourdough, the key to success is warmth. You want to prove between 25–28ºC (77–82ºF), with an active starter. You can fry these on the hob, but be careful. Have a fire blanket or wet tea towel at the ready, and a thermometer handy to check the temperature regularly. Make sure the saucepan is at least twice as high as your oil-fill level, too.

For a dozen big doughnuts:
200g white sourdough starter
250g plain (all-purpose) white flour,
 plus extra for dusting
250g strong white flour
200g milk
50g caster (superfine) sugar, plus extra for coating
8g salt
2 large eggs, at room temperature
100g unsalted butter
vegetable or sunflower oil, for greasing
 and deep frying

For the crème pâtissière:
250g whole milk
3 egg yolks
20g cornflour (cornstarch)
1 tsp vanilla paste or 2 tsp vanilla extract
60g caster (superfine) sugar
40g unsalted butter

If your sourdough starter needs topping up, take it out of the fridge the night before and give it a good feed, leaving it to rise for 8–14 hours. I like to start this recipe in the late morning so that it's ready for early evening, which means the night before is perfect.

Make the dough. Start by weighing together the two flours in a large bowl, then mix in the sugar and salt. Warm the milk (in the microwave) until it feels just warm. Add this, along with your white sourdough starter and eggs. Mix everything until it forms a clump. Cover your bowl with a damp tea towel or a plate and let it sit for 30–40 minutes to autolyse.

Time to knead: mix and mix until your dough passes the windowpane test (see page 44). This will be about 12 minutes by machine, first on speed '1' for 7 minutes, then speed '2' for 5 minutes. By hand, this will be 10–15 minutes (see pages 50–2). Once developed, you should add your butter. If it is cold, heat it (again using the microwave) until soft, almost melted. Use your hands or a mixer to mix your butter in until you've got a homogeneous dough.

Leave your dough for about 4 hours at a warm room temperature. Because of all your development, it should swell at quite a rate. It's quite a dry dough, so it probably won't need any stretching and folding.

Turn the dough out onto a lightly floured surface. Chop into 12 roughly equal lumps of dough using your scraper. If you want to be exact, you can weigh them. Each lump should be 94g, with a little left over. Once you're happy with each, line a tray with non-stick greaseproof baking paper and brush it with a little vegetable or sunflower oil: this will be where the doughnuts prove.

Shape into little balls by repeatedly driving your dough scraper underneath the dough at a roughly 45-degree angle, tucking each side in, just as in pre-shaping loaves (see page 58). You should feel the dough stick slightly to your surface. Otherwise, if you're confident, you can do the same thing using a cupped hand, making gentle circular motions. This action will form the dough into tight balls. Place each one on your prepared paper.

Spray or brush a sheet of cling film (plastic wrap) with some more oil, and gently lay this on top. Alternatively, if you have a stiff plastic bag, you could use this to cover the tray. Leave your doughnuts to rise for 2 hours at a warm room temperature, or until swollen to at least one and a half times their original size. You can then stick them in the fridge, covered, until you're ready to fry.

It's at this stage that I make the crème pat. You could do this up to a day before and chill it until needed, though. In a bowl, whisk together your egg yolks, cornflour (cornstarch), vanilla and sugar until you've got a smooth paste. Pour your milk into a saucepan and bring to a gentle simmer over a low heat. When steaming hot or just bubbling around the edge, pour half into your eggy mix, and whisk together quickly to stop

it scrambling. Pour all of this back into your remaining milk, and place back on the heat. Stir or whisk all the time until you've got a very thick paste, and once it's thick, keep stirring and heating for another couple of minutes. Remove from the heat and whisk in your butter. Cover with cling film touching the surface to prevent a skin from forming, leave to cool and then stick in the fridge until needed.

When ready to fry the doughnuts, set your fryer or heat your oil to 160°C (320°F), over a low-medium heat if using a saucepan. This can take a while, so start 20 minutes before you intend to fry. Prepare a tray or dish that's got plenty of sugar in it. Test the oil with your roughest-looking doughnut – use a slotted spoon to gently prise it from its paper and place it in the saucepan. It should bubble around the edges shortly after it hits the oil. Fry for 3–4 minutes, before turning over and frying for the same length of time on the other side. It might turn itself over, as it becomes top-heavy.

When golden on both sides, use your slotted spoon to lift it from the oil and let it drip for a few seconds. Place it in your sugar and roll around to coat. They can stay here, or you can place them on a plate. Repeat, frying as many doughnuts as you can fit without crowding your saucepan.

Once your doughnuts have cooled, you can fill them with the crème pat. Give the custard a good mix with a whisk so that it's homogeneous (it will go a little gelatinous when cooled) and then scoop into a piping (pastry) bag. Use a knife to make a hole in the side of the doughnut, and then pipe your custard in the centre. Weighing before and after on scales can be helpful if it's your first time. You want about 30–35g of custard per doughnut. They'll keep for a day or two, but are best eaten as fresh as possible.

BRIOCHE

For a long time, brioche to me was a soft, dense, slightly sickly roll that came out of a plastic packet, with chocolate chips or raisins. Nice, but not worth the calories. And boy, what a lot of calories.

It took a cycling trip around France in 2012 for me to experience proper brioche for the first time. Naturally leavened, well-fired brioche. This little bakery, in a little village called Le Vast in north-east Normandy, was conspicuous compared to others because we saw people driving from villages all around, each with their own good bakeries, to pick up the brioche. They'd buy brioche, and only brioche, then leave.

The brioche had a flaky, eggy crust. It was not squidgy; when sliced, it didn't squelch together, but had a firm and extremely open structure that a sharp knife could slice without deforming. Eating the dough was like eating savoury candy floss: first it felt dry and web-like, but then dissolved. Complex and interesting. It came into its own when lightly toasted over our camping stove and slathered with good jam.

I strive, in recipe form, to re-create this life-affirming brioche for you. To hit the right spot in terms of flavour and acidity, one of your fermentations needs to be long and cool (but not too cold), and I'd make it your first one, if possible. This makes shaping easier. You'll need to get the heat cranked up during the second prove.

My brioche formula is quite simple and quite easy remember, for those who like bread formulae (see page 81): 100% flour, 50% egg, 40% butter, 40% starter, 30% milk, 10% sugar, 2% salt.

For 2 shallow tins of brioche, or 12 wee 'à tête':
200g white sourdough starter
500g strong white flour
10g table salt
50g caster (superfine) sugar
5 large eggs, at room temperature
150g milk
200g unsalted butter, softened,
  plus extra for greasing
1 egg, beaten with a pinch of salt, for brushing
butter, for greasing

Check your sourdough starter about 8–14 hours before you want to bake. It should be very active. If it isn't, take it out of the fridge, give it a feed and see how it does. In any case, let your starter warm up for a couple of hours before using.

In a large bowl, weigh your flour. Add your salt and sugar, and then mix these in using your fingers. Add in

your sourdough starter, and then break in your eggs. Warm your milk until it is tepid-warm and mix everything together until you've got a very rough dough. Leave it to sit for 30–40 minutes somewhere warm.

Mix your dough – preferably in an electric mixer. If it's sticky, that's OK. You want it to get to the point where it passes the windowpane test (see page 49). Once it has, you can add the butter, which should be soft. If it isn't, give it a blast in the microwave (it doesn't matter if it's a bit melted). Mix your butter in and keep working until the dough is shiny, smooth and consistent.

Cover your bowl with a plate or damp tea towel and leave it at room temperature for 3–4 hours. This will further develop your gluten and begin to form some aeration. You could move straight to shaping after this step, but I prefer to let the flavour develop for a little longer. Stick it in the fridge, covered, or somewhere cool, and leave it to prove for another 8–12 hours.

At some point, grease either two 900g (2lb) loaf tins or 12 small brioche tins with butter.

Following your cold prove, you'll find the dough a rather solid lump, and this is fine. This makes it more tenacious, less extensible and less elastic. Divide into two lumps. Shape into balls just as you would normally pre-shape (see page 58) using your dough scraper. Place these balls in your baking tins – either stacked side by side in 900g (2lb) loaf tins or in your brioche tins. If you've got brioche tins and you like the little ball on top, you'll need to split off little lumps of dough to go on top. Shape these just like you'd pre-shape any loaf (see page 58).

Place the tins in a plastic bag. Leave to prove in a warm place for 2–3 more hours – you want them to grow significantly. If you see little activity, get more heat on it. With the warming up from the fridge, it could take 4–5 hours if your house is cool. About 20 minutes before you think they will be ready, preheat your oven to 250ºC (480ºF)/230ºC (450ºF) fan/Gas 9. Preheat for longer if you're using a baking stone underneath your tins.

Brush the egg wash over the top of your risen brioche. You could sprinkle on sesame seeds if you're feeling fancy, but I don't. Stick your tins in the oven and turn it down to 220ºC (430ºF)/200ºC (400ºF) fan/Gas 7. Bake for about 40 minutes, or until they're not burnt, but getting very dark. Check on them after 30 minutes and turn down the oven by 20ºC/10ºF/two gas marks if you're worried they're colouring too fast. Leave to cool in the tins for at least half an hour, then bash them out to finish cooling on a rack – and they must cool completely before slicing, so don't be tempted to do so sooner.

PANDORO AND PANETTONE

Some might call it sacrilegious to lump these two iconic breads into one recipe. Or naïve, considering their geographically related but misaligned history. I can't help but recommend using the same dough for both, though. They're both soft, fluffy-centred and heavily enriched doughs where we aim for the lightest of light textures. They're both celebration centrepieces: the pandoro (*pan d'oro* – golden bread) was enjoyed by the nobility of historic Verona and the panettone by Milanese high society.

Modern *pandori* tend to be a little drier, firm and brioche-like, whereas *panettoni* makers strive to maintain their fluffy, soft origins. The pandoro is simpler: all the ingredients are purchasable in your local small supermarket. If you don't have a pandoro tin, you can use a tall cake tin. The panettone, if you want to present or gift it, requires you to purchase paper moulds, a specific extract and, for an authentic loaf, you'll need Italian candied citrus peel. At a push, you can substitute orange blossom water and supermarket mixed peel.

Both loaves will last for a very long time following baking, and make ideal Christmas gifts. And both require plenty of baking itself, so it helps to take it steadily and not get the oven too hot: because of their shape, the centre takes a long time to heat up compared with a traditional loaf. If you have a thermometer, I'd double check that the middle has reached 96ºC/205ºF before removing them from the oven.

I've already written one recipe for panettone, and this was in my last bread book. That was based on a very traditional commercial method, and this one is better for home use. With a greater understanding of bread science, I feel that the processes can be consolidated into fewer steps. Despite this, this dough requires that you follow all of the tenets of sourdough (see page 15). It is notoriously difficult. You want to push your gluten development to the maximum without causing it to break. It really helps to have an electric mixer.

For 1 loaf, or 1 traditional panettone case or pandoro tin:

For the autolyse:
60g very active white sourdough starter
250g strong white flour
70g tepid-warm water
6 large egg yolks, at room temperature

For stage 1:
85g caster (superfine) sugar
15g good-quality runny honey
   (Scottish heather honey is best)
3g salt

For stage 2:
125g unsalted butter, softened
vegetable or other flavourless oil, for shaping

For pandoro (after stage 2):
1 vanilla pod or 1 tsp vanilla bean paste

For panettone (after stage 2):
1 tsp good vanilla extract, ½ tsp vanilla paste
   or seeds scraped from ½ a split vanilla
   pod (bean)
1 tsp Aroma Panettone, or orange blossom
   water as a substitute
100g sultanas
100g Italian candied citrus peel
2 wooden skewers

Around 8–12 hours before you bake, take your white sourdough starter out of the fridge. Give it a feed, then leave at room temperature for this time. If it isn't very active after this, delay baking by another day and give it another feed that evening. You should only use it if it's very active.

In a large bowl, weigh your autolyse ingredients. Mix them together until combined into a rough but homogeneous dough. Cover your bowl and leave it somewhere warm for an hour or so.

Now add the 'stage 1' ingredients to your bowl. Mix everything together, and then knead vigorously for 10–15 minutes. You want your dough to windowpane properly (see page 49). Anything less isn't enough, and therefore if you have a mixer, use it.

Leave your dough to prove for 3 hours, preferably some-where warm. It's a slow-proving dough, so it should be showing some signs of activity at this point, but not be doubled or tripled in size.

Add in your 'stage 2' butter. Again, it's time to use your electric mixer if you have it. If not, it's going to take a wee while for you to combine the butter into your dough by kneading. Once the butter is combined, add the vanilla for pandoro, or vanilla, Aroma Panettone, sultanas and peel for panettone. Mix some more until these are completely combined.

Cover and prove for another 4–6 hours, or until you're noticing it has risen a little more. Stretch and fold (page 55) at this point, then cover and stick in the fridge. Prove here for anything between 12 and 24 hours. At some point while it is proving, you want to grease your pandoro tin with plenty of butter, or prepare your panettone case by poking two wooden skewers in line with the base: this allows you to hang your panettone upside down.

Turn your dough out onto your work surface. Divide into the number of loaves you require, and pre-shape

as per the guide on page 58, using a little extra water, or even a little vegetable or other flavourless oil to help you. Once pre-shaped, bench rest for an hour. After 30 minutes, if the dough has spread significantly, pre-shape again and leave for the remaining time.

Shape, using a little oil, as you would for boules (see pages 60–1). Because of the relatively low gluten content in this recipe, this can be quite difficult. Place the dough in your prepared tin or case.

This final prove is very important because it gives you an idea of your potential for rise. Don't worry if your dough, so far, sits quite low in your tin or case. It will rise, probably tripling in size. Then the oven spring should be magnificent. Allow to prove somewhere warm, such as near a heater, for 3–5 hours.

After this time, your loaf will be ready to bake. It helps to put the tin or case on a baking stone for even greater oven spring; preheat this to at least 220ºC (430ºF/200ºC (400ºF) fan/Gas 7. You want to do this at least 45 minutes before baking.

If making panettone, score the top in a cross shape. For pandoro, don't bother. Transfer your proved loaves to the oven and add steam by placing a cast-iron pan filled with water in the bottom of the oven. Turn your oven down to 190ºC (375ºF)/170ºC (340ºF) fan/Gas 5. Bake for 1 hour, or until a deep, dark brown on top. If you have a digital probe thermometer, check the centre: you want it to be over 96ºC (205ºF).

For cooling, your pandoro can sit and cool as it stands in its tin. For your panettone, it should be cooled upside down. You can pile up books, or use two Kilner (Mason) jars: those wooden skewers should hold your bread upside down to prevent shrinkage as it cools.

If storing, store in a tin (an old shop-bought panettone tin works, obviously), an airtight container, or wrapped in cling film (plastic wrap).

CHUGELHOPF (CHERRY KUGELHOPF)

I was never that sold on *kugelhopf*. It felt like a lesser Austrian version of panettone, or a *baba au rhum* lacking that all-important slug of booze. The examples I've eaten had been dense, dry or cake-like, and not ultra-light and fluffy as I always expected.

Yet here it is, a further festive loaf. The reasons are threefold. The first is simple – it's just too awesome to leave out. This isn't your traditional *kugelhopf*; the kirsch is a blunt, sweet force that, with the help of the cherries, allows the bread to stand alone without accompaniment, but for a fine dusting of sugar. Second, there are very few *kugelhopf* recipes out there for those inclined to ferment using sourdough – this to me is a good enough reason for inclusion alone. The third is that this is an excuse to use an unusual vintage Bundt tin I found on eBay.

For 1 chugelhopf:
75g white sourdough starter
65g milk, warmed
250g plain (all-purpose) white flour
5g salt
2 large eggs
25g caster (superfine) sugar
½ tsp rosewater
100g unsalted butter, softened,
  plus extra for greasing
50g dark chocolate chips (optional)
10–12 whole almonds, for finishing
icing (confectioners') sugar, for dusting

For the cherries:
100g dried cherries (preferably sour cherries)
100g kirsch

Start the night before you actually want to be doing stuff. In a bowl, mix your cherries with the kirsch (you can use another liqueur if you don't like kirsch). Cover with cling film (plastic wrap) or a plate and leave to infuse. Take your sourdough starter out of the fridge, give it a feed and get it going overnight.

In the morning, or 8–10 hours after feeding your starter, you can mix together your dough ingredients. Warm your milk in a microwave until it is just tepid-warm, and then add all the ingredients except your butter (and chocolate chips, if using) into a large bowl. Mix everything together, and then cover and leave for 30 minutes to autolyse.

Knead your ingredients together until they have formed a smooth and silky dough. Windowpaning (see page 49) is preferred, though not essential. When you're there, add in the butter and continue kneading to combine it. It helps if you have a mixer. Your butter should be soft to help it amalgamate – if it's hard and cold, give it a buzz in the microwave beforehand. Once your butter is combined, add your kirsch-soaked cherries. If you like chocolate, add the chocolate chips.

If you're going to retard either prove for more flavour, I'd extend this first one. Cover your bowl with a plate or damp tea towel and leave it at room temperature for 4–5 hours. If retarding, stick this in the fridge, covered, and leave it to prove for another 8–16 hours. Towards the end of this, grease a bundt tin with plenty of butter, and arrange your whole raw almonds at the bottom of it.

How you shape your kugelhopf will depend on how it feels. If it's feeling fairly solid and tenacious, carefully shape without disturbing its delicate bubbles. If it is fairly floppy and extensible, you'll want to pre-shape first (see page 58), or at least do a wee stretch and fold in your bowl (see page 55). Follow this with a 30-minute rest.

I would make some effort to create a little tension within the dough and shape as you would for a long, blunt batard (see pages 62–3), but do this without removing the aeration you've already created. Then you can simply curl the dough into a ring shape and place in your tin on top of your almonds.

Place the dough-filled tin in a plastic bag. Leave to prove back in a warm place for 2–4 hours. If your dough has been cold, it will take a while to heat up and will be closer to the longer time. You want it to rise to nearly double its original size. If you see little growth, get more heat on it. At least 20 minutes before you think it will be ready, preheat your oven to 220ºC (430ºF)/200ºC (400ºF) fan/Gas 7.

Turn your oven down just before you stick the tin in. Go for 200ºC (400ºF)/180ºC (350ºF) fan/Gas 6. Bake for about 35–40 minutes, or until the top is a deep golden brown. Once baked, let cool for 5 minutes in the tin and then turn out onto a cooling rack – it should plop out easily, but if not, carefully run a knife around the edge. I like to dust with icing sugar first when hot, and then again once it's cool to completely cover. Serve with coffee or tea.

THE ENRICHED VEGAN PLAIT

This recipe isn't conceited at all. Plaits (braids) are seen by some as a bit of a novelty: part of a bakery display a generation ago. If I was ever to own a trendy bakery, I'd have a single loaf of that day's batch in the window, sliced in half to reveal the crumb. No plaits or wreaths in sight.

Part of the reason that you rarely see sourdough plaits is that it's actually quite difficult. The slow prove creates a dough that is so extensible and sticky that when you try to roll out the strands, they flop and stick everywhere. And then when you successfully plait your loaf, it tends to amalgamate into a wet doughy mush.

I hope this loaf doesn't. It introduces a practice that I've been scornful about in the rest of this book: low hydration. You can make a delicious sourdough with an open crumb, but you have to be prepared to give it a long autolyse. This fully hydrates your flour and allows for a good breakdown of some of the longer proteins and starches.

I've not included any step-by-step photos here because actually, though it might look complicated, this plait is really easy. It's basically a three-strand plait, which is just like plaiting hair. However, instead of turning one strand over the over, it's two. This creates the illusion that this loaf is much harder to make than it really is.

This is a mildly enriched loaf; less so than others that don't make it into this chapter. But it makes an excellent breakfast bread, served with jam. Otherwise, serve with beer or wine; either way, break bread and be happy.

For 2 large plaits:

For the levain:
100g white sourdough starter
150g unsweetened almond milk
300g strong white flour

For the autolyse:
650g strong white flour
1 x 425g can pumpkin purée
100g unsweetened almond milk, plus a little
for brushing the plait

For stage 2:
10g table salt
50g caster (superfine) sugar
100g cold-pressed (extra virgin) rapeseed oil

This recipe uses a levain, so you can use your sourdough starter straight from the fridge if you like. The night before you want to bake your loaf, mix the ingredients for your levain in a large bowl, cover your bowl and leave it at room temperature for 8–12 hours.

In a separate bowl, just after (or just before) you mix your levain, mix together the autolyse ingredients. You want a rough dough. Don't knead. Cover this bowl, and leave it at room temperature, too. Leave this for as long as you leave your levain – 8–12 hours.

The next day, add your autolyse to your levain, or vice versa – it really helps to have a stand mixer here. Mix together until completely combined and looking fairly smooth. Then, add your salt and sugar, and mix things together for a minute or two: your dough shouldn't feel grainy, but it's okay if the salt and sugar haven't fully dissolved. Finally, add your oil. Mix your dough until it is fully combined and the dough is looking very shiny.

Cover your bowl with a plate or damp tea towel and leave it at room temperature for 3–4 hours – you'll want to stretch and fold (see page 55) a couple of times during this time. As with Brioche (see page 221), you can retard the prove in the fridge following this for extra flavour and even more extensibility.

Following your first prove, you'll find that your rather dry dough is more aerated and malleable. This is required for the shaping. You want to turn it out onto an unfloured surface, and use a dough scraper to divide it into six equal pieces. Use a scale if you're unsure: to pull off this loaf, getting your strands to look the same is essential. Pre-shape each equal lump lightly using your dough scraper (see page 58), keeping them oblong if you can. Leave to bench rest for 20–30 minutes.

The next step is to shape each dough into a long sausage shape – if you can, try and do it as you did for baguettes (see pages 146–7). This is good practice for baguette shaping, as it's repeated. If you can't be bothered, it's OK to roll your lumps of dough into extended sausage shapes, each 40–50cm (16–20in) long and each exactly equal to the last. The edges should be slightly tapered.

Separate your strands into pairs and place on a tray. Pinch each pair together at one end so that you've effectively got three strands (each made up of two, side by side) facing you. Plait (braid) each pair over one another just as you would plait hair: fold the left-most strand over the middle one, and then repeat with the right side. Repeat until you've got a plaited loaf all the way down. Don't stretch your dough too much, and try to apply equal pressure all the way down the dough. It's okay if it's a bit thicker in the middle.

Leave to prove for a further 2–3 hours at room temperature. Alternatively, fridge it after a couple of hours, covering the tray with a plastic bag. About 20 minutes before you want to bake, (or 40–50 if using a baking stone) preheat your oven to 240°C (460°F)/220°C (430°F) fan/Gas 8.

In a cup, measure a few tablespoons of almond milk. Brush this over the top of your risen plait. Stick your tray in the oven and turn it down to 220°C (430°F)/200°C (400°F) fan/Gas 7. Bake for about 40 minutes, or until very dark indeed, but not quite burnt. Leave to cool before enjoying.

FRANGIPANE RAISIN KÄNELLANGD

This tear 'n' share tribute to a sweet Swedish loaf is the bready answer to the *pain aux raisins*, a sophisticated riposte to the Chelsea bun and, most importantly, a sublime retort to all of life's troubles.

It utilises a non-traditional brioche-like dough. The frangipane stays moist and distinct. The raisins and cinnamon give you an excuse to make it and eat it in the morning when it's an entirely inappropriate breakfast food.

I made this loaf again and again, trying to find a suitable icing or syrup or caramel to top it with. Out of many syrup recipes I tried, one prevailed: pure golden syrup. The rest were too sweet or caused sogginess of the crisp, flaky crust, or both.

I found one addition, though, that caused me unimaginable happiness. This changed it from something nice to something insane: clotted cream. Good clotted cream with this bread, which had been allowed to cool but not yet become dry, stops life still. It's the Insta-showpiece of a chain of bakeries I've yet to start. Now you've got the recipe, feel free to start said chain – I won't be unhappy. I'll be first in line.

For 1 large loaf or a dozen buns:
150g white sourdough starter
400g strong white flour, plus extra for dusting
8g table salt
50g caster (superfine) sugar
100g milk, warmed until tepid in the microwave
3 large eggs, at room temperature
100g unsalted butter

For the frangipane:
110g unsalted butter
110g caster (superfine) sugar
2 large eggs
130g ground almonds
250g good-quality raisins
100g golden syrup

This recipe works quite a lot like the buns from the Relaxed Recipes chapter – see page 113 – but with a bit of kneading. Start by taking your sourdough starter out of the fridge the night before. If it wasn't fed before being put in there and it's been more than a week, give it a good feed and leave it to rise for 8–14 hours.

Bung all the dough ingredients in a large bowl, except the butter – there's no advantage in being precious here. Give it a good mix until the ingredients are all combined and there are no lumps. Cover your bowl and let it sit for 30 minutes to autolyse.

Give your dough a mix. Knead for about 10 minutes, or until silky and brioche-like. If it doesn't windowpane (see page 49) don't worry, but this would be good. Then heat your butter if it's coming out of the fridge (I use a microwave) until soft, then add this to your rested dough. Use your hand or a dough hook to combine the butter until smooth. Cover your dough and leave it for about 4 hours, at warm room temperature – about 25ºC (77ºF). You should see it swell, but not quite double in size.

In the meantime, you can make your frangipane. If your butter is cold, weigh what you need in a bowl and stick it in the microwave until it's somewhere between melted and soft. Add in your sugar, eggs and ground almonds, and beat using a stiff spoon until combined and there are no buttery lumps. That's it. Cover and leave at room temperature until needed.

Soak your raisins – this is an optional step, but it stops them burning so easily in the oven. While you could use alcohol, I'd just measure your raisins into a bowl and pour over 2 tablespoons of just-boiled water. Slosh it about and cover. At some point, you should find your biggest baking tray and line it with some non-stick, greaseproof baking paper.

When your dough is done, turn it out onto a floured surface and dust with plenty more flour. Stretch (see page 56) and then roll it out into a large rectangle. You want the rectangle to be about 50cm (20in) wide by as high as your biggest baking tray is long – usually, at least 30–35cm (12–14in) high. The shorter edge will be the length of your loaf. Use more flour to stop it sticking.

Spread your frangipane over your dough, nearly to the edge. It might seem quite thin and this is fine. Drain your raisins, then sprinkle over as evenly as you can.

You want to roll up your dough along its short-edge, like a Swiss (jelly) roll, creating a fatter, shorter sausage rather than a long, thin one. Roll or lift this onto your lined baking tray. Use your dough scraper to divide it into 12 slices, but don't slice quite through the last layer of each bun. Instead, flop these buns onto their side. One should flop left, and the next right, so you've got what looks like lots of buns sitting just on top of each other.

Place your tray inside a plastic bag, or cover it with some lightly oiled cling film (plastic wrap). Leave it for 1½–2 hours in a warm place; alternatively, you could retard the second prove after an hour or so. About 30 minutes prior to baking, preheat your oven to 200ºC (400ºF)/180ºC (350ºF) fan/Gas 6.

Remove the tray from the plastic bag (or remove the cling film), and place in the oven. Add steam by filling a cast-iron pan with water and sitting it in the bottom of the oven, and bake for about 35 minutes. You want it golden brown and delicious-looking, but none of the raisins should be burnt.

As soon as the loaf is out of the oven, pour the golden syrup into a saucepan and heat gently until it has turned a little more liquid. Brush this over your hot, swollen loaf. Use it all. Observe its wonderment and let it cool until barely warm; at least 1 hour. At this point, tear and serve with tea and clotted cream.

LEFTOVER STARTER

Since switching to keeping my sourdough starter in the fridge, and baking at least a couple of times a week, I never have any spare sourdough starter. This makes me sad because it means that I rarely get a chance to use these recipes.

I used to keep my sourdough starter out of the fridge and feed it daily. This led to lots of forgotten feeds and dough procrastination, and I often had surplus. These recipes are intended for those times, but occasionally I'll feed my starter more so that I have an excuse. Most can be adapted to use any sort of sourdough starter you want – whether it's wholemeal (wholewheat), rye or white.

BANANA PANCAKES

Sourdough starter, especially old, overripe sourdough starter, is very acidic. This is great, because it means that it reacts with bicarbonate of soda to produce a lot of CO_2. A lot. So, in things like cakes or scones that rely on chemical leavening, you can produce some almighty reactions.

I've found that one of the best places for this is in pancakes – not crêpes, but US or Scottish-style airy pancakes. The healthy dose of starter gives a slight muffin-like firmness to the dough and a lingering tang, as well as a complexity of flavour that balances well with the banana.

The same can't be said for cake or banana bread, in my experience – maybe that's because cake is best left unadulterated.

You can add sourdough starter to any of your pancake recipes – just add an extra ½ tsp of bicarb (baking soda) for every 50g sourdough starter added on top of your usual ingredients. Proportionally, there's a little more bicarb in the recipe below because the overripe bananas are also a bit acidic.

For about 12 pancakes:
80g white sourdough starter
120g plain (all-purpose) white flour
pinch of table salt
1 tsp bicarbonate of soda (baking soda)
2 overripe bananas, mashed
2 medium eggs
butter, for frying

Ideally, your starter should be over-mature – a day old if left at room temperature, or a week old (or more) if left in the fridge. Start by preheating a thick-bottomed frying pan (skillet) over a low heat. Don't add any butter.

In a large bowl, weigh your flour. Add your salt and bicarb (baking soda) and mix in. Then, add in your ripe bananas, starter and eggs. Mix everything together until it is combined into a lumpy but gloopy dough.

Add a few wee knobs of butter to your pan. If it instantly sizzles and spits, it's probably too hot and going to burn; remove the pan from the heat and stick it on a lower ring. Once your butter is melted, take 1 tablespoon of dough from your batch and let it drop onto your greased pan. Use this as a tester. Fry for 2 minutes or so on each side, or until golden brown.

Repeat with the rest of the dough, keeping the pan topped up with butter all the time to stop sticking and add flavour. Fry up to four pancakes at a time, or however many you can fit in your pan. When each batch is done, stick them on a clean tea towel, folding it over to keep them warm.

Serve with whatever you fancy. My favourite is natural (plain) yoghurt, honey and blueberries.

CRUMPETS

Crumpets are the go-to leftover-starter recipe sweeping Instagram and Pinterest for their ridiculously easy method and few ingredients. When you've not got any eggs in the fridge, they're pretty much the best lazy lie-in weekend brunch to make when you want something special but can't be bothered heading to the shops. Thickly filled with butter, there's little better.

This recipe takes advantage of the reaction between the acid in the starter and the alkaline bicarbonate of soda (sodium bicarbonate, or baking soda). The key is creating enough heat to accompany this vigorous reaction, but not using so much that the crumpet or the butter burns. The next most important thing is using plenty of butter on your crumpet ring, or you'll definitely have very stuck crumpets. Some places sell non-stick versions, but I don't have them.

And if you don't have crumpet rings, don't worry. If you like tuna, their cans make perfect crumpet rings. Remove the labels (obviously) and then open the tins at both ends, making sure that your tin opener makes its cut in the side of the can rather than the top. My editors also oblige you to use a file to soften the cut edges of your cans and then scrub thoroughly with a scourer before attempting this. I recommend you don't cut yourself, and use loads of butter.

For 3–4 crumpets:
200g mature white sourdough starter
½ tsp table salt
2 tsp caster (superfine) sugar
½ tsp bicarbonate of soda (baking soda)
butter, for greasing, frying and serving

Start by preheating your heaviest-bottomed frying pan (skillet) over a low heat on a medium ring. Despite the low heat, you want the pan preheated for your initial lift. Grease your crumpet rings with loads of butter. Loads.

Weigh out your sourdough starter. To be quite honest, the quantities don't need to be precise: as long as you've got enough bicarb (baking soda) for a decent reaction, you'll be fine. Add in the salt and the sugar and stir these in gently to combine. Leave your starter for 2–3 minutes.

Add in your bicarb (baking soda) and stir. It will bubble vigorously if all is well. As soon as the bicarb is combined, add a good, chunky knob of butter to your pan and tilt the pan to cover it. Add in your crumpet rings and fill each crumpet ring with your bubbly starter until you're just under halfway up. Don't fill any more than this.

Wait, wait and wait some more. It will feel like it's taking ages. Don't be tempted to turn up the heat. After about 6–8 minutes, or when the crumpets are coming away from the sides of the rings and are looking like they're cooked all but for the middle, gently prise the rings away and turn them over. You can turn them over, rings and all, if they won't easily come away.

Fry for another 2–3 minutes on the other side, before removing from the pan to rest. Re-grease your rings, wipe the pan clean using kitchen paper (paper towels) and add some more butter if you've got some mix left. You can then do the next batch. Cooked, they'll keep in an airtight container for a few days – toast before eating and apply butter as generously as you dare.

CORNBREAD

Cornbread is a cake-like southern US bread. Many in the Deep South think they invented it, but their ancestors appear to have stolen it from their Native American compatriots' ancestors. Besides, related breads have long been made in the corn-rich south west of France since before the US was a country.

My first cornbread renaissance was in 2013. I met with my book team at Lockhart – the London restaurant where American chef Brad McDonald cooked. The fluffy cornbread was soaked in honey butter and epic in every way.

The second cornbread revelation came in my own home. Trying to replicate the awesomeness of the cornbread, I tried, once, using the recipe below with a little added sourdough starter. And just this once, things worked out as they should have. I've made it again and again since, without changing a thing.

The fat you use can be any sort – I keep and use bacon fat because there is not a fat that compares, and I always feel bad throwing it away. I imagine any sort of pig fat would work well, including lard.

For one 20cm- (8in-) diameter bread:
1 tbsp bacon fat, for greasing (butter or lard will do)
200g coarse polenta (cornmeal)
50g plain (all-purpose) flour
50g light brown soft sugar
3g table salt
6g bicarbonate of soda (baking soda)
25g salted butter
200g buttermilk
2 medium eggs
100g sourdough starter

For the honey butter:
50g salted butter, softened
20g runny honey

Start by preheating your oven to 220ºC (430ºF) /200ºC (400ºF) fan/Gas 7. Seek out a large, heavy cast-iron frying pan (skillet). At a push, an ovenproof frying pan will do. Stick your pan over a medium-low heat with your bacon fat to melt.

In a large bowl, weigh your polenta (cornmeal), flour, brown sugar, salt and bicarb (baking soda). Mix these together with your fingers until evenly combined.

Soften your butter in the microwave so that it just melts but no more, and add this to your flour, swiftly followed by your buttermilk, eggs and starter. Mix everything together with a wooden spoon quickly until you've got a homogeneous mixture.

If your pan isn't yet hot with your bacon fat melted, sizzling gently and smelling delicious, turn it up a little so that it is. Add your batter all at once, and then transfer your pan to the oven.

Bake for 20 minutes, or a little longer, until a light golden brown and torn magnificently open. It should bounce back when pressed gently. While it's baking, you should take your remaining softened butter and mix it with your honey. As soon as the cornbread is out of the oven, serve it in its pan, with the honey-butter spread and melting over the top. Enjoy with chicken wings, barbecue and collard greens.

SOURDOUGH PAPPARDELLE

Fresh, homemade egg pasta is a wonderful thing and easily achievable on a weeknight as a quick and simple dinner, especially if you've got an electric mixer. And I don't mean one with a pasta attachment; I make this recipe often, and I don't own any specialist equipment. The addition of the sourdough starter actually makes this task easier – it really adds to the extensibility of the dough, meaning it is much less work to roll out and aids in giving you a stronger gluten development.

Pappardelle is pretty much the result of a home chef or amateurish restaurateur not being bothered to slice their ribbons of pasta into the thinner tagliatelle. They're just thick ribbons. Quite right, too: spend any extra time you have rolling your dough extra-thin. We've served it with a basic beef ragù, but I like it just as much with truffle oil and Parmesan.

To feed 4:
200g fine semolina
100g strong white flour (preferably Italian '00' pizza or ciabatta flour)
50g sourdough starter, preferably wholemeal (wholewheat)
3 medium eggs
table salt, for boiling

Start at least 50 minutes before you want to eat. In a large bowl, mix your semolina, flour, starter and eggs. Note there's no salt in the dough. Mix these together until combined, and then knead vigorously until smooth. It will come together eventually – it's best to use an electric mixer. Give it a good 10 minutes.

Stick your smooth dough in the fridge and let it rest for 30 minutes. Meanwhile, you can make whatever sauce you plan on serving it with.

Stick a large pan of water – about 2 litres – on to boil. Add at least 2 tbsp table salt. As it heats, take your rested dough and tip it onto a fairly well-floured surface. Add more flour on top and begin to roll out your pasta dough. You want to make it into as big a rectangle as you can manage. It should be about as thin as a 5p (10c) piece – this is very thin. If you are struggling, you can wrap the dough around your rolling pin and stick it in the fridge for a couple of minutes to relax.

When your rough rectangle of dough is as thin as you can bear, roll it up into a big sausage shape. Use a pizza cutter or your dough scraper to cut your folded pasta into 1cm (½in) wide strips. Then, when they are all cut, use your hands to lift them all up in the air in a big bunch. Repeat this, mixing with any remaining flour on your bench in order for them to separate from their neighbouring pasta ribbons or their folds.

When your water is at a rolling boil, add your pasta. After a minute, use a slotted spoon to gently prod and separate any ribbons that have stuck together. Cook for another minute. Drain through a colander, catching the pasta-water in your pasta saucepan if you can.

Let drain, and then add your cooked pasta into your sauce. Mix and mix until all the pasta is coated. Add up to 4 tablespoons of your original pasta water to loosen. Serve.

SAUERDOUGHKRAUT

I keep my sourdough starters in my ceramic fermentation jars. These jars have an airlock that lets any gas escape from fermentations, and allows you to add some water to prevent any oxygen from getting back in.

There are fermentation jars of every sort and shape – most contain some kind of airlock system like mine. This makes them perfect for storing starters, as it keeps the starter moist while avoiding the complications of jar explosions.

When I want to use my jar for fermentations, such as kimchi or sauerkraut, I use a silicone spatula to remove all that's practically possible of my starter and transfer it to another jar. Then when I go to make pickle, I'm not worried that the vegetables I've bought aren't rich enough in the wonderful bacteria needed to ferment them. I'm also not worried for my own health, and I don't need to buy any special cultures.

One note with this: I'd only do this with a fresh starter. Obviously, don't use a pink/blue/mouldy starter for this purpose. Make sure your starter is rising and falling as expected. This technique can be used with any vegetables to make your fermentations more reliable. If it ever seems suspect despite this, don't risk it.

For 1 large jar:
1 fermentation jar, emptied of sourdough starter
  but not cleaned
1 pale cabbage (Savoy is nice too)
3 tbsp good-quality sea salt
½ tsp caraway seeds

Start by removing your sourdough starter from your fermentation jar, as above. Wipe it clean using a silicone spatula, but don't rinse it and don't go to any great lengths. It can look almost entirely clean and still have a significant effect – that's why it's *micro*biology.

Chop your cabbage – finely. Be conscientious. Actually, that's a stupid thing to say. Be conscientious if you like your sauerkraut to be easily spoonable. Don't be if you prefer it chunky.

Stick your chopped cabbage in a large bowl with your salt and your caraway. Use one hand to massage your salt into your cabbage, turning your bowl and getting the cabbage right at the bottom each time. Think of this like kneading bread. Keep working until you're starting to get some watery film over most of the cabbage. At this point, leave for 5 minutes.

Fill your fermentation jar with the cabbage and any excess brine, too. Press down so that you can fit as much cabbage in it as possible. After anywhere between 30 minutes to 1 hour, use a spoon to agitate your cabbage, stirring to disseminate any bugs from the edge of the jar. Pat down again to remove as much air as possible.

Place the airlocked lid on your jar and leave at room temperature for 1-3 weeks. After a few days, it will smell terrible and this is normal. The airlock will bubble quickly because of the vast amount of yeast present compared to normal sauerkraut. Taste it after a week, and then every few days until it is sour enough for you. Then fridge it. It will keep for a while in the fridge – you can eat it as long as it isn't mouldy. About 4 months is safe.

INDEX

A

Acme Bread 198
active fermentation 78, 82
Agas 31
air 98
all whole wheat 179
almond milk: the enriched vegan
   plait 231–2
almonds
   chugelhopf 227–8
   frangipane raisin känellangd
   233–4
anchovies: fougasse 149–50
ancient Einkorn batard 187–9
Aroma Panettone: panettone 225–6
ascorbic acid 99
Aspergillus species 101–2
autolyse 23, 48, 78, 79–80, 179

B

baba au rhum 227
bacteria 92
bagels galore 166–9
baguettes 34, 110
   baking 69
   demi-baguettes à l'ancienne
   143–7
   shaping and scoring 65, 146–7
bakers' percentages 81
baking 68–9
   par-baking 70, 143
baking stones 31, 34
banana pancakes 238
bannetons 32
baps, unbleached 121–2
barley 23, 27, 84
basil
   Neapolitan-style pizza 127–8
   Rome-style pizza 195–6
baskets, proving 32, 34, 64
batards
   ancient Einkorn batard 187–9
   lemon and poppy seed loaf 207–8
   scoring 65
   shaping 62–3
batons 34

fresh spelt batons 181–2
   scoring 65
Bertinet, Richard 12, 13, 49
Bertinet method *see* slap and fold
   method
bicarbonate of soda 163
bird's eye bubbles 109–10
bitty breads 190–215
   crispbread 211–12
   Danish rye 203–4
   ficelle with olives 213–14
   lemon and poppy seed loaf 207–8
   Rome-style pizza 195–6
   sandwich seeded 193–4
   walnut levain 198–201
bolillos, salty 155
boules, shaping 60–1
bran 23
bread
   bread formulae 81
   cooling 70
   denseness 106
   how to bake 68–9
   how to make 46–73
   troubleshooting 104–11
Bread Ahead 219
Bread Lines 94
brewer's yeast 92
brioche 108, 157–8, 217, 221–2
brotforms 32
bubbles
   lack of 109
   large 111
buckwheat 27
bugs 26, 82
bulk prove 46, 53
buns
   burger buns 157–8
   epic buns 123–6
   hot dog buns 161
   unbleached baps 121–2
burger buns 157–8
burnt loaves 108
butter 30
   brioche 221–2
   burger buns 157–8
   chugelhopf 227–8
   cornbread 243
   frangipane raisin känellangd

233–4
   pandoro and panettone 225–6
   the world's best doughnuts
   219–20
buttermilk: cornbread 243
butyric acid 102

C

cabbage: sauerdoughkraut 246
Cake and Bake Show 13
Candida 93, 99
   C. milleri 93
capers: ficelle with olives 213–14
caramelisation 108
caraway seeds: sauerdoughkraut
   246
carbohydrates, low-carb diets 89
carbon dioxide 26, 30, 41, 53, 68–9,
   98, 107, 110
cast-iron pots 34
ceramic cloches 35
cereals 27
cheat's starter 99
cheese 30
   fougasse 149–50
   Neapolitan-style pizza 127–8
   Rome-style pizza 195–6
   see also cream cheese; ricotta
cherry kugelhopf 227–8
chocolate: *chugelhopf* 227–8
chugelhopf 227–8
ciabatta 34, 137–9
   baking 69
ciabatta flour
   Rome-style pizza 195–6
   sourdough pappardelle 244
cinnamon 30
   epic buns 123–6
citrus juice 99
citrus peel: panettone 225–6
cloches 31, 34, 35, 69
Clostridium butyricum 94
Coca-Cola 94, 99
Coeliac disease 85, 87
competitive inhibition 92
cooling bread 70
corn flour 27
cornbread 243
couches 34, 143

crackers, crispbread 211–12
cream cheese: epic buns 123–6
crème pâtissiere 219–20
crispbread 211–12
crooked English muffins 171
crumb 10
  lack of bubbles 109
  proving and 53
  raw or doughy 108
crumpets 241
crust 10
  bubbles in the 109–10
  bubbles under the 111
  formation of 69
  gluten and 108
  pale, thick and tough crusts 108
  proving and 53
  steam and 69
culture mediums 92

D
Danish rye 203–4
darker breads 172–89
  all whole wheat 179
  ancient Einkorn batard 187–9
  fresh spelt batons 181–2
  leftover-bread bread 186
  miche d'ecosse 175–6
  overnight oat sourdough 185
  pane rimacinato 178
deflation, dough 107–8
demi-baguettes à l'ancienne 143–4
dense bread 106
  denseness at the bottom of the
  loaf 111
dextrins 89
diabetes 89
doneness, checking dough 64
double hydration mixing 137
dough
  autolyse 79–80
  deflation 107–8
  dense 106
  elasticity 78
  extensibility 78
  first prove 46, 53
  good dough strength 16
  high hydration 12, 16, 78
  hydration 32

increasing strength 106–7
  kneading 49–52, 54–6, 78
  lack of rise 106
  levain 81–2
  low-hydration doughs 78
  overproving 79, 108, 110, 111
  perfect dough structure 76–9
  pre-shaping 18, 57, 58–9, 78, 79,
  107
  retarding 16, 18, 53, 64, 78, 79, 109
  rheology 13, 76
  scoring 18, 35, 57, 65–7
  second prove 64
  shaping 18, 57, 78, 79, 107
  splitting 57, 58–9
  temperature 28–9, 107
  tenacity 78
  troubleshooting 106–7
  understanding 74–89
  wet dough 107
  what dough does to you 85–9
  when to add salt 80
  when to stop proving 64
dough hooks 78
dough scrapers 31–2, 49, 79
doughnuts 217
  the world's best 219–20
dried fruit 30, 99
  frangipane raisin känellangd
  233–4
  panettone 225–6
drying starters 99, 103
durum wheat 27
Dutch ovens 34, 110

E
E. Coli 102
'ears' 65, 110
eggs
  banana pancakes 238
  brioche 221–2
  crème pâtissiere 219–20
  frangipane raisin känellangd
  233–4
  pandoro and panettone 225–6
  sourdough pappardelle 244
Einkorn flour 27, 84
  ancient Einkorn batard 187–9
elasticity 16, 78

electric ovens 31
Emmer 84
English knead 49, 52
English muffins, crooked 171
enriched breads 216–35
  brioche 221–2
  burger buns 157–8
  chugelhopf 227–8
  the enriched vegan plait 231–2
  frangipane raisin känellangd
  233–4
  pain de mie au levain 133
  pandoro 225–6
  panettone 225–6
  the world's best doughnuts
  219–20
epic buns 123–6
equipment 19, 31–7, 82
  for starters 95, 97
exploding starters 103
extensibility 16, 78

F
fan ovens 31, 69, 108
fat 30
feeding your starter 44
fermentation 10
  active 78, 82
  retarders 53, 94
  spontaneous 11
ficelle with olives 213–14
firm dough 16
flatbreads
  baking 69
  focaccia integrale 117–18
  proving 64
flavour 30
  lack of 109
flax seeds
  Danish rye 203–4
  sandwich seeded 193–4
flies 103
floppy dough 106–7
flour 19, 23–6
  French flour system 143
  for rye sourdough starters 42
  sourdough starters 42, 95
  starter inactivity and 101
  strength 26

focaccia 29
  baking 69
  focaccia integrale 117–18
folding 16
formulae, bread 81
fougasse 149–50
frangipane raisin känellangd 233–4
freezing
  bread 70
  starters 99, 103
French flour system 143
fruit
  dried fruit 30
  fresh fruit 99
fruit juice 94, 98, 99
  rye sourdough starters 41, 42

G

garlic: Rome-style pizza 195–6
gas ovens 31
germ 23
gliadin 23, 76
gluten 16, 23, 26, 29, 30, 179
  active fermentation and 78
  crusts and 108
  deflation and 107
  dense bread and 106
  developing in starters 98
  developing with mixers 36
  effects of baking on 69
  intolerance of 85, 87–8
  kneading and 49, 53, 76, 78
  overdevelopment of 110
  perfect dough structure and 76, 78
  proving and 53
  salt and 80
  sloppy dough and 107
  strength and 54
  windowpane test 49, 76
glutenin 23, 76
golden syrup: frangipane raisin känellangd 233–4
grains, home milling 82–4
granite slabs 31
greasing loaf tins 64
Great British Bake Off 12–13, 166
growths, random 110

H

Hamelman, Jeffrey 115
hands, cleaning after kneading 49
Hawos 84
health, sourdough and 85, 88
herbs 30
  ficelle with olives 213–14
  focaccia integrale 117–18
  fougasse 149–50
high hydration doughs 12, 16, 78
Hollywood, Paul 13
honey
  cornbread 243
  pandoro and panettone 225–6
hooch 101
hot dog buns 161
hydration 28, 32
  gluten development and 76

I

idli 92
inactivity 101
ingredients 19, 23–30
Irritable Bowel Syndrome (IBS) 85, 87
Italian peel: panettone 225–6

K

Kamut 84
känellangd, frangipane raisin 233–4
ketones 89
ketotic 89
Khorasan 27
kirsch: *chugelhopf* 227–8
knäckebröd 211
kneading dough 16, 49–52, 54–6, 78
  English knead 49, 52
  gluten and 49, 53, 76, 78
  lamination method 54, 56
  slap and fold method 49, 50–1
  stretch and fold method 49, 54–5, 76, 78
knives, scoring bread 35
Komo Fidibus mills 84
kugelhopf, cherry 227–8

L

lactic acid 92, 93
Lactobacillus 93, 99, 102
L. sanfranciscensus 93
lames 35
lamination method 54, 56
Lammas Fayre 84
The Lancet Public Health 89
Le Vast 221
leftover-bread bread 186
leftover starter 236–47
  banana pancakes 238
  cornbread 243
  crumpets 241
  sauerdoughkraut 246
  sourdough pappardelle 244
lemon and poppy seed loaf 207–8
lethargic starters 102–3
Letts, John 84
Leuconostoc species 92
levain 10, 46, 81–2
  walnut levain 198–201
little breads 152–71
  bagels galore 166–9
  burger buns 157–8
  crooked English muffins 171
  hot dog buns 161
  pretzels 163–4
  salty bolillos 155
loaf tins 35
  baking 69
  greasing 64
  second proves in 64
  shaping for 62–3
The Lockhart 243
low-carb diets 89
low-hydration doughs 78
lye 163

M

Maillard reaction 163
malted barley 27
maltose 93
miche d'ecosse 175–6
milk
  chugelhopf 227–8
  crème pâtissiere 219–20
  epic buns 123–6
  frangipane raisin känellangd 233–4
  the world's best doughnuts 219–20

milling grains 82–4
mills 82, 84
mixers 35–6
mixing dough 16, 49, 78
Mockmills 84
mother dough 10
moulds 101–2
mozzarella
   Neapolitan-style pizza 127–8
   Rome-style pizza 195–6
muffins, crooked English 171
mycotoxins 102

N
Neapolitan-style pizza 127–8, 195
Nutrimills 84
nuts 30
   crispbread 211–12

O
oats: overnight oat sourdough 185
oil 30
olives
   ficelle with olives 213–14
   fougasse 149–50
orange blossom water: panettone
   225–6
oven spring 65, 68–9, 79
   irregular 110
   poor 110
ovens 31, 69
   preheating 68
   temperature 108
overnight oat sourdough 185
oxygen 98

P
pain au levain 38–73
   how to make 46–73
   rye sourdough starters 41–5
pain de mie au levain 133
pale crusts 108
pancakes, banana 238
pandoro 225–6
pane rimacinato 178
panettone 225–6, 227
par-baking 70, 143
pasta: sourdough pappardelle 244
pavé rustique 115–16

peels 35, 65
pineapple juice method 94
pizza
   Neapolitan-style pizza 127–8, 195
   proving 64
   Rome-style pizza 195–6
plait, the enriched vegan 231–2
polenta: cornbread 243
poppy seeds 30
   bagels galore 166–9
   lemon and poppy seed loaf 207–8
   unbleached baps 121–2
potato flour 27
pots 31, 34, 69, 110
pre-shaping dough 18, 57, 58–9, 78,
   79, 107
pretzels 29, 163–4
proteases 76
proving 12, 16, 18
   first prove 46, 53
   flavour and 109
   overproving 79, 106, 108, 110, 111
   proving schedules 72–3
   second prove 64
   when to stop 64
proving baskets 32, 34, 64
pumpernickel, seeded 203–4
pumpkin puree: the enriched vegan
   plait 231–2
pumpkin seeds: bagels galore
   166–9

R
raisins 99
   frangipane raisin känellangd
   233–4
   raisin-water 99
rapeseed oil: the enriched vegan
   plait 231–2
Rayburns 31
razor blades 35
relaxed recipes 113–29
   epic buns 123–6
   focaccia integrale 117–18
   Neapolitan-style pizza 127–8
   pavé rustique 115–16
   unbleached baps 121–2
retarders 18, 53
   dough 16, 18, 53, 64, 78, 79, 109

starters 93
Revival bread 186
rheology 13, 76
rice flour 27
   tiger bread 141
ricotta: Rome-style pizza 195–6
Rivet 84
Robertson, Chad 12
   Tartine 82
roller-ground flour 26
rolls
   burger buns 157–8
   unbleached baps 121–2
Rome-style pizza 195–6
rosewater: *chugelhopf* 227–8
routine 19
rugbrød 203–4
rye 23, 27
   Danish rye 203–4
rye flakes: Danish rye 203–4
rye flour 106
   crispbread 211–12
   miche d'ecosse 175–6
rye sourdough starters 106
   Danish rye 203–4
   feeding 44, 46, 48
   focaccia integrale 117–18
   how to start 41–5
   leftover-bread bread 186
   miche d'ecosse 175–6
   overnight oat sourdough 185
   pain au levain 46–7
   pavé rustique 115–16
   sandwich seeded 193–4
   unbleached baps 121–2
   walnut levain 198–201

S
Saccharomyces 99
   S. cerevisiae 92
salt 29, 32, 49
   bread longevity and 109
   focaccia integrale 117–18
   salty bolillos 155
   sauerdoughkraut 246
   when to add 80
San Francisco white sourdough
   135–6
sandwich seeded 193–4

sauerdoughkraut 246
scales 32
Schnitzers 84
scoring 18, 35, 57, 65–7
    baguettes 146–7
    unopened scores 110
Scotch scraper 31
scrapers, dough 31–2, 49, 79
seeds 30
    bagels galore 166–9
    crispbread 211–12
    Danish rye 203–4
    lemon and poppy seed loaf 207–8
    sandwich seeded 193–4
    seeded pumpernickel 203–4
    unbleached baps 121–2
semolina 27
    ciabatta 137–9
    dusting with 35, 65
    pane rimacinato 178
    sourdough pappardelle 244
separation 101
sesame seeds 30
    bagels galore 166–9
    Danish rye 203–4
    sandwich seeded 193–4
settling, starters 101
shaping dough 16, 18, 57, 78, 79, 107
    baguettes 146–7
    batards 62–3
    boules 60–1
shelf life 70, 108–9
slap and fold method 49, 50–1
sloppy dough 107
smell 102
smørrebrød 203
soft drinks 99
sour sourdough 106
sourdough
    10 tenets of 14–19
    basic process 16–19
    circle of life 17
    cooling 70
    definition of 10–13
    healthiness of 85, 88
    how to bake 68–9
    how to make 46–73
sourdough pappardelle 244

sourdough starters 10, 16
    air 98
    bacteria in 92–4
    black, red or blue starters 101–2
    cheat's starter 99
    drying and freezing 99, 103
    exploding 103
    failed 94–5
    feeding 44, 46, 48, 93
    flies in 103
    flour 95
    how to start a rye sourdough
    starter 41–5
    inactivity 101
    keeping your starter happy 95–9
    leftover starter 236–47
    lethargic 102–3
    retarding 93
    separation 101
    smell 102
    sour sourdough 106
    starter starters 98–9
    stiff versus sloppy 98
    storage 95–7
    temperature 97–8, 103
    troubleshooting 101–3
    understanding 95–9
    using fruit juice 94–5, 98, 99
spelt 23, 26, 27, 84
    fresh spelt batons 181–2
spices 30
splitting dough 57, 58–9
spontaneous fermentation 11
springy dough 16
stagnant fermentation 78
stale bread 108–9
starches 76, 89
starters 10, 16
    air 98
    bacteria in 92–4
    black, red or blue starters 101–2
    cheat's starter 99
    drying and freezing 99, 103
    exploding 103
    failed 94–5
    feeding 44, 46, 48, 93
    flies in 103
    flour 95
    how to start a rye sourdough

    starter 41–5
    inactivity 101
    keeping your starter happy 95–103
    leftover starter 236–47
    lethargic 102–3
    retarding 93
    separation 101
    smell 102
    sour sourdough 106
    starter starters 98–9
    stiff versus sloppy 98
    storage 95–7
    temperature 97–8, 103
    troubleshooting 101–3
    understanding 90–103
    using fruit juice 94–5, 98, 99
steam 18–19, 31, 34, 69, 108, 110
stoneground flour 26
stones, baking 31, 34
strength 54
    good dough 16
    increasing dough 106–7
stretching 16
    stretch and fold method 49, 54–5, 76, 78
strong flour 23, 26
sugar 29–30, 108
sultanas: panettone 225–6
sunflower seeds
    bagels galore 166–9
    Danish rye 203–4
    sandwich seeded 193–4
    unbleached baps 121–2

T

T. Thermophilus 102
tap water 28
tapenade: ficelle with olives 213–14
tapioca flour 27
temperature
    dense bread and 106
    dough and 107
    oven 68, 108
    proving 16, 18, 53
    starters 44, 97, 103
    water 28–9
tenacity 16, 78
thefreshloaf.com 94

tiger bread 141
tins 34
tomatoes
   fougasse 149–50
   Neapolitan-style pizza 127–8
   Rome-style pizza 195–6
trays 34, 35
troubleshooting
   bread 104–11
   starters 101–3
Type 2 diabetes 89

U

unbleached baps 121–2
urad dal 92

V

vanilla
   crème patissiere 219–20
   pandoro 225–6
   panettone 225–6
Varimixer 36
vegan plait, the enriched 231–2
vegetables 30
vitamin C 94, 99
vomit smell 102

W

walnut levain 198–201
water 28–9
   temperature 28–9
'Welsh' baking stones 34
wet dough 16, 107
wheat 23, 26, 27, 106
wheatgerm: crispbread 211–12
white breads for sharing 48
   ciabatta 137–9
   demi-baguettes à l'ancienne
   143–7
   fougasse 149–50
   pain de mie au levain 133
   San Francisco white sourdough
   135–6
   tiger bread 141
white flour 19, 23, 27
   ancient Einkorn batard 187–9
   bagels galore 166–9
   banana pancakes 238
   brioche 221–2

burger buns 157–8
chugelhopf 227–8
ciabatta 137–9
crispbread 211–12
crooked English muffins 171
demi-baguettes à l'ancienne
143–7
the enriched vegan plait 231–2
epic buns 123–6
ficelle with olives 213–14
focaccia integrale 117–18
fougasse 149–50
frangipane raisin känellangd
233–4
fresh spelt batons 181–2
hot dog buns 161
leftover-bread bread 186
lemon and poppy seed loaf 207–8
miche d'ecosse 175–6
Neapolitan-style pizza 127–8
overnight oat sourdough 185
pain au levain 46–7
pain de mie au levain 133
pandoro and panettone 225–6
pane rimacinato 178
pavé rustique 115–16
pretzels 163–4
Rome-style pizza 195–6
salty bolillos 155
San Francisco white sourdough
135–6
sandwich seeded 193–4
sourdough pappardelle 244
tiger bread 141
unbleached baps 121–2
walnut levain 198–201
the world's best doughnuts
219–20
white sourdough starter
   ancient Einkorn batard 187–9
   bagels galore 166–9
   banana pancakes 238
   brioche 221–2
   burger buns 157–8
   chugelhopf 227–8
   ciabatta 137–9
   crispbread 211–12
   crooked English muffins 171
   crumpets 241

demi-baguettes à l'ancienne
143–4
the enriched vegan plait 231–2
ficelle with olives 213–14
fougasse 149–50
frangipane raisin känellangd
233–4
fresh spelt batons 181–2
hot dog buns 161
lemon and poppy seed loaf 207–8
Neapolitan-style pizza 127–8
pain de mie au levain 133
pandoro and panettone 225–6
pane rimacinato 178
pavé rustique 115–16
pretzels 163–4
Rome-style pizza 195–6
salty bolillos 155
San Francisco white sourdough
135–6
tiger bread 141
the world's best doughnuts
219–20
wholemeal Einkorn flour: ancient
Einkorn batard 187–9
wholemeal (wholewheat) flour 23
   all whole wheat 179
   miche d'ecosse 175–6
   pavé rustique 115–16
wholemeal (wholewheat) rye flour
211
   Danish rye 203–4
wholemeal (wholewheat) sourdough starter 106
   all whole wheat 179
   epic buns 123–6
   focaccia integrale 117–18
   overnight oat sourdough 185
   sandwich seeded 193–4
   unbleached baps 121–2
   walnut levain 198–201
windowpane test 49, 76
Wink, Debra 94

Y

yeasts 68, 92, 93, 107
   dense bread and 106
   starting starters 99

ACKNOWLEDGEMENTS

I will forever be grateful to the wonderful **Sarah Lavelle**, for her continued faith and encouragement and enthusiasm. That goes for her wonderful family, too: **Tilly, Elliott** and **James**, who are collectively some of the most remarkable people. Thank you for looking after me.

This book is dedicated to **Tim Hayward, Alison Wright** and **Liberty Wright**, who for three weeks plied us with much wine and allowed us to disassemble their kitchen, leaving every surface in a blanket of flour and a crusting of dough.

For five books **Will Webb** has done an awesome design job under considerable duress and pressure from author and editor. Thank you. And you, the reader, wouldn't have any idea of what I'm on about without the photographic mastery of **Andy Sewell** who, like all the above, is an inspiration himself.

Fenella, my wife, without whom none of this would get done. The family, for your love and support despite the geography: **Magnus** (and family), **Martha, Dad, Mum, Sandy** (and family), **David** (and family). Work colleagues, especially **Gordon, Diane, Mark, Allan, Katy, Jill, Becca, Suzanne** and all the practice staff.

SUPPLIERS

The wonderful bowls, plates and fermentation jars you see are handcrafted by **Natalie Smith**, who you can find at @throwing_pots on Insta and you can email her for orders on throwingpots@posteo.uk

BakeryBits.co.uk is where I get most of my baking stuff. It has everything, including wonderful unbleached **Gilchester's** flour and the tricky but flavourful **Lammas Fayre** biodiverse selection of ancient grains. For the majority of the recipes in this book we used **Marriage's** strong white flour, supplied by **Fitzbillies** bakery in Cambridge. Head there for the quintessential Chelsea Bun.

The best electric mixer I've used and owned comes from Denmark, and it is the **Varimixer** Teddy (varimixer.com). It strengthens dough in a comparable way to many stretches and folds. The specific dough scrapers used in the shoot are '**Campbell's Dough Knives**', and you can find him on Insta @campbell2664 or rackmaster.co.uk. They're excellent. Thank you to **Joel Black**, for your wonderful knives, and to the many other craftsmen and craftswomen who inspire.